Advance praise for *Kind of a Miracle*

Doug Wilhelm has skillfully chronicled the creation and development of the Community College of Vermont — one of the most important stories of Vermont higher education. Surprisingly, it's also one of the least known. Until now.

Employing historical research, dozens of personal interviews, and engaging writing, Wilhelm gives us the history and impact of a statewide grass-roots college made by Vermonters for Vermonters. It's a school no one believed could survive, but one that has, over the last half-century, deeply enriched the cultural life and economic vitality of this small state.

It's an important story — and a fascinating read.

— Tom Slayton, former editor of *Vermont Life*
and author of *Finding Vermont* and
Searching for Thoreau

Kind of a Miracle is the inspiring story of an institution built from the ground up — and of the value in adhering to a clear mission, of experimentation, and of leaders and teachers who are from and for the communities they serve. Always under-resourced financially but long on talent and innovation, CCV has been a pioneer in competency-based education, credit for prior learning, distributed libraries, serving refugees, dual enrollment, distance education, and stackable credentials.

This book deserves to become a classic in the higher education literature.

— Dr. Barbara Brittingham, president emerita
New England Commission of Higher Education

In an age where the unexpected becomes routine and foundational things are shaken to their core, this book is a crucial reminder that good things disappear if not defended. Good things disappear if the wrong people lead. Good things disappear if change is not embraced, something Doug makes central to the CCV story.

— Emerson Lynn, editor and publisher emeritus
St. Albans (Vt.) *Messenger* (from the Introduction)

Kind of a
Miracle

Kind of a Miracle

The Unlikely Story of the Community College of Vermont

Doug Wilhelm

Long Stride Books

Copyright © 2024, Doug Wilhelm

LONG STRIDE BOOKS
Middlebury, Vermont
longstridebooks.com

All rights reserved. No part of this book may be reproduced or utilized in any form or by any means, electronic or mechanical, including photocopying, recording, or by any information storage and retrieval system, without permission in writing from the publisher.

Book design and production: Laughing Bear Associates, Montpelier, VT
Cover illustration: Detail of 1979 editorial cartoon by Jeff Danziger

When CCV celebrated its 50th anniversary at the Vermont State House in January 2020, many who attended, including Governor Phil Scott, wore a sticker that read: "Ask me about my CCV story."

ISBN: 978-0-9857836-6-2

We were the rebels tunneling under the walls and into the halls of the higher education establishment... and if we had to drive through blizzards to attend these regional meetings, well, all the better to prove ourselves worthy of our great and noble cause. We'd stumble into the back rooms of local restaurants, shake off the snow, pull off our boots, and take up the business of creating a college that could change the world.

— David Buchdahl, academic dean from 1994-2012,
  on the early years of the Community College of Vermont

Contents

Introduction: The Power of People Who Refused to Give Up
by Emerson Lynn 9

Part One. Inventing a College: 1969–1979 13
1. If There Were No Examples, We Had to Create One ... 15
2. What Do You Want to Learn? 29
3. Finding the Money and Claiming a Place 54
4. Giving Education Back to the Learner 68
5. Building Credibility and Surviving 82
6. Voices from the Field 95
7. A Turbulent End to a Pioneering Time 103

Part Two. A Lifetime of Learning: 1979–2001 113
8. We've Got to Save This 115
9. Where Vermonters Go to College 138
10. To Produce Profound Change 185
11. What Are We Growing Into? 205

Part Three. Inventing the Future: 2001–Now 241
12. On a Big Playing Field Now 243
13. Changing Lives, One at a Time 305

Afterword 368
Acknowledgments 370

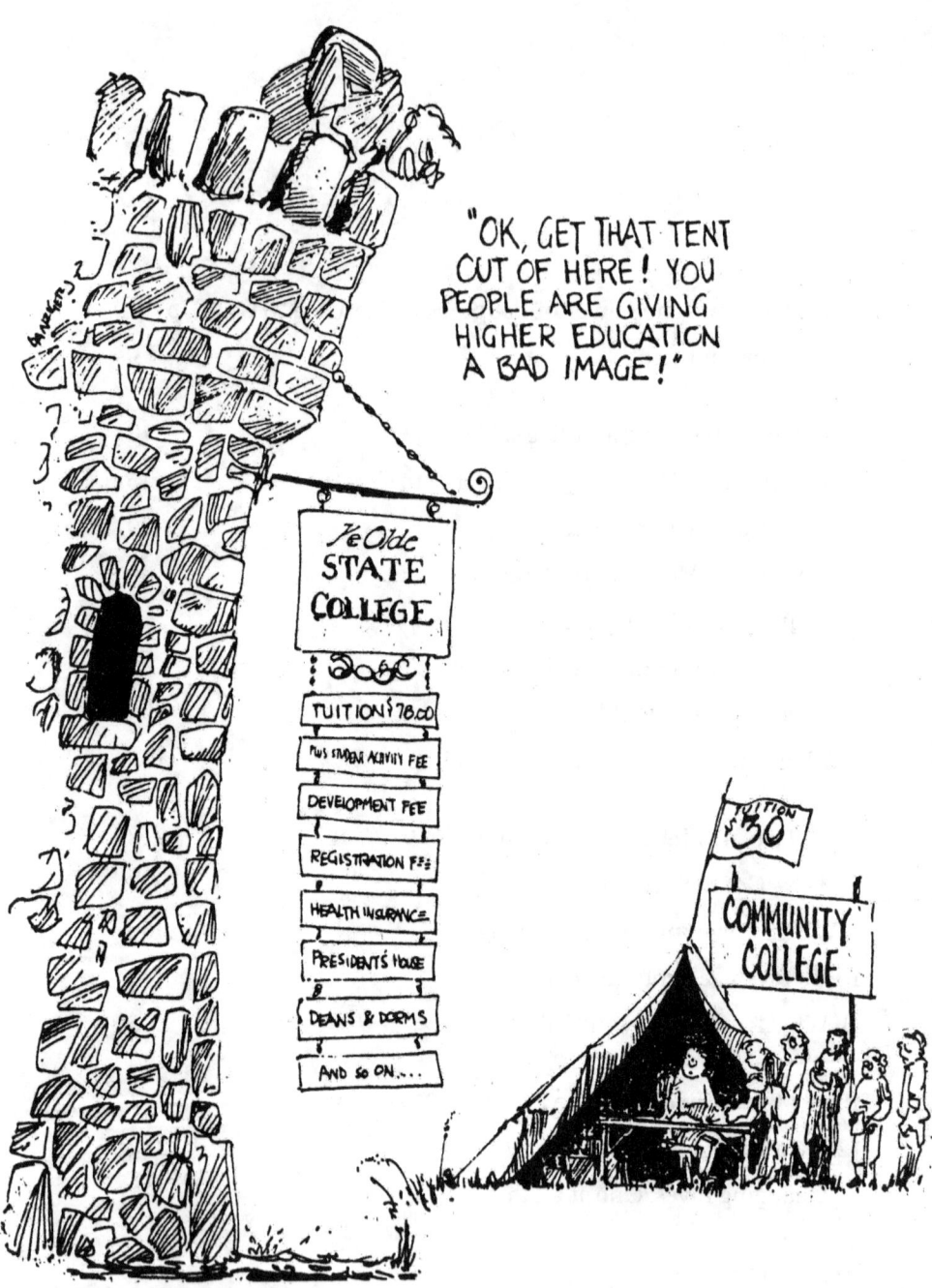

From Vermont editorial cartoonist Jeff Danziger: a memorable comment on the 1979 effort in the State Legislature to kill off CCV.

Introduction

The Power of People Who Refused to Give Up

Emerson Lynn

Doug Wilhelm's *Kind of a Miracle* is perhaps less a story about how the Community College of Vermont came to be than it is about the power of people who refused to give up — people whose thirst to turn the educational model upside down could not be quenched, and people who prevailed when all others told them they were wrong, or they did not belong.

This is a book inspirational to Vermonters, because for the past half century CCV has been woven into our individual communities in a way nothing else in higher education has. As Vermonters, we know them. They know us. CCV is centered on the belief that it is only as strong as its community relationships are deep, the operating philosophy of current President Joyce Judy. It's a belief and a practice that has made CCV the second-largest higher-ed presence in Vermont, and the one within the Vermont State College system that is strongest and most envied.

CCV's relationships are personal, especially so for this writer. I came to Vermont a decade after Peter Smith, the soothsayer, began this "experiment" in higher education in 1970. I was the new owner/publisher/editor of the *St. Albans Messenger* and CCV had recently opened its doors at a small store on the city's main street. It was there I met Pixley Hill and David Buchdahl, local tour de forces for CCV and people I'd remain friends with for decades. (Pixley was my next door neighbor.) It was through them that I met the irrepressible Peter, the founding president of CCV, who was then a state senator and who would soon become the state's lieutenant governor, then congressman, and a lifelong friend.

In this book Peter characterizes what has transpired at CCV as "a very unlikely story." Indeed. It was, and is, a story that rewrites people's lives.

The college gave those without the resources the opportunity, followed by the thirst, to learn. It served as a pillar to the community, something to be defended, encouraged and celebrated. A half-century later that same sense of belonging, and importance, remains at the center of its 12 academic centers statewide. Doug Wilhelm's book explains why, and does so through testimonials and interviews with new CCV disciples as well as those who have been there through the half-century-plus experience.

In an age where the unexpected becomes routine and foundational things are shaken to their core, this book is a crucial reminder that good things disappear if not defended. Good things disappear if the wrong people lead. Good things disappear if change is not embraced, something Doug makes central to the CCV story.

The college has been extraordinarily fortunate to have been led by CCV "insiders" like Barbara Murphy, Tim Donovan and Joyce Judy — people who were pivotal in its evolution, who were ahead of their times in understanding that students' needs were, and still are, the focus of their mission. And, as Doug ably portrays, these people are simply marvelous human beings.

The expression "Run till you're tackled," which appears more than once in this book, will be familiar to Vermonters old and new who have taken part in making this uncommon college work so well.

INTRODUCTION

The phrase best describes CCV's philosophy, and it explains why the college's leadership has prevailed against the forces that resist change. It conveys why it's never acceptable to rest in neutral while change erupts around us — and it hints at why CCV's educational model is essential to Vermont's future.

Thank you, Doug. The story of the Community College of Vermont is a tale very much worth telling.

Emerson Lynn was the owner, editor and publisher of the St. Albans Messenger *from 1981 to 2019. He continues to write the paper's editorials as editor emeritus.*

"I ran an extension cord into the window of a soon-to-be-demolished hotel room. The owner-landlord let me have it for literally no money. That was the first office."

– Peter Smith

Part One

Inventing a College

Peter Smith, 1969–1979

Chapter 1

If There Were No Examples, We Had to Create One

It's not uncommon to think of the late 1960s as a time of peaceable idealism — but the pivotal year 1968 saw angry, even violent upheaval across much of the United States. College campuses roiled with demonstrations against the Vietnam War; in the civil rights movement, frustrated young people were growing more militant; and the nightly TV news brought the trauma of battles far and near into American living rooms. Then in the spring, the assassinations of Dr. Martin Luther King Jr. and Robert F. Kennedy set cities aflame and threatened to tear the country apart.

By the time Richard Nixon won the presidency that November, thousands of young Americans were leaving suburbs and cities for rural places in hopes of finding a way of life that made more sense to them. In Vermont, they found a state that was changing — or parts of it were.

The construction from 1960 to '65 of nearly 350 miles of interstates 89 and 91 had cut through long-isolated farm communities and opened new access for visitors, new supply routes for businesses, and swifter pathways for people moving in. Ski areas were growing into destination resorts. After IBM leader Thomas Watson Jr. visited Stowe in 1956, his company built a manufacturing center in Essex Junction that by the late '60s had begun to make the integrated-circuit chips that would revolutionize the growing world of information technology.

But in much of Vermont, especially its many rural areas separated from the new highways by distance and mountains, opportunities to earn a decent livelihood were scarce for natives and newcomers alike. The traditional farm economy was suffering, as small dairies struggled to survive or gave up the ghost — and both job training and higher education lay an often-forbidding distance away.

Yet "there was great potential for growth in Vermont ... all that was necessary was to train people for jobs," wrote Larry Daloz, then a young educator and Peace Corps veteran who would soon become a key contributor to the early development of the Community College of Vermont, in an unpublished history of the college's first years.

"Community colleges were springing up all across the nation to fill that need for 'middle-level manpower,'" he wrote. "Why not here?"

President Lyndon Johnson's Great Society initiative had created a number of antipoverty programs. Vermont had a new state Office of Economic Opportunity (OEO) that had federal dollars to invest, and the New England Regional Commission, organized in 1967, was also parceling out funds for economic development. In 1968, that commission gave Vermont's government a small grant, just $15,700, for a feasibility study that would look at whether the state — already home at its geographic center to the two-year Vermont Technical College — might develop another technical college somewhere.

A different idea

To conduct the study, liberal Democratic Governor Philip Hoff created the Vermont Technical Commission. To chair it, he appointed the state's commissioner of education, Harvey Scribner, a progressive-minded educator — Daloz called him a "maverick" — who had earlier overseen the integration of schools in Teaneck, New Jersey.

Joining Scribner on the panel were executives from major corporations with Vermont facilities: IBM in Essex Junction, General

Electric in Burlington, Union Carbide in Bennington, and the Jones & Lamson Machine Tool Company in Springfield, plus the business-school chair from the University of Vermont, a retired Standard Oil exec, a top state official, and the president of Vermont College, an independent two-year school in Montpelier.

The commission's January 1969 report noted "a mounting interest in, and demand for, adult education programs among Vermonters eager to acquire new or improved employment skills," with "an extensive equal need for technical education." Yet creating a new "technical institute," the report concluded, "would not meet state needs," because "a public education facility limited by location will serve a limited local purpose."

Instead, the commission proposed a different idea: "the establishment of the Vermont Regional Community College System."

Scribner's group was somewhat vague about what this system would be. Its report advised only that the state should organize something "tailored both to our needs and our capacity," with "a flexible comprehensive program in vocational, technical and liberal arts arenas. Both credit and non-credit courses would be offered contingent on demand." Classes would be scheduled between 4 p.m. and midnight, with instructors "recruited from Vermont industry, particularly for courses in the vocational and technical field."

It was an interesting idea, for a rural state.

For a while it went nowhere.

'Let's do something with this'

"This thing got no attention at all," remembers Peter P. Smith, who was then the young scion of a prominent Vermont banking family and was working for Scribner as an intern.

The state's new governor, sworn in that January, was Republican Deane C. Davis, a conservative former CEO of the National Life Insurance Company in Montpelier. Davis took no action on the proposal from Scribner's group.

"The idea did not go over with the Legislature" either, wrote Daloz. "Scribner was looked on by many as excessively liberal ... By June 1969, the idea was politically dead."

Peter Smith in the '70s.

But then Scribner delivered the keynote speech at a late 1969 conference in Stowe sponsored by New Careers, a federally funded employment training program. He told the gathering that "there remained a need for post-secondary job training for Vermonters — especially in the area of Human Services, where significant growth was projected in those waning days of the '60s," Daloz wrote.

"He held the [commission] report up in the air; and at lunchtime," Daloz wrote, "a small group, including one of his aides, a young Vermonter named Peter Smith, schooled at Andover and Princeton, sat down to write the letter of intent."

Recalled Smith: "A guy named Chuck Butler, who was Dean Davis's chief of civil and military affairs and a good friend of mine, and I got talking with a couple of other people and Lloyd Lagrow, who ran New Careers out of his St. Albans office." Lagrow was director of the Champlain Valley Work Training Programs, an umbrella group of youth and job-training programs in northwest Vermont.

"We had a little conversation," Smith remembered. "We said, 'Let's get a college that goes to the end of the road, and deals with adults and does all these cool things.' And of course we all said, 'Absolutely, let's do that.' So about five of us ended up sitting in the board room at the Department of Education on State Street [in Montpelier], writing a grant to OEO."

The proposal to the OEO asked for $60,000, Smith said, "to conduct a study for a rural, community-based community college that would take education to the learner, meet learners' needs, and do so with existing resources."

And "lo and behold, the grant came through" — for $59,716.

The founding head of the Vermont OEO, appointed by Gov. Hoff, was Thomas C. Davis, a Democrat who would later serve as state director for U.S. Senator Patrick Leahy. Tom Davis was the new governor's son.

"So Tom says to Dad, 'Let's do something with this,'" Smith recalled.

'Nobody thought it would work'

"In August 1970, Gov. Deane C. Davis issued Executive Order No. 27 creating the Vermont Regional Community College Commission to oversee the planning phase of an OEO grant to establish a Community College demonstration model," said a report on the project that was prepared the next year for the State Legislature. "Dr. William G. Craig, president of Johnson State [College], was appointed President of the Commission, and in November 1970, Mr. Peter P. Smith was appointed the project director."

Smith had by then completed his post-Princeton internship with Scribner. "I had started a street academy in Montpelier for dropouts called the Montpelier Educational Facility, but I'm still working with some of these other guys on this idea," he said. "I remember sitting in a meeting, talking about advertising the [director's] job — because now it's August, it's a one-year grant and the clock's ticking and we don't even have an executive director.

"They were talking about the job description, and I was, you know, holding court: 'If you guys advertise for a community college president, you're going to get a college president and that's not what this state needs. We need something more like the Ag Extension Service, but an educational institute.'

"Topper McFaun [Francis McFaun of Barre Town, then with the Central Vermont Community Action Council, later a Republican state representative] turned around at one point and said to me, 'If you're so damned smart, why don't you apply for the job?' I said, 'Really?' He said, 'Peter, we've got ten and a half months and $59,000.'

"There were three finalists, of which I was one, and I was probably the strongest candidate of the three, which tells you something about the quality of the pool," Smith said with a laugh. "Basically nobody thought it would work, so I got it."

He was twenty-four years old.

"I started on the first of October [1970] in the old Montpelier Tavern, in a section that was closed for demolition," Smith said.

A 1932-vintage hotel on State Street, the Tavern Motor Inn was a short walk from the State House. "I ran an extension cord into the window of a soon-to-be-demolished hotel room. The owner-landlord let me have it for literally no money. That was the first office — it was in a condemned building with an extension cord, and I didn't even have a telephone."

Smith's first hire was one of the other finalists for his job, "a community organizer named John Chater from the Northeast Kingdom, a guy I knew and a good guy. The commission was put together with Bill Craig as the head. We had educators and public [agency] people and low-income advocates on the commission, and we met monthly. This was still fall 1970."

Craig, the commission chair, was president of Johnson State, one of the four established Vermont State Colleges. He held an education doctorate from Harvard and had directed training for the Peace Corps in its early 1960s beginnings. He would later become chancellor of the Vermont State Colleges System, then chancellor of the California Community Colleges.

Craig was, Smith said, a "stout defender" of this new concept: a college that would have no facilities and didn't plan to build any. Instead, it would bring higher education and job training to learners in communities all over this rural state, simply by taking advantage of the resources that communities already had.

"I started to do some research, and very quickly found out that there was no model for what we had said we wanted to do. There were no no-campus colleges in the country," Smith said. "There were no operating models of a community-based community college that used the existing human, physical and programmatic resources of the community to meet learners' needs. So with the commission's approval, we chose to simply go get some learners and begin.

"If there were no examples, we had to create one."

Community colleges and the "great transformation"

The nation's first two-year or junior college opened in 1901 as an extension of a high school in Joliet, Illinois, outside Chicago. Some leaders of U.S. higher education looked down on this innovation, but others promoted it; and the idea began to grow that schools like this, granting a new credential called the associate degree, could become true "people's colleges," opening up access to higher education for more Americans than had ever had a chance at college before.

As of 2023, more than twelve million students, from a very broad diversity of backgrounds and a wide range of ages, were attending nearly 1,200 associate degree-granting institutions in the United States, according to the American Association of Community Colleges. The associate degree is commonly earned over two years of full-time study, and the name *community college,* introduced in San Francisco in the 1930s, reflects what these colleges have generally become: learning centers that connect closely, in a variety of ways, with the communities they serve.

Along with the land grant movement of the late nineteenth century, which gave rise to many of the nation's public universities, the community college is one of "the two great innovations in higher education in the United States," wrote Clark Kerr, the influential former president of the University of California and member of the Carnegie Commission on Higher Education, in a foreword to the 1985 book *Renewing the American Community College: Priorities and Strategies for Effective Leadership* (Hoboken, NJ: Jossey-Bass).

"The community college movement began the great transformation" of the nation, Kerr wrote, "into a learning society in which every person who wishes to do so can study almost any subject in almost any geographic community."

"For more than a decade, the majority of all degree-credit students entering the system of higher education have done so in a two-year institution," wrote Yale professor Steven Brint and University of California

▶

Berkeley professor Jerome Karabel in a 1989 history, *The Diverted Dream: Community Colleges and the Promise of Educational Opportunity in America, 1900–1985* (New York: Oxford University Press).

"The community college has a crucial role to play," they said. "It is, after all, the most common point of entry into college for those groups that have traditionally been excluded from higher education."

Yet during the early decades of the twentieth century, even as the number of public two-year colleges grew steadily in other parts of the country — most notably in California, the South and the industrial Midwest — the movement made no inroads at all in New England. By 1940, one American student in ten was enrolled at a two-year school, but "not a single public [two-year] institution had been opened in New England," wrote Brint and Karabel.

"In the Northeast, the first junior colleges were exclusively private," they wrote, and were often schools for women that "typically sought to provide cultural finishing for the daughters of the well-to-do."

It wasn't until 1962 that a Vermont public institution began offering the associate degree. That year the Legislature authorized the renaming of what had been the Vermont School of Agriculture (and briefly the Vermont Agriculture and Technical Institute), in Randolph Center, as Vermont Technical College, with A.D. programs in agricultural and technical fields.

'The junior college is properly a community college'

Across the country, students entering junior colleges in the early and mid-twentieth century were often encouraged to choose vocational programs for fields that only required an associate degree. Yet most of those students had other ideas: Consistently from year to year, significant majorities wanted to go on to colleges and universities that granted a bachelor's degree.

Outcomes proved how often they deserved that chance.

"A 1924 study of more than 9,000 California junior college students revealed that 80 percent of them intended to go on to four-year colleges and universities," wrote Brint and Karabel. In the late 1920s, "comparisons of the academic performance of junior college transfers and 'native students' at nine universities" showed only one case, they wrote, "in which junior college students performed significantly less well." At all the other schools, "the grades of transfer students were on average higher."

Enrollment in the nation's two-year colleges saw three big twentieth-century surges: after World War I, as veterans returned home; during the Great Depression, when many Americans sought affordable education and job training; and most dramatically after World War II, when the G.I. Bill of 1944 provided financial aid to millions of vets. In 1946, the influential report of the President's Commission on Higher Education, widely known as the Truman Commission, emphasized its vision in italics: "*Free and universal access to education, in terms of the interest, ability, and need of the student, must be a major goal in American education.*"

"The Commission's call for equality of opportunity was followed by a proposal for the massive expansion of higher education," Brint and Karabel wrote. "The junior college was central to the Commission's plans for expanding educational opportunity."

By then, a new approach — and what seems to have been the first use of the term *community college* — had been field-tested at San Francisco Junior College. Under President A. J. Cloud, that college "set about to serve the instructional interests of many community groups, not just college-age students," wrote Brint and Karabel. "During most of the 1930s the college had no regular campus, and instead offered an extraordinarily wide range of services at over 20 centers scattered throughout the city."

"The junior college is properly a community college," A. J. Cloud wrote in 1940. "It seeks to make a continuous study of community needs … developing types of instruction and training that will meet such needs."

"Cloud's ideas had little immediate impact on the movement," noted Brint and Karabel, "but they were revised and became an important influence in the 1960s."

To reach 95 percent of the people

By the late 1960s, nearly three in ten Americans enrolled in higher education were studying at a junior or community college. "By 1970 the proportion had grown to more than 40 percent," Brint and Karabel wrote. "The two-year college had spread to virtually every state in the union and, in so doing, had become an integral part of the system of higher education."

"Financial well-being was visible in [community] colleges that were the pride of local communities," wrote William L. Deegan, a Florida State University professor, and Dale Tillery, professor emeritus at the University of California, Berkeley, in their 1985 book *Renewing the American Community College*.

"The year 1970 was one of great confidence in the community colleges," Deegan and Tillery wrote. "Their campuses were among the best in the land, and as community centers they served a large segment of the public. The faculty and administrators were well-educated, and many of their leaders were graduates of major university leadership programs. Federal policies and groups, such as the Carnegie Commission on Higher Education, encouraged continued but disciplined expansion."

The Carnegie Commission had been created in 1967, to build a vision and plan for American higher education "at a time of great social and political upheaval on the nation's campuses and in society at large," Brint and Karabel noted. In its widely read 1970 report *The Open-Door College: Policies for Community Colleges*, the commission proposed that all community colleges should be "open-door" institutions, with very low or no tuition fees, and admitting "all applicants who are high school graduates or are persons over 18 years of age who are capable of benefiting from continuing education."

The Carnegie Commission also proposed that by 1980, America's network of community colleges should have so greatly expanded that 95 percent of all Americans could commute to one. To reach that goal, it recommended the building of between 230 and 280 new two-year colleges across the nation.

In Vermont, the state's mountainous geography and hardscrabble economy made it plainly impossible to build enough new colleges to bring higher education to 95 percent of its people. So in 1970, Peter Smith and his collaborators in the Vermont Regional Community College Commission were getting set to try something quite different: doing away with the campus altogether.

Instead, they would take an approach that was similar to the one San Francisco Junior College had tried, without much notice, over three decades before.

•••

INVENTING A COLLEGE

'To be able to invent'

"It was completely unpredicted, unpredictable, and in some regards bizarre that I would end up at age twenty-four being the executive director of this commission that was going to start a college," recalled Peter Smith. "But what took me there were experiences I had in Outward Bound and the National Outdoor Leadership School, post-high school and before I graduated from college. I was going to be an outdoor experiential educator, because I had really fallen in love with the notion of how much you learn when you're actually doing things."

After graduating from Princeton with a history degree in spring 1968, Smith began graduate studies in education at Harvard. But "when I did my student teaching, I was put off by the way high school was structured," he said. "I found the whole thing, for me personally, very stifling. So I came back to Vermont and did an internship with then-Commissioner of Education Harvey Scribner.

"At his request I created something called DUO, Do Unto Others. It was a high school experiential learning program in which kids could get a semester off, sophomores or juniors, to do work in the community and then return to school. We ended up with something like twelve or fifteen high schools doing it.

"After I finished my internship, I started a street academy in Montpelier for dropouts. There was no faculty, it was a storefront school. I did that for about four months. Along came the community college opportunity, the commission, and I signed up for that.

"I wanted to be able to invent, but the whole point was to come up with an approach to curriculum that was activity-based, outcomes-based. We were going to use the resources of the community. In other words, we weren't going to have the usual inputs that tell you — or told you theoretically — there was quality in a college. We had to have *outcomes, results, consequences* that would *prove* that somebody knew what we said they knew.

"We just decided to do it. That's how it happened. It was a very unlikely story."

KIND OF A MIRACLE

'You better do something with this time'

Smith had grown up in an old Vermont family with a background of privilege. His father, grandfather and great-grandfather each served as president of the Burlington Savings Bank, and his great-uncle was a lieutenant governor. After finishing college at the height of the Vietnam War, Smith applied to Officer Candidate School to serve in the military, "but I got turned down because I had some fundamental problems with my body, my physical structure. So I got drafted.

"I'm on a bus to Albany to have my physical the following week, and I took my X-rays with me of my faulty joints, hips and shoulders. I showed them at the end of the day to a doctor, and he said, 'Oh no, we can't draft you — you can't fall on your elbows. Your body won't take it.'

"So I'm riding home on the bus and I'm sitting in the back, looking out a window, and I said to myself, 'Goddammit Peter, you are going to know people — I already had several friends who had been drafted and were in the front lines — you are going to know people who died. You better do something with this time.'"

When the opportunity arose to direct the community college experiment, "what I saw immediately was that this was a large unregulated area," he said. "We could start classes without being a college.

"I think it's honest and fair to say that my privilege, my Princeton and Harvard degrees, my family having been in Vermont since 1812 or something — I think that helped. We needed to buy three or four years" to get started, "and everybody thought we were going to fail anyway, so why waste any energy on these guys? Why bother with Peter Smith, he'll take care of himself. I think my background cleared the way for people to deal with the idea on its merits, because they knew me.

"I was the first employee of the Vermont Regional Community College Commission, and I literally drew on my living floor a flowchart of how I thought the learner experience should go. The essence of it was that *time* was going to be a variable and *learning* was going to be what we paid attention to. 'What is it you need to know, and how can we help you learn it in a community-based setting?'

"It was very different, in 1970, to be talking like that, and to be assessing prior experiential learning — saying, 'What you bring with you matters. We're going to help you understand that, and we're going to build on that.'"

'Let's see what happens'

"If you would ask me what was the hallmark of Peter Smith, it was that he encouraged experimentation," said Ken Hood, a well-regarded educator who had been superintendent of two Vermont school supervisory unions before becoming Smith's de facto chief of staff in 1972. "Peter didn't fear new ideas, and he didn't fear other people having new ideas. 'Let's see what happens.' I see that as his strength."

"Peter seemed to be one of those people who was completely fearless, with little doubt about what he could accomplish when he set his mind to it," observed Dick Eisele, who began teaching for the college in 1970, joined its administrative staff in 1975, and continued to teach courses for nearly fifty years. "So when he decided to do something, he just went ahead and did it, confident that it would work out."

"Instead of developing an elaborate plan to get this new 'college' underway," Eisele said, "he decided to jump right in and offer courses in the community, see what happens, and do the planning later. Let people see that it works right from the start."

"Peter's gift was the ability to put the human together with the leadership. He always had a good sense of humor about himself," said John Turner, who opened the new college's Brattleboro site in 1971. "The image I have is one time, when trying to impress some respectable people with the professionalism of the college, in the process of making a point he fell over backwards in his chair."

The experimental project officially became the Community College of Vermont in 1973, and Smith served as its founding president until 1978. He went on to earn a doctorate from the Harvard Graduate School of Education and served as a Vermont state senator (1981–1983), lieutenant governor (1983–1986), and the state's representative in the U.S. Congress (1989–1990).

After his single term in Congress, Smith became dean of George Washington University's Graduate School of Education, founding president of California State University, Monterey, then assistant director general for education at UNESCO, the United Nations Educational, Scientific and Cultural Organization. Currently a professor of innovative practices in higher education at the University of Maryland's online-focused University College, he is the author of four books on higher education and learning in today's changing world. The two most recent are *Free-Range Learning in the Digital Age: The Emerging Revolution in College, Career and Education* (New York: SelectBooks, 2018) and *Stories from the Educational Underground: The New Frontier for Learning and Work* (Dubuque: IA: Kendall Hunt, 2021).

People who worked closely with Smith in CCV's earliest days often mention the seemingly undentable optimism that he brought to a time for the college that was exciting and creative — but stacked high with challenges, resistance and uncertainty.

"Peter had a way of declaring victory," said Ken Hood. "He was great that way."

Chapter 2

What Do You Want to Learn?

"That's the thing about a community-based institution: You have to be in sync with the needs of the people in the community," Smith observed in an interview. "You can't sit up on your hill and decide what's important for other people — you have to continually listen and adapt and adopt. If I'm proud of one thing other than being around in the beginning, it's that we started a culture of putting the learner and learning and the community first, and building all our resources around that."

When Smith became the director — and briefly, the only employee — of the Vermont Regional Community College Commission (VRCC) in November 1970, "there was no model we could copy to do what we wanted to do, so we hired a bunch of people and started," he said. "That December we started planning, and in January of 1971 we had sixty students in the Northeast Kingdom and in Montpelier at U-32 High School. It was 'What do you want to learn and how can we help you?'"

Having given the project that modest start-up grant of just under $60,000 in 1970, the Vermont OEO extended its financial lifeline in 1971, awarding the VRCC a two-year, federally funded grant of

$496,268. State government was not providing any other funding, and wouldn't until 1973. The OEO funding kept the shaky experiment just barely off the ground.

"To call this unlikely by any logic would be an understatement. I look back in wonderment," Smith said. "The real heroes are Margery Walker, John Chater, Tom Yahn, John Turner, Nancy Chard and all sorts of people. I'm sitting downtown in Montpelier dreaming big dreams and writing grants, trying to determine where true north is and trying to handle the politics; but they're out in the street with real people, saying, 'Would you like to go to college?' 'Well, what college is it?' 'Well, we're just sort of starting it.'

"And that takes incredible courage."

Setting up shop

The commission's office in Montpelier soon moved from its condemned second-floor hotel room to a brick building on State Street that was next door to the Pavilion building, home to the governor's office and the Vermont Historical Society Museum.

"We were on the first floor," Smith recalled, "and something called Bad Acid, which is a drug prevention program that I had started with a couple of other people, was on the second floor. Bad Acid is 223-ACID [local phone number], we thought we were so frickin' clever. Anyway, we were there for a year and a half, and then we moved to Langdon Street," above Onion River Sports, a shop selling outdoor sports equipment.

The first regional sites, as they were called, soon opened: in December 1970 at Union 32 High School in East Montpelier, for Central Vermont; in spring 1971 for the Northeast Kingdom, Vermont's northeasternmost region, in Barton, St. Johnsbury and Newport; and in August 1971 in Bellows Falls, for Windham and Windsor counties in the southeast.

"Each regional site was staffed by a coordinator, assistant coordinator, counselor, counselor aides and a secretary," said the September 1971 report the Regional College Commission prepared for the Legislature. "The Commission feels that by actually operating in the field during the planning phase of the [OEO] grant, the Commission can, in fact, test the potential demand for its educational services, and encounter the major operational problems and obstacles of a community college system."

These first courses were offered in spring '71:

- In Central Vermont: typing, child development, consumer protection, art appreciation, "Career Opportunity Program," "Understanding Human Behavior."

- In the Northeast Kingdom: child development, community leadership, cosmetology, Canadian studies, "Industrial Arts & Crafts," "Learner & Learning Process."

Total students enrolled: 150. Total who completed their courses: 101.

The first courses were free, and would be for some time. The teachers, generally community members who had expertise they wanted to share, all volunteered their time.

"We have found many people with the capacity for effective teaching who may not have ordinary teaching backgrounds," said the report to the Legislature. To create a system for evaluating courses, the commission recruited a consulting team that included two UVM professors, the planning director at the state Department of Education, and the administrative assistant to Robert Babcock, provost (and de facto CEO) of the Vermont State Colleges.

Those first students were all adults, all older than traditional college ages. The great majority were women. And their numbers grew fast.

"One simple measure of VRCC achievement is the steadily increasing number of students attending the college, from roughly 100 during the first trimester to over 700 during the fourth," said the commission's first annual report, sent to Gov. Davis in August 1972. "During the past year, demand for VRCC services by potential students exceeded VRCC available courses by nearly two to one."

That first annual report divided the initial "18-month developmental period" of the Regional Community College Commission into two phases:

The first phase saw the Commission staff identifying problems, and asking questions pertinent to the operation of a non-campus, open-access college in Vermont.

KIND OF A MIRACLE

> *By December 1971, the staff had identified an operating structure which would allow local flexibility while ensuring the delivery of quality educational services to VRCCC students. This structure included the development of curriculum, learning support for teachers and students, management and planning at all levels, internal information systems, and staff training.*
>
> *... The second phase included field testing some of the ideas and solutions generated during phase one ... and increasing the professionalism of staff. This phase ended on July 31, 1972. Thus, when the Community College opens in the fall, 1972, a trained staff will be operating a field-tested model.*

Hiring by intuition, casting for ideas

"Smith's first move was to hire the runner-up for his job," wrote Larry Daloz, who would soon join the central office staff.

John Chater, that first hire, had been director of the Barton Parent Child Center and "was the son of a Protestant minister and a Goddard [College] graduate," Daloz wrote. "Immersed in the perspective of the community action and Head Start programs of the mid-Sixties, Chater forged early links with poverty programs in the central and northeastern parts of the state.... Chater knew most of the leadership of the low-income associations personally, and was liked by them. His presence proved of fundamental importance during the first, early years."

John Chater

"In hiring their staff, Smith and Chater never attempted to define needed job skills ... relying primarily on their intuition and hiring 'people we liked, felt comfortable with,'" Daloz continued. "They knew they wanted people who could 'relate to low-income people,' who were open to unconventional approaches and — perhaps most important — whom they felt they could trust. Formal academic qualifications were of secondary importance and, in fact, were somewhat suspect.

INVENTING A COLLEGE

"Smith and his team cast about wildly for ideas, writing dozens of letters," Daloz wrote in "Radicals," his unpublished 1978 account of the college's creation. They wrote to Donald Rumsfeld, then head of the federal Office of Economic Opportunity, who ignored them. They wrote to Clark Kerr of the Carnegie Commission on Higher Education. "Kerr's response.... was to say that what they had described was not a college at all, would never work, and that they ought to refund the money and forget the whole thing."

Larry Daloz

From "Radicals":

"It was devastating," recalls Smith. "But what happened was that I gave up the whole notion that I could go someplace and find the answer.... So we said the hell with it; we're not going to ask anyone else."

The early months of the college seem to have been a passionate mix of earnest talk and impulsive action. Turbulent philosophical disputes surged back and forth among the more articulate staff members while the others sat back frustrated, dreaming, or simply puzzled. Friere, Holt, Kozol, Horton, Illich, Dewey, Chickering, Postman — these were the books on their shelves in those days.

At about that time, Chater moved out to the northeastern part of the state and began bringing together small clusters of low-income people to help them articulate their needs. Community, he believed, was an integral part of the adult student's life. Education must not take the student out of the community but rather must help learners understand the role and meaning of community in their own lives. That was the whole problem with academic education, he would argue: it separated people from their contexts instead of helping them make connections. Once a person got an education, they would turn their back on their communities, cast off friends, and head for the big city.

> *Courses must be* relevant *to the lives and needs of the learners where they lived. The first course he organized was "Hairdressing." Twenty-five people in Barton, a town with a population of less than a thousand, signed up.*

'We knew very well what we were up against'

Joining the start-up as a planner was Stephen F. Hochschild, who was doing a field study for the doctorate he earned in 1971 at Harvard.

"Steve's role was as planner with a capital P," said Daloz, who soon would also join the staff. "Steve was the rationalist and the system thinker. He was the guy that brought a kind of a crisp, hard-edged planning consciousness, accountability consciousness to this conversation, which was sort of theoretical and fourteen feet off the ground in those early years.

"I played, I think maybe it's fair to say, a kind of a medial role between Steve's hardcore planning on the one hand and Peter's blue-sky, fast-talking, highly creative, iconoclastic vision and imagination."

Daloz would play a central role in developing the new college's approach to teaching and learning. He had grown up in Boston, where his father and grandfather owned a dry-cleaning business. He graduated from a traditional prep school, "very patriarchal and straitlaced," earned a bachelor's degree at Williams College and a master's in teaching English at Harvard — then spent two years in the Peace Corps, teaching English in eastern Nepal. Reentering Harvard for a doctorate in educational planning, he did two years of fieldwork in Papua New Guinea.

"That kind of yanked me out of traditional educational models, the combination of Nepal and Papua New Guinea," Daloz remembered. Back from overseas, he and his wife moved to Glover, a small town in the Northeast Kingdom. They began building a geodesic dome for their home, "because we'd become part of what became known as the back-to-the-land movement." At Harvard he had come to know Hochschild, and now the two "got talking about this project that he'd become involved with."

Daloz joined the project for six months as a consultant in 1971, to put together a system for supporting its volunteer teachers. The college had, he explained, "developed the idea of 'regional site teams' — groups

INVENTING A COLLEGE

From the Regional Community College Commission's first bulletin, autumn 1971.

of teacher and student support professionals whose primary job is to bring together those who need information with those who have it," Daloz wrote in "Giving Education Back to the Learner," a 1975 article in the *International Journal of Career and Continuing Education*.

"So for six months I traveled around, talking with other teacher-support people around the state," Daloz said. After that he joined the staff. "I was called the coordinator of learning services because it was 'flat.' I was the academic dean, in fact, but we would never have used that term in those days."

"Those were times of sharp reassessment of our institutions — from hospitals to churches to college," Daloz said in a 1992 talk to the CCV faculty. "We knew very well what we were up against: grades, credits, immobile classrooms, entrenched faculties, textbooks.... We were less clear what we stood for, but we knew that the individual was important.... We were trying to invent a college from the ground up, and the idea of individualized, self-directed learning was central.

"We dusted off an old term and brought it forth into Vermont in the back-to-the-land Seventies: *self-reliant learning*. In fact, it was not a bad idea."

The Central Vermont Region staff, 1973. Front row, left to right: Barbara Ploof, Karen Saudek, John Chater. Back row, left to right: Judy Cyprian, Jan Garber-Hanke, Ivy Freeman, Carol Brasswell, Sylvia Walker, Don Hooper, Clo Pitkin, Howard Fisher, Judy Tomasi, Terry Knight.

INVENTING A COLLEGE

'It began to turn some heads': Memories from the first regional sites

Here are recollections from some of those who worked at the regional sites in the college's start-up years:

Dick Eisele

Dick taught one of the very first courses in Montpelier. He continued teaching, and then joined the staff in 1975 to manage a new summer program in Central Vermont. He remained on the college staff until 2005 and taught CCV courses until 2018.

The following is from "CCV Stories," a collection of reminiscences gathered by Mary Ellen Lowe and Megan Tucker for the college's website. This piece was posted on November 19, 2013.

I was hired by Charlie Parker to teach a class in Understanding Human Behavior to twelve adults, mostly women. Charlie (known commonly as Parker man) was one of the first employees hired by founding President Peter Smith to help get classes for adult learners started in central Vermont....

My first class was held in the basement of the Bethany Church in downtown Montpelier. All CCV classes, at that time, were held wherever free or cheap space could be found.... At that time there was no formal registration, no tuition, no teacher pay, no grades, and no credits. This amazing experiment in community education was strictly a matter of matching adults in the community who wanted to learn something with other people from the same community who had the appropriate talents to teach them. How cool was that?... From that first class on, I was hooked on teaching adults.

The typical student in my early Montpelier classes ... was a married or recently divorced adult woman who had suspended her educational goals to raise a family and, in some cases, find part-time work. These women (of course there were also a few men in my early CCV classes, and there were lots of men in early classes like welding) were smart and highly motivated. CCV was providing the opportunity for them to ease back into formal education at the college level and do it locally. I could tell this was an incredible innovative experiment that had the potential to fill a large gap in Vermont's existing system of higher educational offerings.... However, even the best situations often have a down-side somewhere. More than a few of the women students, in my early classes, expressed to me that their enthusiasm for learning and the changes they were experiencing were not appreciated at home. In effect, their participation in college courses served to disrupt their marriages, especially marriages that may have been somewhat fragile to begin with....

I quickly came to realize that CCV, still in its infancy, was right near the forefront of adult higher education in the country. Clo Pitkin and Mary Wade were the "brains" behind the counseling program, Don Hooper and Tim Welch supported the Central Vermont teachers and were the creators of the first teacher handbook (*Educational Wampum*), and Margery Walker directed the Central Vermont program. Ken Hood, former Superintendent of the Washington West school district, came in to help Peter with the management side of the college. Scott Bassage was the registrar who led the college's effort to organize, institutionalize and articulate registration procedures and incorporate a record-keeping system. In the sites some of the key figures that come to mind were Tom Yahn, John Turner, Nancy Chard, and Priscilla Newell in the Southern Region, John Findlay in the NEK, and Peggy Williams, Susan Smallwood, and Pixley Hill in the Northwest.

Ken Hood

Ken joined the central office staff in 1972, serving as Peter Smith's de facto chief of staff until 1977. He worked in administration at Johnson State College from 1977 to 1978, and then became an assistant professor of education and associate dean of the College of Education at the University of Vermont.

I was a school superintendent in two different districts in Vermont. When I was superintendent at Washington West, Peter had just begun the community college, and he came over to me about offering courses. I asked him, "Peter, what can you do for me that I can't do for myself?" His answer was, "Damned if I know." That's Peter. I went full-time with him in 1972.

I think in retrospect that it began to turn some heads — that maybe this thing called the community college had some validity to it. The validity really was built by people like Tom Yahn in Southern Vermont, Clo Pitkin in Central Vermont — people like that. Their relationship to people out in the field was the critical part of building it. Tom had an uncanny knack of getting people who had a local influence to be okay with this new idea. He created a lot of comfort in people.

And Peter really let people experiment a lot. It would be an error on my part if I said the site in Springfield was the same as the site in Central Vermont. They were pretty different from each other. At the same time, given their audiences, in retrospect they were very effective.

It was the best educational experience I've ever had. There were a lot of experiments — and even though a few of them failed, I don't think many people thought of them as failures. We thought, "Yeah, that didn't work, but we learned a lot, and let's move on." I think that was the general attitude at CCV.

Don Hooper

Don was the first coordinator of instruction at the Central Vermont site. He then served as regional director in the late 1970s. He was later a member of the Vermont House of Representatives, and served as Vermont secretary of state and as Northeast regional representative for the National Wildlife Federation.

After Harvard I went in the Peace Corps to Botswana, and I spent three years teaching school and building the school where I taught. At the end of those three years, in 1971, I came back to get a master's degree at Harvard. One of the case studies at the Harvard Grad School of Education was on CCV. Stephen Hochschild, a bright bright guy, was getting his doctorate by being the planner who kind of charted the course for Smith and the other insurgents who began the college.

I was so dubious when he presented this case study in some administration course I was taking. I said, "This is such a crock of shit. You guys are elitists, you think you know what the working class wants. This is just a pipe dream." He said, "Well, if you feel that way, why don't you come up and take a look?" So I did!

I stayed overnight with Steve and went to a weekend [CCV] program — and I was so impressed. They were teaching people how to balance a checkbook, how to shop for groceries that weren't all garbage ... this was a special program for people who generally didn't have a GED. It was the original adult education. They didn't make any distinction between people who were trying to get a degree; there was none of that. We wanted to teach courses that would help people improve their skills, to get more money to have a more sustainable lifestyle.

I was so attracted by this thing, and they said, "We are looking for a site coordinator here in Central Vermont. Why don't you put an application in?" Well, they hired me. I had been looking for a place that had the same sort of community as Botswana did, and Vermont impressed me in that way.

We called ourselves coordinators of instruction. We were sort of back-to-the-land hippie types. The curriculum we put together in Central Vermont consisted of about fifty to seventy courses a term, for three times a year — a summer session, a fall and a spring. The courses generally speaking went for fifteen weeks, one night a week, three hours. My job was to hire teachers to teach for free, in church basements, high school auditoriums, wherever we could find. I used the Christ Church every single night in Montpelier, the Methodist Church, wherever. Allan Mackey taught a history of rock 'n' roll in the Thrush Tavern. Billy Brauer taught a course in life drawing in Applegate Horse Stables — a jockey's room or something. We used any place we could find.

INVENTING A COLLEGE

An early class, in the back stockroom of a hardware store.

You've got to go back to the '60s — this was our community service. We were going to turn the world upside down. We were going to be the generation that made a difference. So we just appealed to other people to make the same difference, and son of a gun, they stepped up.

Typically, we'd start [a class] with fifteen students, and if it was a good teacher, end with a dozen. My job as coordinator of instruction was to go out every night and visit those classes that we thought were maybe in trouble and see if I could see what might be going wrong. They were just teaching their skill, doing the thing that they do. We didn't have any kind of infrastructure for training them, even presuming we could. So our job was to determine from the students, particularly, who was succeeding. Then we would bring [those teachers] back.

We were dead set against grading. What we did instead was say, to each student, "You have a goal for taking this class. Help the teacher understand what that goal is on night number one. You establish what will be the goal that you're working toward, what will be the completion requirements, and what will be the methods you and the teacher together are going to use to get there. At the end of all that, the teacher's going to write, and you are too, a narrative evaluation of whether you succeeded."

We got a guy to teach welding in Montpelier. Francis Brooks, who was a chemistry teacher at Montpelier High School, taught chemistry. I had a guy in Barre who taught auto body repair; I made him a fleet of sawhorses. Marsh Gardner taught a course in tuning up your engine.

We had five or six counselors on our Montpelier staff. Margery Walker was our captain. They worked with students to design a program for each of them that was individualized, so they had some sense of continuity and integrity to what it was they were going to take, if they wanted to achieve something as lofty as a two-year degree.

Jeff Danziger

After serving in Vietnam with the U.S. Army from 1967 to 1971, Jeff taught English for eleven years at Union 32 High School in East Montpelier and became one of CCV's first Central Vermont instructors. He began to draw cartoons, political and otherwise, for the Vermont press in 1971. Now a nationally syndicated editorial cartoonist, he won the 2006 Herblock Prize and the 2008 Thomas Nast Prize for his work.

I taught a course in literature of the world wars and a course in home plumbing. In the old days in Vermont, you did your own plumbing. It just seemed like a community thing.

I don't think they ever cancelled a class at the early CCV just because only four people showed up. It was enjoyable; it was fun. It was Vermont, where people basically want to have a group effort. They want to talk, have a confab. So it wasn't that you're the teacher and you're the great knowledgeable person.

You met some very good people, you got to spend an evening — you've got to remember, this was back before cable. Everybody brought cookies and cider and milk and enjoyed themselves.

INVENTING A COLLEGE

Peggy Williams

Peggy became regional director in St. Albans for the Northern Region, including Franklin, Grand Isle, Lamoille, Orleans and Essex counties. She went on to serve as president of Vermont's Lyndon State College, then became the first woman president of Ithaca College in New York.

In the fall of '72 I started the Lamoille [County] office with a colleague. I literally responded to an ad in the newspaper. There was a region in Washington County, and the idea was to expand to Lamoille — and the key here is, we were invited. Bill Craig, the president of Johnson State College, said to Peter Smith, "Come here and set up shop." The notion of having an office on one of the college campuses was really radical, but Bill Craig was a very, very smart man, and so we started. We literally had a table, two chairs and a telephone in the lobby of one of the residence halls.

Peggy Williams

We were in Cambridge at the VFW building, we were in Morrisville at a church, in Hyde Park at Lamoille Union [High School], in People's Academy in Morrisville and Stowe High School. We did everything, from recruiting to hiring the faculty to negotiating all of these spaces and places. You know, there is an amazing amount of talent around.

We said that students aren't going to pay anything. We used to give people mail-in envelopes; you put money in if you want. And we had no registration — we registered people on a blank piece of paper.

CCV when it started out was really intended for the adult learners. We were not looking to recruit students out of high school — we didn't have much to offer them. We were selling it as a community service, as an important way to provide access to adult learners, to get started or to finish their college career. I think we just kept making that argument as to why we believed that this kind of place was, you know, important.

If you've ever taught adult learners, they're fabulous because they're very active. They sit in the front row and they bring their experience to the table, and you're lucky if you get to say anything — versus a lecture to lovely eighteen-year-olds who are waiting for you to teach them something and maybe they'll respond. My husband taught one of his courses in our living room.

We built policies because we needed them, not because you needed a fat book sitting on the table. They say in the world of organizational development "policy follows practice," and in many ways we were the epitome of that.

The thing that was so important for my own development was that at a very young age I was a member of the President's Council. I reported directly to Peter Smith, and I sat around the table with him and the other regional directors and the CFO and the head of academics and hammered these things out. We were a very agreeable group, a bright group, all willing to be kind of part of this experiment — and Peter just had incredible energy and vision. He was best when he left things alone: "Let's agree to do that, now you just go ahead." But he was accessible, and he was fun.

In all of our offices we had what was called a CIA, coordinator of instruction and advisement. They recruited the faculty, they recruited the students, they provided student support services. Day in, day out, they were the face of the institution.

INVENTING A COLLEGE

John Findlay

A native of Lyndonville, John was on the CCV staff from 1973 to 1979, first as a coordinator of learner support and then as Northeast Kingdom regional director. He went on to teach history at Lyndon Graded School, and then at Lyndon Town School, until he retired in 2009.

I graduated from Lyndon State in 1971, major in history, minor in education, and I was all excited about teaching, but we'd glutted the market — I couldn't get a job. The community college was getting into providing education for low-income people. They had an opening and darned if I didn't get the job.

I got hired in '73. In '74 they ran out of money, and they closed the Northeast Kingdom offices, but they kept two of us. When they decided to reopen the site, I got the job of director, and we hired a new staff and went on from there. When I started our office was in St. Johnsbury, but then we were on the campus of Lyndon State [in Lyndonville]. We had another office in Newport.

You know, college was a big deal — and a lot of people had grown up with the idea, especially if they were low income, that they weren't "college material." So we had a lot to overcome, just repeatedly meeting with them, sometimes individually, sometimes in groups. We'd set up classes, and there were usually very few people in the class. I did tours of historic sites around the Northeast Kingdom, and I had a big group of people who were not the usual community college students. But by becoming involved, they learned that we weren't the bad guys.

The other state colleges were really resistant, particularly at Lyndon. But some faculty members, including someone named June Elliot, gave us a home up there in her learning center. Then eventually I decided it was too hostile on the campus at Lyndon State, and a local superintendent took us into a spare room in his office. That was on Church Street in Lyndonville. It wasn't until a few years later that [the state college] began to see us as a feeder institution. We sent some of our students to them, and they began to see the other side.

A lot of [newly recruited instructors] thought, "Oh, teaching — that would be kind of cool." One particular guy was on the school board in Lyndon. He had a department store, but he was also a CPA. He was very opposed to us even being in the superintendent's office, but he was a good listener — so he said, "Oh, so that's what you're trying to do." He had a couple of students that he knew would like to take his accounting course. So not only did we get a teacher, but it was excellent public relations: All of a sudden the school-board guy, who was seen as kind of a high-powered guy around town, was a big supporter. He recommended his friends to help us teach other courses.

We got in with a welding supply company in St. J, and then we opened a whole new branch, had guys taking welding courses, and then they told their friends. Then we did typing — and all of a sudden typing, accounting and welding all took off in different directions. So we went recruiting and building, and things got bigger and bigger.

We had offices in Island Pond, in Newport. I think we had a branch in Canaan — that's remote even by Northeast Kingdom standards! I kept doing more and more, but I used to joke with Peter Smith: I think I'm approaching the Peter Principle, where I'm doing beyond what I'm capable of. Meanwhile, I was working in the superintendent's office, and he said, "You know, we're going to have an opening this year for a history teacher at Lyndon Graded School."

Nancy Fried

After she had earned a degree in English at the University of Michigan and taught English for a year at the American International School in Vienna, Nancy and her husband, Kim, moved in 1971 to Newark, a very small town in northeastern Vermont.

I started in '73 at the community college — at that time it was really the bare beginnings. Our first office was in the back of the superintendent's office on Church Street in Lyndonville. After that we were next to the employment office in St. Johnsbury, then we went upstairs over the bank in St. Johnsbury. We didn't have big offices.

I was the coordinator of instruction, getting all the courses together. I worked with Larry Daloz; he was up in Glover. We depended on the community — our classes were in schools, high schools, we had some in churches, all community buildings.

I was lucky. So many people moved up to Vermont at that period who were just so talented and educated. We had this great vision for a community-based college, so for the instructors I was able to get people like Topher Waring from Northeast Kingdom Mental Health, who ran the woodworking courses we did for the area. They had woodworking shops, and he did courses up in Glover. We had Mark Craven — he taught a lot of courses that were very popular, psychology and philosophy courses. We did a history of the blues course; this guy Dave Davis had one of the best collections of records, and they did it in the Drawing Room, a coffeehouse that was under the bridge in St. Johnsbury.

Larry Daloz had a whole program for students where they could get credit for life experience. They had to develop a portfolio. I think we even did an auto mechanics course at one point. Benji Tessier, who was the head of the business department at Lyndon Institute [Lyndonville's high school], taught tons of courses for us, in bookkeeping and typing. So many of the teachers were just such talented people.

I worked with students to help them develop their portfolios on life experiences. For a lot of Vermonters, it gave them an opportunity to come to school. People who were so talented in their professions and maybe couldn't afford to go to college before were able to document their life learning. And all the community college people, working across the state — it was such a great mix of people.

I stayed with the college for four years. When I got pregnant with my second child, I took a couple of years off, then I went back for my master's degree in education and counseling. After that I did thirty years of counseling for the St. Johnsbury school district.

Tom Yahn

Tom directed the Windham/Windsor regional site from 1971 to 1977 and ran the college's Summer Residency Program in 1978. He became a core faculty member in the Adult Degree Program at Goddard College, and in the mid-'80s he founded the Brattleboro Center of Vermont College, serving as center director until 2002. As New England regional program director for the Foundation for Excellent Schools, he developed programs that encouraged high school students to aim for college, and he served until his retirement as director of the Collegiate High School, a dual high school–college enrollment program at Brattleboro Union High School.

Like so many of us, I went to an Ivy League school, Dartmouth, and didn't learn much except for a lot of useless information. Then I went to New York City because I had a girlfriend down there. I got involved with the Welfare Department; I had a caseload of like ninety people on the Lower East Side. Got connected with a couple of community action groups; we started something called the University of the Streets. We had educational programs for these kids that were taught by people like Miles Davis, for example — people that looked like them, that they trusted. I learned a lot about starting *with* kids, rather than starting with what you think kids need.

I just decided one day I had to get out. I took a trip to Vermont, just hanging out, and I bumped into Peter Smith on the streets of Montpelier. I think the Vermont Regional Community College Commission had been around for about a year. He was looking for somebody to run the [Windsor/Windham] operation. It's how we operated in those days: Don't check with anybody, don't see if they really can do what they say they can do, just hire 'em and hope for the best. I wanted to be in Vermont and my wife wanted to be in Vermont, so why not?

We had to get courses out there, somehow get them advertised, and get people to sign up. We asked the community to volunteer to teach. I remember having community meetings

INVENTING A COLLEGE

Throughout the early years, women were in the great majority as CCV students.

that Peter helped us set up — kind of like town hall meetings, where we talked both about becoming a teacher and becoming a student. Because we were square one: Come one, come all.

Shortly after that we came up with a course list. We created these great courses and advertised them to the community in this open-ended way. I think we had mimeographed course lists that we put around in restaurants and pinned up in store windows. But we had no constituency. We had no student body per se, the first few times around.

And I can remember many a night waiting, with a teacher who had put their heart and soul into designing a course, for people to show up. And nobody would. Then I would say, "Well how about if we do this again next week, same time same place?" We would just keep trying.

We were staffed by lawyers, all kinds of cool people from the community that were part of that whole radical chic thing. We had an office in Windsor, and I can tell you a long tale about setting up courses in Windsor prison that became very successful, very well-attended. People couldn't miss class!

One of our big clientele were Head Start workers, who were mainly women. They had a lot of what I call tacit knowledge: knowledge that they have but don't know how they have it. How do you unearth that? That kind of reflective practice is really key to education with adults. Help them reflect on their own experiences and make meaning out of their stories.

We were turning learning upside down. There was a vast amount of knowledge in the experiences of people that were coming to us; it was now our job to turn that experience into meaning, through our coursework, where they said, "Oh, Freud said that! I understand what he's talking about now, or I understand why that happened to me."

John Turner

John served in the Peace Corps in the Philippines, and then worked for CCV in Brattleboro from 1971 to 1976. After leaving CCV, he returned to the Philippines to do community development work for two years in remote, indigenous communities. Back in Vermont, he became a management training consultant for the Vermont Department of Human Resources, and then director of human resources at the state Department of Education from 2000–2012. He taught CCV courses for fifteen years in Montpelier.

John's narrative below is drawn in part from a "CCV Stories" interview, conducted circa December 1977 and published on the CCV website on July 15, 2013. The rest is from an interview with the author.

Peter was traveling around the state looking to expand the program. He hired me and four other people to start it in Windsor County. This was the late summer of '71.

I was in Brattleboro. We invited Peter to come down and talk. We invited the whole community to come learn about the Community College of Vermont.... Three people showed up. Peter got into a long discussion with a woman. It spilled out into the street, and just as they were ready to part, the woman, who later graduated from CCV, said to Peter, "By the way, what do you do with CCV?" ...

The first time we went into Brattleboro, we invited the editor of the newspaper and all the civic leaders. The five of us stood up front like a lineup and proceeded to tell these very sophisticated, very tough-minded people we're going to start a college in your town. We're not going to pay teachers any salary; we're not going to build a campus; we're going to have a community faculty, and students don't have to pay anything. All I remember was the manager of the local radio station saying as politely as he could, "You people will not be around a year from now," and the editor saying it was a rip-off of the taxpayers' money.

...[O]ne of the first courses when we started to get a "respectable" crowd, some of the mainstream Brattleboro society instead of the commune-hippie crowd, was an American Literature course. The guy who taught it was living in a commune in Putney. We decided to have the course out at his place. So I remember driving these four straight Presbyterian women up to the course. He said, "Why don't we meet outdoors?" He didn't have any shoes on... and he had purple nail polish on. So he begins outlining the course and these women are sitting on a wagon, and he's talking. Out of the farmhouse bounce four people with a volleyball, who proceed to play in front of the class ... totally nude. It was the last time I saw any of those women ever again.

In the early days it was mostly women, a lot of single women, struggling to survive. There was one woman who told me she wanted a course on literature — any kind of literature. She just wanted to read something. So I went to the public library in Brattleboro and said, "Can we use your room on Tuesday night?" They said sure, so we scheduled the time — and when the night came, the woman didn't show up. I went back to her and said, "I thought you wanted this. How come you didn't show up?" She said, "Oh, I didn't believe you."

I thought, I get it — why should you believe me? Here I come asking what you want to learn; you're a single mom with a couple of kids, you haven't had a lot of breaks in your life, so why should you believe me? So I said to her, "I get it. Okay, let me ask you the question again: What do you want to learn?"

It's really a question of developing credibility with people, especially people that traditionally have not been listened to.

It takes time, developing credibility that you're really going to make an attempt to match what they say they need with what you can offer them. So that was my driving fire for the five years I spent developing the program in Brattleboro.

There was a teacher of poetry who ran away once with one of our student's poetry....

We had a couple teaching Irish literature who quit in the middle of the summer; we never heard from them again....

Ron Krupp did yoga headstands during staff meetings while trying to do needs assessment. Staff members would disappear for forty minutes a day to meditate.

Once we printed up a thousand Certificates of Achievement with the word *achievement* misspelled....

There was an excessive need for meetings in those days. My best decision was to suggest that every time we failed to make a decision, we had to take off a piece of clothing.

A woman took a consciousness-raising course, having been married for forty years, during which she'd never been away from her husband for a single night. After the group she spent a night in a motel in Brattleboro alone. She came back to the class and said, "It was like going around the world. I was scared, but I made it back."

There was another forty-five-year-old woman who had put two or three daughters through school and had zero confidence in herself. She kept saying she couldn't do anything. She turned out to be one of the best early students we had. She went on to Antioch and now has a master's degree. She still tells me, "It was at CCV where I began to believe in myself."...

I always saw it as basically very revolutionary. I figured if we can give these people an opportunity to take control of their own learning, to have a major voice in what they learn and how they learn it, it has to run over into other aspects of their lives. That's important in our increasingly regimented society. It's romantic, but the alternative doesn't impress me.

'You want a vote of confidence?'

The purpose of the Vermont Regional Community College Commission was explained yesterday to a group of area citizens.
  Thomas Yahn, regional site coordinator for the commission, said the project hopes to develop an "outreach program" to provide college-level subjects for people in the Windham-Windsor County area.... The program is already underway in northern Vermont, Yahn said. Courses already taught include jewelry-making, early childhood development, basic automobile maintenance, and journalism.... The commission's major task in this area now, he said, is to see what courses are wanted by people, and to get them set up.

— Brattleboro Reformer, September 1971

If you want to learn something the College will try to find someone qualified to teach it. Classes are kept small and the teacher and students mutually decide what goals they want to reach and how they'll do it.

— Sam Hemingway, *Lamoille County Weekly*, July 1972

"*I met with the Chamber of Commerce to develop a relationship. At the end, the chair said, 'You want a vote of confidence?'*
  'Yes, sir.'
  'Well, you didn't get it.'"

— John Turner, first staff member in Brattleboro

Chapter 3

Finding the Money and Claiming a Place

For Peter Smith and his leadership team, the first two and a half years of steering and shaping this college-without-a-campus brought a tense scramble for enough money to keep going — and some close, very skeptical scrutiny from Vermont's higher education establishment.

The project survived both. In the process, it got through what Smith called two "near-death experiences," each of which nearly ended the experiment before it could find solid ground.

Interest among Vermonters was growing: The college's enrollment doubled between July 1972 and spring 1973, from 635 students to more than 1,200. "Demand for services continues to outweigh the College's capacity to provide services," its 1973 annual report said that September.

But from 1970 through early 1973, no state funds were allotted to the college, which was still charging no tuition. Without an income stream of its own, what was then the Vermont Regional Community College Commission had to survive on whatever grant money its leaders could bring in.

That took some persistent digging around.

"If I was good at something," Smith mused years later, "it was winding my way through the weeds to create the stability that we had to have in order to have a chance of being successful."

The first two grants of federal funds through the state Office of Economic Opportunity — $59,716 in 1970 and $496,268 in 1971 — enabled the project to deliver its initial hodgepodge of courses in communities from Brattleboro to the Northeast Kingdom. Then in mid-1972, after a two-day visit by a team from the Carnegie Foundation of New York City, that foundation awarded the VRCCC almost $100,000 to expand its operations and strengthen its field staff.

The Carnegie grant was also important "because it got written up in educational magazines," Smith said. "One called *Change* did a lead editorial on us."

"It would be sheer folly for Vermont to now drop the ball on this highly creative forward step, so essential to its citizens' survival in the Seventies," declared the editorial in the June 1973 issue of *Change*. "Vermonters, of all people, appreciate good work at a fair price, and they have it here in spades."

But with enrollment and demand rising, college leaders needed to find more funding — a lot more, and quickly. Then a day came when it appeared their quest would fail. It was, Smith later said, "the only moment when I was ever in despair."

In spring 1973, he made a fund-seeking trip to Washington, D.C., with Larry Daloz and Stephen Hochschild of the leadership team.

"What became the National Institute of Education, NIE, was just about to be formed," Smith recalled, "and the guy who was running it was Tom Glennan, the son of the man who first headed NASA, so a big name in Washington. We went down there to talk to OEO; we were just at the point where that money was ending. We needed to get more federal money, and NIE was our target.

"We sat down with this guy, and at the end of about thirty minutes he said, 'We are not interested in what you're doing. Don't even bother to send us a proposal.'

"We walked out, and Larry and Steve had to sit me down on a bench. It was like I almost lost control of my body. I'll never forget it: I thought, 'This is it. I can't see a path forward.' They were patting my back, saying,

'It's going to be okay, Peter' — and I was saying, 'No it's not! I don't see, I don't know how we're going to do this.'

"But we went over to see the people at OEO who had been taking care of us, Jane Hannaway, Carol Stoel and Chuck Bunting," Smith said. "They told us, 'Carol and Chuck are going to this new group called the Fund for the Improvement of Post-Secondary Education. Let's talk to them.'"

'You who have ideas, come to us'

Congress had recently passed and Richard Nixon had signed a package of education legislation that would have far-reaching impacts. Those 1972 amendments to the U.S. Higher Education Act included Title IX, which opened a new era in women's athletics by mandating that no one could be excluded based on gender from any education program receiving federal assistance. The amendments also created the Pell Grants, providing financial aid to undergraduate students from low-income families.

And although this got far less attention than those advances received, the legislation also set up a new federal initiative called FIPSE, the Fund for the Improvement of Post-Secondary Education.

"The fund and the Pell Grants were in response to the student unrest" of the time, said Carol Stoel, who became a FIPSE program officer. "The fund was charged with improvement: 'You who have ideas, come to us.'

"The first director of the fund was a woman named Virginia Smith," she said. "She came from the Carnegie Commission on Higher Education, so there was a lot of coming together of ideas and concerns. There was Pell money now, so students could apply for that and use it for their education. So the system had changed."

> ### Chuck Bunting
>
> *Chuck served with FIPSE from 1973 to 1980 as planning officer, deputy director and then acting director. He would later become chancellor of the Vermont State Colleges System.*
>
> We were given this money, about $10 million, and we had a very few months to spend it. We had a very talented group working in

Washington. We sent out some sort of broad guidelines looking for improvement projects — and we were completely inundated. We absolutely caught the feel of higher education at just the right time, in the 1970s, when it started really opening up in terms of access and broadening.

I remember I went to speak about the program at one professional conference in the first couple of years of FIPSE, and I was introduced by a guy from the University of Pennsylvania who was pretty stodgy. He said, "You know they call this thing the Fund for the Improvement of Post-Secondary Education. I think I would call it the Fund for the *Expansion* of Post-Secondary Education." He took that as a negative, that the doors were opening wider to people.

I would call the 1970s the most hopeful decade for higher education at least since World War II. So anyway, we were inundated with proposals — but one really stood out.

Here was a proposal to create a statewide community college. Almost all the other projects were important and significant but much smaller in dimension. So it definitely got our attention, but it scared us because it was going to be by far the largest grant we made. How could we check this thing out? How could we make sure we weren't going to fall completely flat on our faces?

So we figured, "We better reach the powers that be in this little state of Vermont and see what the future will be of this thing if it works."

"FIPSE sent three people up to do an assessment of us and what we needed," Smith said. "One was a woman named Kate Patricia Cross, who was a very well-known author on low-income access, outcomes-based education, assessment of prior learning, and all that stuff."

By then the college had started to develop an associate degree program (see the next section), which in its case included an effort to assign value to what students had learned through work and life experience. That initiative would become a major feature of Vermont's community college — but at this point it had only just begun.

"I'll never forget Pat Cross walking into my office, and I'm holding up a file which says something like 'Assessment of Prior Learning,'" Smith said. "She opens the file, and there's nothing in it.

"She looks at me and I say, 'Well, Dr. Cross, it's a work in progress!'"

While they were in Vermont, FIPSE's envoys "interviewed the chair of the House Appropriations Committee, Emery Hebbard, and Bill Craig, who was head of the Vermont State Colleges, and a couple of other people," Smith recalled. "They said, 'If we fund these guys, are you going to support them? Because we're not going to give this money if you're not going to support them.' And they all said, 'Yes.'"

But even as FIPSE weighed its decision, Smith learned that the state university in Burlington was preparing an action that would have blocked the grant, and could have ended the community college project. The University of Vermont had created its Division of Continuing Education (now called Professional and Continuing Education) in 1968, and by now some at UVM were unhappy that, as they saw it, the new community college was luring away adult learners from their university's program.

Peter Smith

[Democrat] Tom Salmon has just been elected governor, and a guy named Norris Hoyt was his tax commissioner. I found out that Ray Phillip [UVM's first dean of Continuing Education] was putting together a FIPSE grant. He knew that all they had to do was submit it because FIPSE had said, "If there are two proposals from the same state, we will disallow them both because that means the state doesn't know what it's doing."

So that would kill us cold, we're done — there's nowhere near the money we need to operate. I went to Norrie, who went to Tom Salmon, and we ended up at an eight o'clock [a.m.] meeting in the governor's office in the state capital with a guy named Wayne Patterson, who was the vice president for administration at the University of Vermont, Norrie Hoyt, the governor and me.

The governor said, "I understand that you're looking for this money, and these guys are already in business and if two grants are submitted, neither of them will be funded and these guys will be out of business, and I hope you'll reconsider."

Paterson looked at him and said, "Surely the governor of the State of Vermont is not telling the University of Vermont what it should do academically?"

Salmon looked out the window. He folded his hands and looked back at Wayne, and he said, "Oh, the governor of the State of Vermont would never tell the University of Vermont what it should do. But he would also want the university to know that if the first institution to come to Springfield, Bellows Falls and Brattleboro and serve the needs of working people — if the University of Vermont allowed or helped to put that institution out of business, the governor would be very, very sorry."

They withdrew the grant.

FIPSE gave the community college $750,000. It was by far the largest grant that it made in 1973. The college was saved.

"You could not believe the intensity and the rapid-fire success of things," said Smith of that period. "By the third year, we had more than a million dollars in funding, our annual budget was probably half a million, and we had joined the Vermont State Colleges almost before anybody knew it."

'Removing the blinders of traditionalism'

The path to becoming Vermont's fifth state college, with more or less secure state funding, had several key stages and culminated in a dramatic State House vote.

The leader of the Vermont State Colleges (VSC) was Robert Babcock, a Republican who had been Vermont's lieutenant governor from 1959 to 1961. He had been appointed by Gov. Philip Hoff to be the first provost, effectively the CEO, of the VSC System, which at that point included four schools: Castleton, Johnson and Lyndon state colleges and Vermont Technical College in Randolph Center.

"Bob Babcock and his wife and their family were absolutely the closest family to my family, socially and politically," Peter Smith said.

"He was a mentor to me starting when I was ten years old, and he's in charge of the Vermont State Colleges because Phil Hoff put him in charge. So I walk into the room saying, 'Hi Bob — I've got an interesting proposition for you.'"

Smith's proposal was that the state college system consider making a place for VRCCC. In response, Babcock and the VSC set in motion a careful process of inquiry into the fledgling experiment.

In September 1971, a joint committee drawn from the boards of both UVM and VSC, chaired by Dr. Frank Smallwood of the Vermont State Colleges board, published a report on the history and future needs of Vermont higher education, called "Higher Education in Vermont: Past, Present, and Future." Its "Strategies for the Future" included this paragraph:

> *This new community college effort represents an extremely valuable addition to the postsecondary educational offerings available to the people of Vermont. It is particularly significant that this program is designed to provide new educational opportunities to Vermonters who are not being reached by other institutions because of economic, geographical or other handicaps. In addition, the program has adopted the philosophy of using existing plant facilities — regional vocational centers, union high schools, public and private college, churches and other community buildings — rather than attempting to build new facilities. Any new planning organization designed to coordinate the higher educational effort in Vermont should include the community college concept.*

Then in March 1972, Babcock asked Sister Elizabeth Candon, president of Trinity College in Burlington and of the Vermont Higher Education Council, to lead an evaluation team in a careful assessment of the community college project. Sister Elizabeth's team spent two days at VRCCC sites, talking "with students, instructors, coordinators, aides, counselors, business managers, consultants and trustees" along with the college leadership, said the team's report in May 1972.

"We addressed ourselves," the report said, "to the question stated by Dr. Babcock: 'Is there a reasonable chance that they can do what they have set out to do?'... Our task was difficult and at times confusing, because we were examining a process rather than a product."

The evaluators included one faculty member each from UVM, Castleton State and Vermont Tech, along with Lyndon State's business manager and an assistant to the president at Skidmore College in New York. The team's report said they endorsed the new college's objective "that education be taken to the consumer (with emphasis on the disadvantaged economic groups)," and "agreed that VRCCC had demonstrated a remarkable level of achievement in the coordination and utilization of existing resources.

"...VRCCC has accomplished 'what they set out to do,'" the team concluded. "Our concern is in our hope that VRCCC staff members continue to work on removing the blinders of traditionalism so that stimulating, creative learning will prevail in their classes. We have seen good evidence that such is being accomplished."

'This is about the commitment'

In summer 1972, a subcommittee of the VSC board was assigned to look into the VRCCC's operations "and investigate possible avenues of affiliation," said the college's annual report that year. After several meetings, the committee unanimously recommended that the VRCCC become a part of the Vermont State Colleges — and in September, the state college board accepted the recommendation.

But there was a catch.

The recommendation came with "an understanding, which was explicit," Smith said, that the new enterprise could only become a state college if the Legislature decided to award it state funding.

"That was the 1973 session, and we asked for $50,000," Smith said. "I remember John Boylan, who was a very fiscally conservative senator from the Northeast Kingdom, looking at me and saying, 'Well, you're just going to be back next year asking for more,' and I said, 'You're absolutely right. But I won't be back here next year asking for more if this committee doesn't give me any money this year.'"

That first state appropriation went through in April 1973. When it joined the Vermont State Colleges in mid-1973, the Vermont Regional

Community College Commission became the Community College of Vermont, with Peter Smith as its first president.

Of the new name, Smith said, "I wanted it to be as simple and plain as possible. I thought Community College of Vermont was pretty straightforward." (The college had briefly, in 1972, called itself Vermont Community College.)

"The next year," Smith recalled, "we came back and asked for $150,000. Norm James worked for Governor Salmon. So James comes running up to me — we're in the [State House] cloakroom and the budget is on the [Senate] floor. He says, 'If you take it down to 125, we know we have sixteen votes. If you leave it at 150, we're not sure.'

"I basically said, 'Screw it Norm, it's time for people to decide. I want to go for the 150.'

"He laughed and said, 'Okay.'"

The budget passed the Senate by two votes.

'An innovation that has followed no rule books'

We do not now have a regular budget for paying teachers. However, by not maintaining a regular faculty, and by paying a teacher an outright fee for teaching a course, we calculate that we could anticipate a very low per-student instructional cost. We estimate this per-student cost at between $40–$50.
> — *Present and Future*, Vermont Regional Community College Commission report to the Vermont Legislature, September 1971

[From] ... the Vermont programs ... has come a new, refreshing approach to education which may well revolutionize higher education in the final third of the 20th century.
> — Dr. Benjamin Fine, journalist and author of books on education, North American News Alliance press release, *Vermont Sunday News*, July 23, 1972

It is the policy of the Vermont Regional Community College Commission that all adults are eligible for college programs regardless of age, economic status, or prior educational attainment. Thus a tremendous diversity of students, none of whom are the traditional full-time college student, have taken courses.... Seventy percent of VRCCC students have informed us that they could not otherwise attend college courses without VRCCC services in their area.
> — VRCCC's first annual report, August 1972

A new chapter in American higher education is unfolding ... as Vermont's pioneering statewide non-campus community college system develops.
> — James Worsham, *Boston Globe*, August 1972

▶

KIND OF A MIRACLE

Vermont, with a population of 444,742 spread over the state's nearly 10,000 square miles, is poor on educational resources. The rate of access to higher education is one of the lowest in the country.... But the catching up has now begun. The Regional Community College Commission already serves over 1,300 people, ranging in age from 16-year-olds to those in their 70s. The Commission retains, at no pay, four hundred teachers who bring educational opportunities to dozens of often-remote communities, meeting in churches, schools, private homes and industrial locations at almost any hour of the day or night.

... Efforts such as these will give back to higher education its good name. Vermont's Regional Community College Commission is also an apt illustration of a successful educational innovation which has followed no rulebooks.... They took risks quite untypical of academic people.... Out of sheer energy, idealism, some bad mistakes, and also some good luck, has come an achievement that is going to be around long after many more publicized and politicized efforts in higher education are forgotten.

— *Change* magazine, June 1973

•••

Community College of Vermont
Vermont State Colleges

Upon recommendation of the Review Committee
of the Community College of Vermont,
the Board of Trustees of Vermont State Colleges
has conferred upon

an
Associate Degree
with all the rights and priviledges pertaining thereto,
given this day of

Chairman, Board of Trustees   *President*

The first commencement: 'A watershed day'

With the State House as the backdrop in June 1973, the Community College of Vermont convened its first graduation ceremony on a hot day in Montpelier. Eight people were there to receive their associate degrees.

"My memory of that day is that it was sublime," said Smith, who handed out the diplomas. "That was such a turning-point year, and I remember saying to myself, 'We're going to make it.' And it was because of them — because of those people who were our graduates and our students, who were testifying with their time and their money, to some extent, and their dreams."

The first person to walk across the stage and accept a CCV diploma was Nancy Button. Her then-husband, a dairy farmer, was there, as were their three kids and her parents.

Button had been born and raised in Chelsea. After high school she completed a year at Vermont College in Montpelier, but gave that up when she got married. With three young children, she got a job as a teacher's aide in the local school, helping in the first and second grades. She liked it.

"It ended up that I was pretty much teaching, under the first-grade teacher," she said, "until the Chelsea school board said, 'You really need to get a degree, if you're going to be teaching.'"

When Button learned about CCV, "I didn't anticipate that it was going to help me much," she recalled, "except that I trusted Peter Smith. I went to a meeting where he was doing a chat about the community college. I talked to my husband at the time, and he was in favor of it." She continued working at the school, and borrowed her in-laws' car to get to her college classes.

"We were not wealthy people by any means," she said. Without CCV, Button said, she would "absolutely not" have been able to afford college.

▶

Another of those first graduates was Nora Swiercinski, a mother of six children in Springfield. She and her husband Henry, an engineer, had moved there from Toronto after Henry's firm bought the local Fellows Gear Shaper Company.

Swiercinski also went to a local meeting where Smith was to talk about CCV. "I thought, 'Nothing's going to come of this, but I might as well go along with everybody,'" she said.

"I had decided I wanted to be a teacher. CCV made it possible." She took courses at night, "and by the time I finished, some of my kids were teenagers," she said. "They knew they'd better be home on time because I'd be up, studying."

'It made me feel like a better person'

"What it brings back to me," Smith said of the inaugural commencement, "was the incredible sense of purpose we had. We were purpose-driven — and the purpose was in the lives of those eight people who were graduating."

Of course, because this was the improvisational early CCV, there's a story to go with the memory.

"I had gone to Reid Payne, who was then the [State House] sergeant at arms," Smith recalled, "and I said, 'We would like to do this in front of the Capitol. Can we borrow some chairs?' He said, 'Sure.'

"So, you know, we got about sixty chairs; it wasn't that big a group. It was about ninety degrees that day — so the chairs all sank into the pavement, and all the rubber things on the bottom of the legs came off in the tar.

"It was hilarious, and Reid was just batshit. I said, 'I don't know what to say,' and he said, 'Oh, just don't say anything.'"

With her CCV degree, Nora Swiercinski got a job teaching primary grades in Perkinsville, a small town in Windsor County. She taught there for seventeen years. She also started a program that brought books in Spanish to a school in Honduras.

Nancy Button stayed with her teacher's aide job in Chelsea for several more years. "Then I was offered a head teacher position in Barre

Town for Head Start. Because I had my degree, I could be the head teacher. I had seven or eight people under me, and twenty kids." She stayed in that position for fourteen years.

Button's three children all went to college. Her oldest earned a master's degree in teaching and is the administrator of a primary school in South Carolina. Her second child graduated from Vermont Tech and is a sales rep for Cargill, the global food conglomerate. Her youngest graduated from Champlain College and is the administrator of a childcare center in Wilder, Vermont.

When she was interviewed for this book in early 2020, Button was nearly eighty years old and still working three days a week as a receptionist in Barre. She has six grandkids and one great-grandson.

Was her life different, she was asked, because she found CCV on that day all those years ago?

"Oh, absolutely," she said. "I was just kind of existing, and it changed me. It made me feel like a better person."

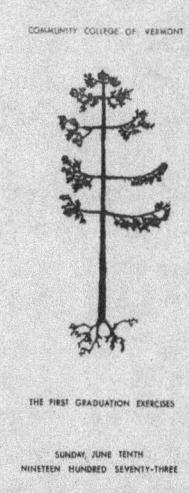

1973: the cover of the first graduation program.

• • •

Chapter 4

Giving Education Back to the Learner

The new college had launched itself on a fresh concept: offering college-level courses that were created in response to local needs and were taught within communities by community members, all of it (at first) for free.

At the core was learning for learning's sake, plus skills and knowledge for better jobs. For completion of the job-skill courses, the college was awarding certificates; but there was, at first, no structure for earning an associate degree.

Then came a reality check.

"I'm up in the Northeast Kingdom," Smith recalled, "and I'm talking to some folks at a community action agency up there, telling them all about how it was going to be cool — no credit, just what do you need to know. This woman stood up and she said, 'You, with your college degree on the wall, are telling me I don't need one? Peter, get real.'

"I got back in the car afterwards and um, she was right. And it just flipped, in my mind anyway: If this is going to be real, it had to be real by the rules of the game, not living outside in some other planetary system."

But even as Smith and his team began thinking about how CCV could award an associate degree, they were committed to staying on the path they had opened — to be centered on learners and what they wanted to learn, rather than building a traditional structure of courses and credits into which students would have to fit.

"We actually saw ourselves as reinventing higher education from scratch," said Larry Daloz, the Peace Corps veteran with a Harvard Ph.D. who joined the college in 1971, to help organize its approach to learning. "We were going to create higher education with a whole new model, because the job of higher education was to marshal the resources necessary for learners to learn what they wanted to learn."

"Would there be a degree? Of course," Daloz later wrote. "But how it would be determined lay before us, a trackless wilderness. It was thrilling."

Larry Daloz

Larry wrote these recollections for "CCV Stories," where they were published on August 28, 2015.

... [C]ourses were to be designed in collaboration with the learners themselves. There were to be no time-based credits: learning would be evaluated in terms of outcomes. Credentials for faculty? Naturally, but it was to be the credentials of earned experience, not mere book learning, that mattered. Want to learn community organizing? We'll hire you a community organizer, not a sociologist.

... For the next six months I worked with each site team to come up with a "learning support system" that delineated each person's roles and the relationships among them. I drew diagrams and maps, typed bullet-points and caveats, spoke of "competencies," "interventions," and "evaluation criteria." Peter thought it was great, Steve [Hochschild] was duly impressed; our resident radical, John Chater, and the site coordinators rolled their eyes, staff shrugged, and I was hired under a fresh Carnegie grant at $12,000 a year to become "Learning Services Coordinator" for the college, its first ... um ... academic dean.

My recollection of those early days features above all else the boisterous and testosterone-soaked Wednesday morning "Management Team" meetings. At one end of the table Peter, wearing his signature leather vest, leans back in his chair, feet defiantly on the table, and exuberantly shreds this or that academic evildoer; beside him Planner Steve Hochschild, necktied and trimly pressed, pleads for a coherent management plan, while Chuck Parker, the Finance Guy, throws out a stream of pecuniary and scatological jargon and warns darkly of fiscal disaster. Meanwhile, as the Site Coordinators argue fiercely for local control, I doodle in my notes my emerging "wagon wheel theory" of administrative order: everyone at the hub wants the spokes to be identical while each spoke, its outer end regularly ground into the mud, demands autonomy....

By late 1972, we had lots of courses running, but still no degree program.... We had declared credits to be the baggage of a moribund system. How, then, did you know when a person merited the degree? "When they are competent, of course," roared the competency-based ideology, but how competent, how do you know that, and at what? What's more, although we were committed to recognizing prior experiential learning, almost every other college who did that (and there were a scant handful at the time) also gave credits. Yet since credits were based on time spent in a classroom, how would we assess the educational value of experience out of the classroom without some academic reference point?

As it happened, Peter had wrangled his way into a coalition of nontraditional colleges under the auspices of the Educational Testing Service to create principles of good practice for assessing experiential learning. Its acronym, CAEL, stood at the time for "Council for the Assessment of Experiential Learning" [now the Council for Adult and Experiential Learning] and, headed by Antioch's venerable Morris Keeton, it was to remain a vital force in nontraditional education for decades. I became the college's academic representative, and over the next several years — we are talking the early '70s here — under steady fire

INVENTING A COLLEGE

Peter Smith in his "signature leather vest."

from our fellow state colleges and their nettled faculties, we wrestled with tough and very real questions: What's the difference between teaching and learning? What is the interplay among assessment, documentation and certification? How do we establish evaluation criteria and assess achievement against standards? The college worked hard to shape a rigorous process of planning, implementing, and evaluating a quality degree program without sacrificing vital student engagement in setting learning outcomes.

The "competency-based" education movement was in ascendance at the time (as it appears to be again today), and it quickly became evident why "credits" were far simpler....

What kinds of competence would make for self-reliant learners? After a year of painstaking conversation with students, teachers, staff, employers and the public, I proudly presented Peter with a list of several dozen clusters of competence. "You've got to be kidding!" he bellowed. "No more than ten — at the most!" I knew he was right, the clusters hit the shredder, and we went back to the scissors and paste. What finally emerged were ten "Areas of Competence": Self-Awareness, Communication, Cultural Awareness, Community Relations, Interpersonal Relationships, Creative Competence, Manual and Physical Competence, Environmental Awareness, Analytical Competence, and (oh yes!) Knowledge. Looking back, I recognize it as clearly a committee scramble, but hey, we were trying to reinvent higher education, weren't we? You could do worse.

So there was one more challenge. How would we decide when a person was ready to graduate? And who would decide? What we came up with is not unlike the portfolio process used today in widely diverse educational settings: students developed a "learning contract" complete with learning goals developed in consultation with CCV staff; they assessed their prior learning against those goals, took courses and independent studies to meet them, and throughout the process met with a "Local Review Committee" made up minimally of a community member, college staff, a fellow student, and faculty. Upon approval, the portfolio went to a college-wide committee for final review.

… Many of those early dreams were simply the stuff of an initial startup, bound to take more substantial form in the rub of the world. And much of it was sheer youthful idealism, some avowedly misguided, an outgrowth of our own '60s counter-dependence. We knew what we were up against, but were less adept at creating something that would reliably replace it.

'Conceived as journeys in individual growth'

"When identifying career needs in rural Vermont, it must be realized that, within his working career, the average person will be changing jobs and needing new career skills," said an early 1970s publication that described CCV's new degree structure. The college, it said, "is therefore committed to educational programs which are not terminal, but in fact are a process enabling the adult to continue learning and adapting to a changing community…. All Community College programs will be conceived as journeys in individual growth, with each student marking out his itinerary in consultation with faculty and staff."

The degree structure the college developed from 1971 to 1975 centered on a broad, integrative approach to competence. It went through three stages of evolution. At first, in 1971 to 1972, "students defined and documented their own competencies within three major areas: Intellectual Competence, Social Competence, and Physical and Manual Competence," said another college publication. "To receive an Associate Degree, a student had to challenge and meet a minimum of 15 competencies (approximately five in each area)."

By 1973, students could aim to earn degrees in three fields of study: human services, general studies and administrative services. Degree candidates now developed what were called Contracts to Complete. "Regional Review Boards of students, teachers and community professionals were established to advise students and evaluate their contracts," the college said.

By 1975, CCV had developed its ten "areas of competence": self-awareness, communication, cultural awareness, community relations, interpersonal relationships, creative competence, manual and physical competence, environmental awareness, analytical competence, and knowledge.

"Students could select almost any field of study for their concentrations," said a college report. "And for the first time, the college recognized the process of developing and validating the contract as a valuable learning experience.

"Classes were established and materials were developed to help students learn the contracting process. Local Review Committees (LRCs) took the place of Regional Review Boards and played a significant role in guiding and evaluating the student's work. Students met with their committees both in the planning stage and upon completion of their programs."

"In contracting for a degree, students spell out skills and knowledge they have and state how they were acquired," said "College Model for the Grassroots," a 1976 profile of CCV in *American Education,* a magazine published by the U.S. Office of Education. *"Evidence —* letters, certificates, recommendation, or other documentation — helps establish how well each was mastered. The contracts are seldom skimpy and some are quite detailed."

"My counselor, Clo Pitkin, was tough," wrote Faire Edwards, a 1975 graduate, in that summer's issue of *Vermont Life* magazine. "She wouldn't always take the first thing I offered her to meet a requirement, but asked for more or better. I ended up with a contract which included 46 pieces of supporting data, reports of activities, letters relating to what I had done, copies of articles I'd written and even a book of photographs.

"The attitude of encouragement plus firm insistence on the student doing all he or she can is built into the programs," she wrote. "In addition, there are so-called 'access courses' which seek to attract people who have become discouraged about schooling and need help to raise their aspirations. This is a very important method of getting people back into the education processes after they have left, and a number of students have taken advantage of these courses."

'So many aspects': Creating contracts for learning

The Local Review Committees generally included a student, a community practitioner (generally someone with practical knowledge of a student's field), a teacher and a CCV staff member, said the first Local Review Committee handbook:

> *When the committee and the student have arrived at agreement about what has been said and what remains to be done, the plan takes on the aspect of a contract among the student, the college, and the committee. The specifics are written in a letter from the committee to the student.*
>
> *With the plan approved, the student is free to work at his or her own rate. Any number or combination of courses, work experiences, or independent studies may be used — as long as the agreed-upon learning takes place.*
>
> *...Throughout the entire process, a CCV counselor is available to help the student. While the exact route taken by each person will vary the journey is the same. It is a process designed first and foremost*

to help the student get where (s)he wants to go. Yet at the same time, the legitimate expectations of the "outside world" are brought into play along with the educational expectations of the college.

"Competency-based education focuses on the outcomes of the learning process — the learning itself — rather than on the inputs to it — the teaching," Daloz wrote in his 1975 article "Giving Education Back to the Learner."

"…While traditional programs tend to prescribe a curriculum of courses to be taken," he wrote, "the CCV curriculum prescribes only learnings to be demonstrated.… As long as a student can demonstrate the required learning, (s)he deserves the degree. It matters not whether (s)he took even a single course."

That doesn't mean it was easy to fulfill all of CCV's expectations.

"As I read through the mechanics that we put together, that we made people go through to get an associate degree, and the level of detail that we were able to write down, it's just astounding," said Tom Yahn, the first regional coordinator in southeast Vermont. "It amazes me that anybody ever got a degree. And that was all on the counselors, to make that happen.

"Larry wrote up the ideas, and then the counselors had to go out and make this happen with students. There were so many aspects of competence that we wanted people to achieve. It was mind-blowing."

Educational Wampum: *The first guide for faculty*

CCV was asking community members to teach what they knew and cared about, to develop courses from scratch — and to do it all for free at first, then for very small compensation. And this was working: The coordinators of instruction and advisement, responsible at the regional sites for recruiting and supporting the faculty, were finding Vermonters who were happy to do all that.

Most of the new instructors had little or no teaching experience. So to help them understand CCV's approach, design an effective course, and carry the process through, staff members Don Hooper and Tim Welsh created a funky, loose-leaf publication in the mid-1970s that they titled *Educational Wampum*.

"Since *Wampum* means exchange," they wrote, "we are hopeful that this notebook can stimulate a sharing of ideas and tips about teaching and learning among CCV instructors."

Before launching into detailed advice, examples, checklists and worksheets on the stages of designing and completing a course, *Wampum* told instructors about the competences "which the college believes are fundamental characteristics of a functioning adult."

"Each degree student selects an area of concentration and writes a plan of study within the framework of the ten broad 'areas of competence,'" the manual said. "… By keeping CCV's competence areas in mind as you produce your course objectives, students can fully integrate your course work with their degree plans."

Wampum also briefed new instructors on who they'd likely be teaching, what students' expectations would be, and how this would be different from a conventional college course and classroom:

> *Average age of students is 30 years. Approximately 2/3 are women. The majority are employed in paying jobs. More than 1/3 list the desire to acquire job-related skills as their primary reason for attending. About 50% are interested in getting an Associate Degree at CCV. 80% have said they have no access to other higher education institutions because of either cost or distance.*
>
> *You'll be faced with a heterogeneous group of motivated adults who will want your course to be as productive as possible. People may have to drop out of your class for reasons which have nothing to do with your teaching or their interest in the subject.… Family and job commitments of students will govern to some extent your pace of instruction and the design of your course.*
>
> *Community College is founded on the conviction that the highest purpose of education is to foster self-reliant learners — people who have learned how to learn. Self-reliant learners are those who can:*
>
> *— assess what they have learned and what they wish to learn*
> *— plan ways to reach their educational goals*
> *— act on their plans*
> *— determine when they have realized their goals.*

> *Underlying this approach is the conviction that learning progresses through the constant interplay of thought, action, theory and practice. People learn both by doing and by reflection on what they have done.*

Assessing prior learning: Joining a larger conversation

"Traditional educational practice had been shaped primarily around the needs of 18- to 22-year-olds who walked into classrooms essentially as blank slates ready to be inscribed by the professoriate," Larry Daloz wrote. "But most adult learners had already achieved a good deal of learning outside of school. To assume that the college classroom was the only legitimate place where college-level learning could be achieved was *prima facie* absurd.

"Fortunately, there were other fellow travelers in those Sixties-fed years. Goddard College, just down the road, had pioneered the assessment of prior learning for credit, and others like Minnesota Metropolitan, Empire State, Thomas Edison, and Antioch were experimenting with their own models."

"Goddard was doing its own very frontier-like assessment of prior learning," Peter Smith agreed. "Tim Pitkin, who was really the guy who founded Goddard, was an advisor and a hugely important mentor to me. We had people on our staff who had been associated with Goddard and the Goddard experimental program in further education, which was working with Head Start mothers."

"In about 1974," Daloz wrote, "the Educational Testing Service convened a group of eight colleges to share what they were learning about the assessment of experiential learning. Smith, hearing about it at the last minute, brought the number to nine. This move to be part of the formative era of CAEL provided invaluable expertise ... about the intersection of competence-based education and prior learning assessment, and put the college into a nationwide conversation about non-traditional higher education.

"At that time, of the relatively few institutions that offered prior-learning assessment, most remained credit-based," Daloz wrote.

"But CCV and several other CAEL members were competence-based, and the challenge of assessment, not to mention the determination of how much was enough for a degree, was very different."

"We had committees of people talking to students and then saying, 'Okay, that's worth ten credits,' except we didn't use credits," Peter Smith said. "But we had a ten-competency associate's degree, and they were putting the experience into the competencies."

After representatives from the federal Fund for the Improvement of Post-Secondary Education (FIPSE) came up to check out the fledgling college in 1972, "they went back and said, 'What they need is to be around and apprenticing with people who know a lot about assessment of prior learning, adults, adult education, etc.'," Smith said. "CAEL was just being formed, and I was on the original board. I say I got my graduate degree at Harvard, but I really got my graduate education from the CAEL board. These were incredible men and women, and I was on that board for the rest of my time at CCV."

Setting standards: 'How much is enough?'

"Ever since we began to work with Local Review Committees to assess the past experience and future learning plans of degree students, we have been confronted with the question: How much learning is enough for the degree?"

That was Daloz and Clotilde Pitkin, a learner-support counselor at the Central Vermont site, writing in a 1976 report published by CAEL titled *Standard Setting by Students and Community — How Much Is Enough?* As they grappled with this question, CCV's leaders discovered through their involvement with CAEL that they were not alone, Daloz and Pitkin wrote:

> As the 'competence-based' movement gains momentum nationally, and as more and more colleges across the country begin to recognize the non-formal learning of millions of adult students, the shortcomings of the time-based credit system spawned in traditional classrooms have become increasingly apparent.

By insisting that community review committees rather than a campus-based faculty decide when a student should receive a degree, the College was affirming that the answer to the question "How much is enough?" must lie in the nexus of the student's own goals, the community's expectations, and the College's requirements.

... Indeed, our "faculty" is part-time and drawn from the community. The task of the College is to provide a framework on which learning can happen. Thus, CCV's consistency and quality control are to be found not in the content of learning, but in the process through which competence is acquired and assessed.

... Through orientation meetings and materials provided by the College, students are advised of the choices available for degree study. When a student decides to enter the process, a meeting is arranged with a counselor to discuss the decision in more detail and to undertake an initial assessment procedure. If the student decides to continue, he or she will most likely join a contracting workshop, led by a college staff or community member.

This group generally meets for a term exploring goals, identifying prior learning, planning future learning, and preparing the study plan for presentation to the committee. During this time, the student will very likely meet with a number of community practitioners to identify skills and knowledge needed in his or her chosen field.

... When the student feels ready, the plan is taken to the [local review] committee for review and discussion. This initial meeting results in a letter of agreement from the committee to the student detailing what remains to be done.

After the initial meeting, the student begins working on the plan negotiated with the committee. This may take anywhere from a few weeks to several years....At some point, when the student believes that the agreed-upon standards have been met, he or she returns to the committee. At this point, the committee reviews all remaining documentation and determines if the terms have been met. If all conditions have been met, the committee recommends the student to the CCV Review Board for a degree.

Learner support:
'Helping them get where they wanted to be'

The staff at each regional site included learner support counselors, who from the beginning — more so than conventional student advisors — were essential to student success.

"I met with people and encouraged them," said Judy Cyprian, who joined the Central Vermont staff in 1975. "It was adults figuring out they needed or wanted an education, so it was talking to them, 'You can do it.' It was really a lot of support. That was probably the biggest thing I did.

"They were mostly females, a lot with kids. Maybe they had graduated high school, or maybe not. They had kids early, and [college] just hadn't crossed their minds. Now their kids were older, and they wanted to go."

"They were not considered very bright," recalled Clo Pitkin, one of the first Central Vermont counselors. "They were homemakers, mostly. And they were very bright."

Pitkin had graduated from and worked at Goddard College, whose unconventional approach to learning had been developed by her father-in-law, Royce "Tim" Pitkin, the college's president from 1938 to 1969.

Goddard was an important influence on the early CCV — and Clo Pitkin said the approach that CCV's counselors took "was the Goddard approach, which was, 'What do you want to do? What's on your mind? Shall we talk about this?' It was the whole idea of just getting to where people were, and helping them get to where they wanted to be."

"I think our students at CCV would never have gone to Goddard," Cyprian said. "They were much more traditional in lifestyles. But a similar approach to education, which is interesting.

"I remember sitting in my office, one little room in Barre, and having students sit by my desk and we would talk about their lives," she said. "What they wanted. How are you going to get there? They took the experiential learning course — you got credit for your life experience, and that was a very big deal. I remember helping students work their way through that. It was amazing for them: 'Oh my God, I really do know about child development! I just never called it that.'"

"That was the excitement, for me," agreed Pitkin, who went on to found the nonprofit organization Woman Centered. "It was exciting in many ways. I remember feeling that mostly what I thought was important about education was the listening. Listening, and getting people to respond to each other, was just so important."

"While most subject classes are conducted in the conventional classroom style, the counseling sessions are usually conducted informally in groups, often at a student's home," wrote '75 graduate Faire Edwards in her *Vermont Life* article about the college. "The quality of interplay and support is fascinating. I believe it reflects a near-missionary calling on the part of the staff."

"It was a very exciting place to work," Cyprian agreed. "And part of what was exciting was not only the concept, but that you could figure it out for yourself.

"And this has nothing to do with the mission of the college, but I remember having a great time with everybody. I just have really fond memories of the staff and just feeling so lucky that I got to work in a place that was so tight and supportive. And fun! We had a lot of fun."

Enrollment: The numbers grow

In spring 1971, about 100 students signed up for the new college's first slate of courses.
- By spring 1972, enrollment had risen to 635.
- Spring 1973: 990.
- Spring 1974: 1,413.

Chapter 5

Building Credibility and Surviving

I had felt for some time that, in education, we were adhering too closely to the methods of the past. I was concerned for people who had been passed by and needed a means to earn a living. I think it's been quite a success.
　　　　　— Gov. Deane C. Davis, quoted by Faire Edwards in "Experience Counts for Credit," *Vermont Life*, summer 1975

Classes are held anywhere space can be had — church basements, libraries, gymnasiums, even auto body shops. Nor does the college have a regular, full-time faculty. Rather, individuals are hired from the community to teach their own career specialties. Its students receive neither grades nor credits. At CCV, two-year degrees are awarded on the basis of demonstrated skills and individual contracts instead of number of courses taken or amount of time spent in study.
　　　　　— Rita Cipalla Bobowski, "College Model for the Grass Roots," *American Education*, June 1976

"You've got to be optimistic when you see what's happening here," Peter Smith told the *Community and Junior College Journal* in 1975. "We have got a success record.... Those who go on to other institutions in the state are easily holding their own with the natives of those institutions.... We feel that for most of our students there is no alternative access route to higher education."

The journal, published by the American Association of Community and Junior Colleges, gave two full pages of its May issue to editor William A. Harper's impressions of CCV. Having spent some time observing this unusual college in action, he was impressed — but, he noted, "there is a constant struggle to maintain the program on a very skimpy budget.

"Smith emphasizes the need to spend money on people in the field who deliver educational services.... He's currently putting out a mere $450,000 for a very lean staff while fighting hard to get the state and other sources to raise the ante."

Free tuition was no more. "Students are given bank-by-mail envelopes to send the tuition of $30 a course directly to the college's bank account," Harper wrote. "Student response has been good — though obviously some simply cannot afford the fee. And they are not penalized for that."

The experiment with voluntary tuition, like a number of others in the early years, did not work so well. CCV had hoped to raise $80,000 from tuition payments during the 1975–1976 academic year; the actual total came to $63,000, and staff members noticed that often the most reliable contributors were the students who could least afford it.

The next year, all students were required to pay the $30-per-course fee. And for the first time, starting in spring '75, instructors were paid: $225 per course.

"Money, while spare, is not the problem it might have been," observed Edwards in *Vermont Life*. "Operating with a budget of $627,000 — of which $430,000 goes for staff and counseling salaries — CCV has little money left for purchasing books and equipment. For a school based on community support, though, the problem is solvable and the solution is clear-cut: CCV borrows everything.

"Public libraries in the three-site area, for instance, have been persuaded to purchase books that are needed in CCV classrooms.

Local high schools provide use of laboratory equipment and classroom space; banks and insurance agencies lend office equipment."

'The last thing we wanted was normalcy'

By the mid-1970s, though, some signs were surfacing that the college might be starting to shift, however subtly, toward operating more like an established institution. One such sign, much noted, came in a brief memo, "The New CCV Look — 'Out with Old and In with the New,'" that Smith sent around to the staff in February '75.

"You have no doubt heard a few comments around the Central Office in regards to wearing blue jeans to work," he wrote. "To clarify the issue I would like to ask all members of the staff to save the 'old, and blue jeans' for the weekend.

"This is not to break any of the free spirit at CCV or to sound like an official edict from the President," added the president. "Although it may seem to be a matter of insignificance, it is also one of importance to our beloved CCV."

Dick Eisele

From "CCV Stories," November 19, 2013.

This trend towards standardization and articulation continued in practically every area of the college's business. I was asked in July '76 to collect a copy of all teacher and staff resumes, to be put on file in the Central Office, and I was even asked to review new teacher resumes prior to contract signing in the sites. I think there was a sense, at least among some, that our survival meant getting our shit (I mean act) together. Another clear sign of this came in an October 76 memo from Ken Hood to the Central Office staff, strongly reminding us of the need for more "orderly arrangement of all work areas, desks, etc." So, we could no longer wear our Levis and we had to clean up our workspace too. It could be argued, although I'm not sure that we realized it at the time, little by little we were inexorably heading toward "normality." But, many of us wondered what we might be sacrificing to get there.... While everybody else wanted us to be normal, the last thing we wanted was normalcy.

At the same time, the leadership and many staff felt assured that CCV had firmly established its unique approach to higher education. The values and dimensions of that were set down in "The CCV Credo," a widely read treatise that Larry Daloz composed and circulated in early '75.

"We assume," Daloz wrote, "that people can continue to learn throughout life and significant learning requires change and growth — change not merely in *what* knowledge is acquired, but also in how people perceive the world and how they act in it. People are not simply at the mercy of the world, they can work to change it." (See pages 91-94 for a "slightly abridged" version of the full Credo.)

It turned out that it was a good thing the college had built this solid a foundation in concept, values and practices — because the mid-to-late '70s would become a time of stress, change and struggle to survive.

'CCV is excess baggage and should be jettisoned'

In its 1975 session, the Legislature cut CCV's allotment of state funds from $400,000 to $350,000 — and an influential senator pushed what would be the first of two attempts within the State House to kill the college altogether.

Graham Newell, a professor at Lyndon State, was chair of the Senate Education Committee and a formidable adversary. Believing, together with a number of his VSC colleagues, that CCV was siphoning off both students and resources that should go to the established state colleges, Newell introduced a bill that would have replaced CCV with an expanded program of continuing education at UVM.

Toward the end of the session, the measure failed in the Senate, twenty to ten. But Newell vowed to try again. "If I get back to the Legislature there will be another bill just like the last," he said.

"Within the state colleges, there was clearly a group of faculty, and to a lesser degree some college administrators, who really didn't want the Community College of Vermont," noted Ken Hood, then Smith's

A 1979 editorial cartoon by Jeff Danziger.

de facto chief of staff. "One of my great memories is going to a meeting, I believe it was in Stowe, where Peter was confronted by probably fifty people about why should we have a community college in Vermont. And Peter in his inimitable way didn't let that set him back at all."

The most intense opposition came from the Vermont State Colleges Faculty Federation, a union chapter of the American Federation of Teachers. At least some, if not most, of its members believed that the money the Legislature was allotting to CCV should be going to the four campus-based colleges, especially toward raises in faculty salaries.

"The CCV administrative pork barrel needs a good flushing," said the Faculty Federation's August '75 newsletter. It decried as "totally unnecessary" the large portion, more than $400,000, of the community college's most recent budget that had gone to maintaining its staff. "Assuming that the same courses continued to be offered throughout the state," the newsletter said, "we maintain that it could be done at a fraction of the cost if it were handled by the existing four campuses as extension courses.

"... We consider CCV's cut-rate education to be no bargain," the faculty union concluded. "In our opinion, CCV is excess baggage and should be jettisoned. The money allocated to CCV ... would go a long way in bolstering the sagging educational facilities on the four campuses."

The Faculty Federation's argument "was filled with inaccuracies and misinformation, which the chancellor pointed out item by item," Eisele said.

That was true: William Craig, who had invited CCV onto the Johnson State campus when he was its president, continued to be strongly supportive as VSC chancellor. "The misinformation being spread about the Community College of Vermont needs to be corrected," he declared in a strongly worded February 1976 memo to the Legislature.

"CCV's total budget level is 18% below the 1975 level; no other college decrease is half that," the chancellor wrote. "CCV has had to cut twice as deeply as any other college. The newsletter forgot to give you these facts."

Plus, he added, "CCV's cost per FTE [full-time equivalent] student is one half that of any of the campus colleges," and "over 80% of CCV enrollment is in Southeast and Central Vermont, where no [other] public colleges exist."

Rather than draw students away from the established state colleges, Craig said the new college had become a feeder institution. "CCV advertises that students can apply for transfer credit at the campus state colleges; the three four-year state colleges have granted full transference," he wrote.

"So all the Union's effort to abolish CCV can achieve," he concluded, "is this: abolition of the opportunity for higher education now available to the 2,400 low-income, job- and home-bound adult students who can only attend college part-time and who live remote from our campus. Is that a good idea?"

'Truly an imaginative and effective approach'

CCV's state funding was in jeopardy, more and more of its students were pressing to transfer their credits to other institutions, and the college's very existence was at risk — so it was vital that the college gain accreditation. Achieving that would establish that CCV's different approach really *was* legitimate higher education.

The college-accrediting institution for the region is the New England Commission of Higher Education, which until 2018 was known as the New England Association of Schools and Colleges, or NEASC. In October 1975, after NEASC had reviewed a very thorough self-study submitted by CCV, it sent a team of experts to observe the college and make a recommendation.

Headed by Harold Shively, president of Bunker Hill Community College, the team included professors and administrators from Harvard and the universities of Massachusetts, New Hampshire and Maine. Its report gives a snapshot of CCV at this key moment in its evolution.

"The financial situation of the College appears to have stabilized," the visiting team reported. "... This (fiscal year 1976).... is the first year that the College's major economic support has come from the State and student tuition.

"Today, the organization is still marked by its apparent simplicity, and it fosters and encourages self-reliance in decision-making from staff, as well as students," the report said. At the same time, "the Evaluation Team is pleased to note that Community College of Vermont has begun a formal process of stabilizing and tightening its organizational structure, regularizing decision-making channels, and moving slowly on plans for the future.

"... Because of its highly decentralized structure and widely dispersed staff, the small groups at each field site tend to see themselves as unique communities and, indeed, they are. This uniqueness is both a strength and a weakness."

The evaluators called for "consistent record keeping, information sharing, definition of authority and the development of a process that involves teachers in the decision-making" — but beyond these process improvements, the team found much to admire in the substance of CCV.

"The learning system concept as described by CCV is truly an imaginative and effective approach of responding to the educational needs of CCV's student population," the report said. "The educational contract system guarantees that the focus for learning rests with the student." It "provides for a process whereby the student learns how to learn" — and combining the contracting with the assessment of prior learning "insures that students take ownership of his or her learning goals and objectives.

"In summary, we find that the learning systems designed for the contracting systems are viable and academically sound."

In late 1975, NEASC granted the college an initial, three-year accreditation. It has renewed CCV's accreditation periodically ever since.

Summer residencies and learning clusters

A big part of the college's curriculum continued to be its nondegree courses that aimed to build job and career skills, often granting certificates. CCV now moved to weave those into its structure of competence-centered learning contracts.

"In mid-'76, the college attempted to clarify and standardize the structure and authority of the LRCs [Local Review Committees] along with the integration of 'vocational' programs into the existing format through an enhanced 'goal statement' and better competency statements," Dick Eisele wrote. "The goal statement and competence statements would also be integrated into the ten competence areas so that both 'vocational' goals and general education requirements (the ten areas) would be met.

"... Also in the summer of 1976, the first CCV weeklong summer residency program was convened at Johnson State College. According to a report written by Kellogg Foundation intern Jayne Shephard, over 30 people attended in each week of the program.... A well-attended evaluation session at the end of each week indicated that CCV and JSC should continue to work together, continue the summer program and even expand it."

Those summer residencies "were amazing for the students," said Judy Cyprian, then a learner support counselor in Central Vermont.

"Students from all over the state would gather at Johnson State, and they would be in classes all day. At night, we would be processing everything — and many of them had never spent a night away from home, so it was super scary. And they had a roommate, on a college campus.

"I just think that was huge," she said. "I remember processing at night with these big circles, of women mostly, talking about what their day was like."

The college also began working with learning clusters, groups of ten to thirty students who all lived in a geographic area that CCV was not at that point serving. The idea was first tried in northwestern Vermont, where CCV in the mid-1970s had no regional site, courses or faculty.

"We started a program in Enosburg at the urging of a local politician," Ken Hood recalled. "Peter and I went there, and all of a sudden there's thirty women in the room. What are we going to do? I went to Peter and said, 'I've talked it over with the people, and we're going to have a clustered group.' Peter's response was, 'What the hell is that?' I said, 'It's a group of people who are learning together, and there'll be a person who goes and facilitates once a week.' He didn't say, 'That's a crazy idea' — and by the way, it worked very well."

This new model enabled the college "to provide cost-effective services to low-income, low-access students in areas that might not support regular classes," staff member Mary Wade wrote in an August 1976 college report. Students from each cluster formed a Learning Support Group that met regularly during the term and helped to define and direct the group's learning experiences: "practicums, workshops, independent studies," Wade wrote. Students also met regularly with a CCV instructor.

The college was also giving students the chance to learn through immersion in an experience, guided by a support counselor but taking place outside the classroom, that could count toward filling a learning contract.

"Through personal reflection on the experience with a counselor," Wade wrote, "students are assisted in developing self-assessment and evaluation skills."

'What education ought to do': The CCV Credo

"The philosophical basis for all of these efforts and for the CCV approach in general was articulated in the famous CCV Credo, which was written in early '75," Dick Eisele wrote in the online "CCV Stories." "The best way to explain the credo is to include a slightly abridged and paraphrased (in places) form of the actual document written by Larry Daloz":

If you find CCV confusing, you're not alone. Many people are bewildered by our jargon, frustrated by our unfamiliar procedures, and even angered by our apparent unwillingness to do things the "normal way."

INSTEAD of giving grades and credits, we evaluate learning in terms of "learning outcomes," require long written evaluations, and even ask students themselves to consider whether or what they have learned.

INSTEAD of simply requiring a number of courses for a degree, we ask students to complete a "contract" based on "competencies."

INSTEAD holding classes on a campus, we hold them in homes, churches, and schools.

INSTEAD of recognizing only classroom learning, we allow students to count work and even life experiences toward the degree.

INSTEAD of having a permanent faculty, we hire people directly from the community to teach specific courses.

▶

...We assume that people can continue to learn throughout life and significant learning requires change and growth — change not merely in what knowledge is acquired, but also in how people perceive the world and how they act in it. People are not simply at the mercy of the world, they can work to change it.

And finally, we affirm that the ultimate purpose of education is to help people take responsibility for their own lives, to the fullest extent of their capacity. Therefore,

WE BELIEVE THAT EDUCATION SHOULD ENCOURAGE ACTIVE PARTICIPATION RATHER THAN PASSIVE ACCEPTANCE.

Education must make learners aware of their own limitations and those imposed by society. As awareness increases, the bonds fall away. To learn actively is to dissolve our limitations. The learner is not simply an empty vessel into which truths are poured.

Real learning means change and change requires active involvement of the learner. The contracting process has been designed specifically to encourage this kind of active participation. We also ask our teachers to help students to engage information actively rather than simply absorbing it. And we encourage teachers to negotiate with students as they plan their courses.

WE BELIEVE THAT EDUCATION SHOULD HELP PEOPLE LEARN HOW TO LEARN AS WELL AS WHAT TO LEARN.

We believe that the process of learning is just as important as the content. Someone who knows how to learn can go on learning long after the teacher has gone. Therefore we provide a "core" of skills basic to the process of learning itself — inquiry, communication, problem solving, analytical, and interpersonal skills. Teachers are encouraged to incorporate these skills into the planning of their courses, and the contracting process places special emphasis on these skills as students plan, carry out, and evaluate their learning.

WE BELIEVE THAT EDUCATION SHOULD LINK THEORY WITH PRACTICE, KNOWING WITH DOING.

A complete learning process involves not merely doing something, but also knowing and understanding the activity. Conversely, knowing is not enough unless it results in action. Knowing and doing go hand in hand. We recognize the value of learning outside of the classroom, and we place strong emphasis on self-evaluation as a means of understanding such learning.

In the contracting process, students identify their experiential learning, for it is the learning that we recognize, not the experience alone. The contract is a way of helping students to know what they know, understand what they can do, and prove it. For the "real world" is both the source and the testing place of ideas.

WE BELIEVE THAT EDUCATION SHOULD ADDRESS THE WHOLE PERSON, NOT MERELY THE INTELLECT.

Learning is not a matter for the mind alone, as though there were no connection with the rest of our being. Intellectual endeavor is no more, and no less, important than other realms of human activity. The capacities to work well with others and to use certain physical skills are also important factors in determining work success and life satisfaction. Therefore,

▶

CCV's competencies are designed to encourage attainment and accomplishment in three broad areas: social, manual/physical, and intellectual competence.

WE BELIEVE THAT EDUCATIONAL QUALITY IS BETTER ASSURED BY FOCUSING ON LEARNING OUTCOMES RATHER THAN INPUTS ALONE.

Traditionally, educational quality control in higher education has focused on such inputs as campus libraries, faculty credentials, and strict entrance requirements. It is assumed that if the teaching conditions are good, the quality of learning will also be good. We prefer to believe that the proof of the pudding is in the eating — that "quality control" should be focused on learning rather than teaching, whether it came from a Ph.D. or a six-year-old, a classroom or a job.

Consequently, we do not require courses. Rather, we require that certain skills and knowledge, called "competencies," be demonstrated. Of any learning experience, we ask these questions: 1. What skills or knowledge were learned? 2. How well were they learned? 3. Under what circumstances were they learned? 4. What is the evidence that they were learned?

The contract and our course evaluation procedures are designed to put the student in charge of this information.

We do not pretend that the way we do things is the only way to act on these beliefs. Nor do we claim exclusive rights to them. But we are convinced that by adhering to these tenets we help people to take greater responsibility for their lives. And that, we think, is what education ought to do.

After CCV, Larry Daloz taught at Harvard and Columbia and wrote extensively on adult education, including the book Mentor: Guiding the Journey of Adult Learners *(San Francisco: Jossey-Bass Publishers, 1999).*

•••

Chapter 6

Voices from the Field

Peggy Williams

In '76, I think, there was another invitation: Franklin, Grand Isle counties invited us to come to the Northwest. There was a group of people in the St. Albans area — no college there. They had some high school adult ed courses, Ag Extension did some workshops, and UVM had some continuing ed courses, but they wanted us to come to (in a sense) fill in the blanks and promote all of that learning as kind of a single piece in a consortium.

So we said yes, and Peter Smith said to me: "Okay, Lamoille is going to break from Washington County, and Lamoille, Franklin, and Grand Isle will become the Northwest region." So we created offices in St. Albans, Enosburg and Grand Isle. We operated out of St. Albans in a four-by-six cubicle in the office of the Ag Extension Services on Main Street. Lamoille remained. I was the regional director; my main office was still in Johnson but I was on the road three days a week because I had to get Franklin-Grand Isle up and running.

Because we said we wouldn't do anything to compete with what was already there, the first thing we did was publish, two or three times a year, the "Franklin-Grand Isle Consortium of Learning" that would list all of the opportunities post–high school that were available in the counties. The goal was for us to become kind of a convener, or curator, and to work with these different agencies. Then also we were in the high school in Fairfax, in St. Albans, in Enosburg, in Richford, in Swanton, the elementary school in Grand Isle — we were all over the place, once again using all of those community facilities. It was very, very fertile ground.

Then a decision was made to create the Northern Region. And I had Franklin, Grand Isle, Lamoille, Orleans and Essex [counties]. Caledonia was added with Orange County and something else; so then we had North, Central and Southern regions. They were all pretty big, and again Chittenden [County, home to Burlington] wasn't in here.

We CIAs did everything in those regions. We did recruiting, we did hiring, we did advising students, we helped them fill out financial aid forms, we found the spaces and the places.

Curriculum was more coordinated across the college by now. We didn't just make up our own courses all the time; we tried to quantify some things and then agree to offer English 101 or whatever.

Eventually, we moved off the Johnson campus to another building the college owned in town, and then eventually relocated to space in Morrisville. Newport was a pretty good site. The non-campus piece was the differentiating factor that allowed us to meet the need in a way that worked here. What ended up, then, was that we didn't always have a lot of similarities to other community colleges.

Kathi Rousselle

Kathi served as coordinator of instruction and advisement in Newport from 1975 to 1988, and became CIA in St. Albans in 1988. When she retired in 2015, she was at the time the longest-served employee in the college's history. Her recollections were published by "CCV Stories" on October 16, 2013.

The office was on Main Street in Newport, over the Passumpsic Bank. Two other people worked there, an office manager and advisor. The office was pretty shabby, and Rosey (my husband) and I laid new flooring and did some painting.

One morning I awoke to hear that there was a fire at the bank. I raced down to check it out. The firemen weren't letting people in the building, but somehow I got in. Maybe I knew the firemen! I needed to get student degree plans out of there. In those days, degree plans were HUGE (some stored in suitcases). There were no duplicates so if they were lost, they were LOST. I got them and headed back out of the building. I took a lot of heat from Rosey when he heard what I'd done!

Kathi Rousselle

Sherry Blankinship

Sherry managed CCV's Bellows Falls office from 1978 to 1979, then served as course coordinator in the Springfield office from 1979 to 1983. These memories are from her contribution to "CCV Stories," January 30, 2014.

I did not choose CCV, it chose me. I was a fairly recent graduate from Keene College [New Hampshire] and Paterson State College [New Jersey]. I had done my course work in New Jersey and when we moved to Saxton's River, I finished my degree in elementary education at Keene State. At the time, there was a big demand for teachers, and I quickly found a wonderful job teaching a small group of kindergarten students who for a number of reasons (emotional, mental, physical or a combination) were not quite ready to enter school. This was a federally funded program, so they had funds to do all sorts of innovative things. I was extremely happy with this position....

In August of 1978, the principal called to tell me that my position was not going to be funded and I was without work. Of course, I was shattered. Only a month until school started — I was a single mom with two kids and now no job. What would I do?

Fortuitously, I qualified for CETA (the Comprehensive Employment and Training Act), which was a government program to train workers and provide them with jobs in public service. The opening closest to my home was at CCV in Bellows Falls, where there was a need for an office manager. So by beginning of the 1978 school year, I had a new job.

CCV was located next to the CETA office, and there was much reciprocal interaction, since many of their clients were our students. The CCV office was pretty rough, and the CETA office only a bit better. We had desks, phones, typewriters and a few bookshelves.

The highlight of the office was the bathroom. It was in the basement. The door was at the farthest end of the office, down the stairs to a dirt basement and then a walk back to the front of the building where there was a wooden enclosure with a toilet. Dark, dank and scary, but [worst] of all were the rats and roaches. We would bang and make lots of noise to scare the rats away, who were pretty much out of sight during the day anyway. We kept the light over the toilet on constantly so that we could see any roaches before stepping up to the toilet. Alternatively, we could go to the CETA office next door, which was marginally better but often had a line and smelled dreadfully. In hindsight, this seems pretty awful, but we just treated it as the way it was.

The various CCV staff certainly made up for the basic environment. They were always encouraging and cheerful to the student as well as supportive of the teachers. At some point the office closed, and I was transferred to Springfield, which was certainly an improvement in terms of office space. By 1980 I became curriculum coordinator, one of the most enjoyable jobs of my entire career in academics....

The staff in each of these offices was small: the office manager, curriculum coordinator and a student counselor. We all became quite close. The secretary at the Springfield Office, Sylvia Myers, supported students, teachers and staff. Her husband cleaned the office and, since they had chickens, kept us in eggs.

Our big break from the daily routine was our trips to Montpelier for meetings with the central office. Typically, Nancy Chard (Southeast regional coordinator) from the Brattleboro office would drive. She would pick us up along the way north. Nancy was full of energy and kept us laughing in the best and worst of times. She worked hard to get the appropriate support for the Southeast. It was also fun to see in person the people with whom we would talk at the most once a day. These were the days of phones where long distance charges were steep, so we had a running tally at the phone of our needs and to whom we wanted to speak. At the appointed time each day (as I recall around 4 p.m.), we would line up to talk about the various issues to the appropriate person in Montpelier.

Once again, CCV interceded in my life and career. I had taken several of the art courses while working there. I loved art and it was a great way to engage with the community, students and teachers. By chance, one of the offerings in Springfield was a design course offered by Stephen Plunkard, a local landscape architect.

He was young, engaging, energetic and enthusiastic. In reality I had little idea exactly what design was but felt that it would be an area to explore. Stephen gave us some pretty interesting challenges, i.e., design an island. After a few assignments, he said to me, "You missed your calling." Well, by the end of the semester, I had to agree.... I decided that I had to pursue this area of my education. I worked for another year at CCV while applying to graduate schools in design. I sold my house to pay for my education and took my two kids with me to North Carolina State, where I eventually received my MFA in Graphic Design.... I continue to design and teach design. I have been able to live all over the world as a design educator. This amazes me as much as anyone I meet, all a result of taking a course offered at CCV.

Judith Tomasi Shailor

Judith started at CCV as an office manager while she got her associate's degree. She went on to serve as the executive assistant to Peter Smith when he was Vermont's lieutenant governor, then as his director of Vermont operations when Smith was in Congress. She later became campaign manager and then community and legislative liaison for Martha Rainville, a retired U.S. Air Force major general who served from 1997 to 2006 as adjutant general of the Vermont National Guard — the first woman in the United States to become a state adjutant general.

I was married and had two babies; I couldn't really afford to go back to school. So I applied for a job at CCV. I thought, I could get my associate's degree and then go on to get my bachelor's. So I first started working there as an office manager in Montpelier. Then I got my associate degree, and I moved into a position as a financial aid counselor, helping people with their financial aid packages at the Central Vermont site.

What I learned, when I started to work there: There was no hierarchical structure in place. Peter set a tone and a philosophy that every single person mattered. It didn't matter whether you were pursuing a degree in mechanics or engineering or early childhood education; if you were the janitor, the financial aid counselor or the president of the college. He expected the staff and students and everyone to realize their value, and to treat each and every person with total respect and fairness.

They were just so open, for people to grow — and that is what gave everyone hope. You felt valued.

Lifelong learning, experiential learning: Every staff meeting we would talk about that. How do you assign credits for life experience? How do you give that person who's had thirty years in the field the same three credits as someone who took two semesters' worth of courses? Totally innovative.

The amazing thing was to see people, sometimes veterans, who thought, "Well, I have the GED, and this will help me get on my feet. I'll get some financial aid." The turnaround of them, to walk through the door and go from wearing a uniform to believing they could do whatever they wanted to — and pursue a degree, say, in finance — was transformational and exciting.

We were seeing those [veterans] who were not feeling good, because people didn't accept them. They hid their service. They were afraid to say, "I was in Vietnam." Then you had the academic world, which tends to be of a liberal mind-set and not necessarily engaged with military, coming together and welcoming these military people with open arms, which they hadn't necessarily felt before, and giving them hope, saying, "You can do this, and we're going to help you do this."

So it was strange bedfellows. And yet it was a perfect match.

"Give them a chance to prove it"

It would be an understatement to say that the Community College of Vermont is nontraditional. Certainly few institutions would accept experience as a service station attendant as counting towards a degree. Or that "teachers" would be selected more in terms of their experience in community organizing than for professional credentials. And that students should sign contracts covering learning goals, methods of reaching them, and ways in which the learning should be evaluated.

And there are a number of other canons — one of which says "thou shalt not have physical facilities" ... the kind of learning they are promoting prospers without a "campus."

— "Community College of Vermont: Some Impressions," Community and Junior College Journal, May 1975

Dr. William Craig, chancellor of the Vermont State Colleges, points out that most systems of education are exclusive while Community College is inclusive. "Older students, of course, involve less risk; they are a serious clientele. We do not try to predict what people are going to do but, rather, give them a chance to prove it. With our small investment per student per class, it's actually cheaper to give them a chance. People are welcome to try. They are accepted for what they are and the purpose is to make them better." He also points out that this inexpensive type of college education pays for itself many times over, just in the taxes from the graduates' higher incomes.

— Faire Edwards, "Experience Counts for Credit," Vermont Life, summer 1975

Chapter 7

A Turbulent End to a Pioneering Time

As the college's first president, Smith accepted an additional assignment from the Chancellor of the Vermont State College System to create the Office of External Programs, which included developing the External Baccalaureate Degree program for non-traditional students and a portfolio assessment program for evaluating students' experiential learning accrued outside of college.

— Victor Rivero, "Because 'We Shall Not Cease from Exploration,'" interview of Peter Smith, *EdTech Digest*, January 15, 2019

Students in the Vermont State Colleges' Assessment Program have gained learning through many diverse activities. For example, one student earned credit for knowledge of geography gained through his traveling experience as a seaman. Another student began carving decoy ducks for sporting purposes and achieved such a level of expertise that he published a book on the subject. A third student, a young French horn player, rose to the first horn position in the Vermont Symphony.

> *After a closer look, we see that "Nagging Doubt Number One" — i.e., Who was responsible for this instruction? — can be answered: no one. It does not matter that the input controls were missing because the source is merely the opportunity for learning to occur; the source is not the learning itself. We can measure prior learning only after the student brings it to us in a format that we can understand and evaluate according to college-level accomplishment criteria.*
>
> — Myrna Miller and Larry Daloz, "Assessment of Prior Learning: Good Practices Assure Congruity Between Work and Education," *Equity & Excellence in Education*, 1988

"There were a dozen or so nontraditional institutions that were doing assessment of experiential learning for credit," Daloz recalled. "Most of these were institutions that were trying to create different ways of promoting learning. Empire State [College] was one of those — that's where Myrna Miller came from.

"Myrna dazzled Peter and me when we were at some conference or other, at which she spoke about what Empire State was doing. She came about the time that I was leaving, but we were delighted to bring her on."

Miller is a gifted and independent-minded administrator with a progressive orientation; Smith hired her to develop and direct the new Office of External Programs for the state college system. Empire State, from which she had come, is a public college in Saratoga Springs, New York, founded in 1971 with the mission of providing flexible, student-defined education to adult learners.

Before long, Miller would play a pivotal role in CCV's evolution.

Dick Eisele

From "CCV Stories," November 19, 2013.

In early '77, the [college's] movement toward "legitimacy" and standardization took a major step with the establishment of a Final Review Committee (FRC) which would authorize final approval for the degree.... The FRC membership included a CCV staff member, a student, the president of Vermont Technical College, Sister Elizabeth Candon, the head of the Agency of Human Services, the superintendent of Montpelier schools, and Dale Gibson of Vermont Tap and Die Company of Lyndonville. This "high-powered" makeup of the FRC was another important step on our journey toward legitimacy, and it was the end of the individual LRC having the final word on "how much was enough."...

At this time in our evolution, we had several alternative learning models (independent studies, field experiences, practicums, internships, degree planning workshops, etc.), and no official college policy that covered them. Evidently we determined that each site establish a small group to help make *credit equivalent determinations* for these "oddball" offerings so that Scott (the registrar) would have something to go by.

Also on the college's agenda in mid '77 was the need for college-wide systems in reporting of class attendance and a policy for dropping from a course. We had to deal with the inadequacy of the "Carnegie umbrella" for contact hours for some courses and for the oddball stuff. And we had to decide just what should go on the cumulative record.

'The other is to know when to leave'

Before Larry Daloz left the central office staff in 1976, he went to see Richard Bjork, the VSC chancellor. Daloz had decided, with a lot of reluctance, to share a concern that Peter Smith might no longer be the best person to lead CCV.

"I remember going to his office basically behind Peter's back, and saying, 'You know, Peter is really not doing what needs to be done now. He's still trying to function like he did when we founded this place, and we're in a different era now.' I basically said, 'You know, I think he needs to leave.'

"I really haven't forgiven myself for that, but I'm not sure that was dumb. There's a whole literature in orientation-development theory about the founder's syndrome — that the founder stays on too long. He was not a consolidator."

"There are two important decisions you make with any job," Smith himself reflected. "One is to want it and to take it if you get it, and the other is to know when to leave.

"In 1977, we had just gotten a new chancellor, who was a tough guy, Richard Bjork, and he didn't like me and I didn't like him, but that's okay. He wanted me to put together a strategic plan and I said, 'Okay.'

"I went back to my office and I said to myself, looking out the window, 'You know how to spell strategic plan, but you don't know how to do one.' It was the fall of '77, and I said to myself, 'You've gotten this place this far; you don't know how to take it to the next level.'

"I was thirty, thirty-one. I was thinking about graduate school, and what happened with graduate school was I got to study why CCV succeeded those first eight years."

Smith announced that he would be leaving the college presidency in January 1978. He went into politics and held a series of elected offices until, as Vermont's lone Congressional representative, he lost his bid for reelection in 1990 to the former mayor of Burlington, Bernie Sanders.

Dick Eisele

From "CCV Stories," November 19, 2013.

Of course the news that Peter was leaving created a little more insecurity about the college's future. And, at the same time, a new chancellor, Richard E. Bjork, was hired by the VSC board and the rumor was that he was going to shake up the whole system. What helped us quite a bit was that before he left, Peter had hired an interim president, Nancy Wylie, a tall, thin blonde woman who was a very interesting person to say the least. She came with only a BA degree but she had a huge brain to make up for any lack of credentials. As I remember it, she caught on to the CCV culture, philosophy, and practices in an amazingly short time. Her understanding of the college was expressed in May of '78, when she wrote a memo to chancellor Bjork titled, The Role and Scope of the Community College of Vermont. This document was a thorough overview and examination of the college's place in the Vermont higher education community. From my perspective, she got everything right.

An acting president is one thing, but a permanent president without an advanced degree was another thing, so the VSC Board established a search committee to do a national search with the chancellor as chairperson. While obviously not mentioned in the official criteria established for the selection process, rumor had it that the board was looking for a president who might be sort of a "grandfather figure," maybe symbolic of the college's continuing maturation as an established institution. By September, after a series of interviews with six finalists, we selected a new president, Dr. George Bilicic.

'Do not close the doors'

George Bilicic came to CCV in late 1978 from the College at Brockport, a part of the State University of New York system, where he had been dean of continuing education. It soon became clear that he had joined CCV with little actual understanding of the institution.

"He came here and literally had no idea there was no campus, no idea there was no faculty, no idea there were no dormitories," recalled Tim Donovan, who had recently joined the chancellor's staff. "In retrospect, I think they hired this guy because they didn't know what to do with CCV."

Before long, the new president had alienated a number of people across the college staff.

"Bilicic's job was to get rid of all the pioneers," said Don Hooper, who was coordinator of instruction for Central Vermont. "They were going to move over to Bjork's conception of what CCV ought to be. He wanted to get rid of the disciples of Peter Smith — so Bilicic started to chop chop chop, and one after another people got fired."

Bilicic asked Hooper to become CCV's new regional director for Central Vermont. "I did that for about six months, and then he became intolerable," Hooper said. "These guys weren't educators. It was like being in the Trump administration — you had to follow orders, you couldn't argue back, they wouldn't listen. So finally, I quit."

Bilicic himself left the college in August 1979. But during his brief time at CCV, he oversaw the college's response to the most serious challenge yet to its survival.

'Save the community college'

"The House Appropriations Committee surprised nearly everyone last week by abruptly cutting the Community College of Vermont out of next year's budget," reported Tom Slayton of the Vermont Press Bureau, which covered the Legislature for the Barre-Montpelier *Times Argus* and *Rutland Herald,* on March 5, 1979.

The committee's 9–2 vote came during a spell of budget-cutting, in a tight time for the state college system. VSC had been rocked by a financial crisis in 1978, leading it to declare bankruptcy when it was unable to make bond payments on time.

"The coming years will be a time of retrenchment for the Vermont State Colleges, according to a report on the system given to legislators," Slayton wrote.

Those legislators were pressing the VSC to make a serious attempt to tighten its fiscal belt; and cutting the funding for CCV "was something we had to do, if for no other reason than to get the attention of the Vermont State Colleges," Rep. Jane Gardner (D-Arlington) told the *Burlington Free Press.*

Republican Governor Richard Snelling opposed axing CCV. And, the *Free Press* reported, two Republican House leaders were "organizing a 'save the community college' drive."

What followed was an upwelling of support for the college in the letters and editorial columns of newspapers around the state, especially from CCV's students. At a hearing on the Appropriations Committee's proposed cut, "we filled the house — like seven, eight hundred people showed up for the hearing," said Peter Smith, who was there. "They [the committee members] all went, 'Oh my God.'"

"The way I understand" the proposed closure, "the places where the classes are held are not high-class enough for education," wrote Barbara Allard of Lyndonville in the St. Johnsbury *Caledonian-Record* of March 8. "I want to state something right now, many of my classes were held around my kitchen table and I am very proud of it.... Do not close the doors of Community College, which means higher education for the poor people."

"Should funds for the college's operation be cut off, thousands of people in the state will be denied access to higher education when they most need it to cope with the complexities of their lives and times," the *Free Press* agreed in a March 20 editorial.

"One wonders how much serious bipartisan effort was made to determine the community college's effects on Vermont life, particularly that in rural areas," opined the *Newport Daily Express*. "How many of the 2,000 students in the college did the committee interview? Does it realize the number of those students who hold down jobs but still have the opportunity for self-improvement and [to] work toward a college degree, thanks to the presence of the community college in their town or city?

"... And do they realize that the no-walls community college, which has proven time and again that one does not need expensive bricks and mortar to provide learning opportunities, has provoked the traditional institutions to open their musty attitudinal attics to new ideas?"

"Community College Funds Restored," said a March 22 headline in the weekly *Barton Chronicle*. "The full House of Representatives restored the appropriation for Community College. By a vote of 105 to 38, the House added $449,000 to the budget proposed by the Appropriations Committee to fund the six-year-old college for another year.

"The vote came after a lengthy debate on the House floor, during which many members told of an enormous amount of pressure put on them by their constituents to restore the college.

"'I never thought I'd see the day when I would be standing up for Community College of Vermont,'" the Northeast Kingdom weekly quoted Rep. Frank Spates of Newport saying. "From the moment it opened I despised it terrible. But I have received a lot of letters and phone calls, and if I didn't vote for it I would not be properly representing the people in my area."

This was CCV's last near-death experience — and it motivated the college to move further along the path toward a more sound institutional structure and footing.

"When public outcry moved the House to rescue the college's funding last session, the message was clear: Get in fiscal shape," the *Free Press* reported in November 1979. "For a college born nine years ago as free, campus-less and liberal, it was a sobering experience."

> ### Rick Hurley
>
> *Rick came to the VSC central office in summer 1978 with new Chancellor Bjork. He had been a junior administrator at New Jersey's Stockton State College, when Bjork was president there.*
>
> I was brought up [to Vermont] as the assistant to the chancellor, so I did whatever he wanted me to do — and I got the liaison responsibility with the community college. His expectation was that I would develop a relationship with the president and understand how it operated. He [Bjork] was a traditionalist, so in his mind [CCV] was a fly-by-night organization. You know, a bunch of hippies walking around over there.
>
> He fired the president [Bilicic] and called me in his office. He said, "Listen, you understand that place better than anybody in this office, so I need you to go home this weekend and prepare for me an organizational chart with job descriptions and have it on my desk Monday morning." That's the way he was. He was old school.
>
> So I did that, and in the process — you can picture me drawing the boxes and the lines and all of that sort of thing — I created the position, underneath the president, of dean of administration. When I presented it to him I said, "That's me."
>
> He was startled to know that I was interested in going to work over there. Anyway, he changed [president] to dean of the college, Myrna Miller, and he downgraded my position to director of administration.

"My phone rang," said Miller. "I picked it up. [Bjork] said to me, 'You're head of the college, I just fired Bilicic.' I went, 'Oh … okay.'"

It was the last month of the 1970s, and it was the end of the improvising, decentralized, scrabbling-for-survival CCV. What was about to begin, under Miller's decisive and often-controversial leadership, would be a new era.

Facts and figures: 1979

From a college one-pager, "Facts about CCV":

- CCV educates 25% of Vermonters in the VSC system.
- CCV's cost per fulltime-equivalent student is $700 per yr. Other VSCs and most campus-based institutions' comparable cost is $1,500 per yr.
- CCV staff salaries are 25% lower than comparable VSC salaries.
- 80% of CCV students are poor or working poor.
- CCV educates over 3,000 Vermonters per year. Our student body has tripled since the fall of '73.
- CCV took an 18% budget cut for FY '76 — largest in the system by twice.
- Over 90% of CCV students polled reported that as a direct result of new knowledge, skills and experiences gained from CCV, they were able to do one or more of the following:
    1. Secure employment
    2. Find a better job
    3. Do better at their present job
    4. Save money or earn extra money outside of their job.

Graduates

Year	Total
1973	8
1974	48
1975	61
1976	118
1977	66
1978	96
1979	19

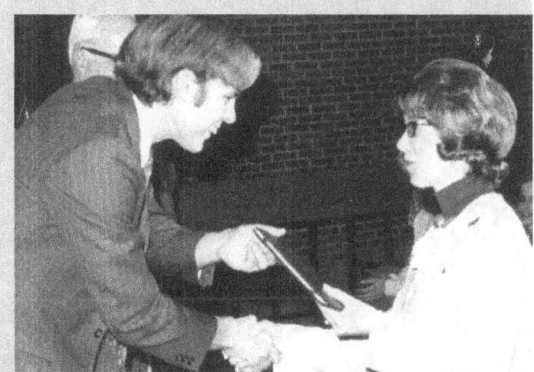

Peter Smith awards a diploma at the college's first graduation.

> "There was always the desire to prove ourselves, but not at the expense of the creativity and imagination that made CCV work."
>
> — Bette Matkowski

Part Two

A Lifetime of Learning

1979–2001

Chapter 8

We've Got to Save This

Myrna Miller, 1979-1982

Our president, Myrna Miller, in heels and rustling silks, moved among us like a monarch.
— Roger Cranse

Myrna Ring Miller came from a very different background than Peter Smith had, but they shared a conviction that higher education should — and could — be made more accessible to people of all ages, backgrounds and situations in life.

A native of Chicago's South Side whose father and grandfather serviced Pullman railroad cars, Miller came to Vermont in 1975 from Empire State College in the State University of New York system. Offering an individualized, flexible degree program to students who had responsibilities outside school, Empire State was one of the nation's first colleges to offer credit for the learning its students had gained in work and life. Miller met Smith through CAEL, the Council for Adult and Experiential Learning.

"I had no idea what CCV was or what it did," Miller recalled. "Peter and I served on this CAEL thing and I knew he was doing something innovative, so when he wanted someone to set up an assessment of prior learning program, I jumped on that. That's what

I love to do, develop programs from scratch without anyone messing in your head about what you can and cannot do."

Myrna Miller

Smith had secured a new federal FIPSE grant to create a Vermont initiative that would assign college credit for prior learning. In autumn 1975, he put Miller in charge of setting up an Office of External Programs, which was soon authorized by the Vermont State Colleges Board of Trustees. Starting in 1976, adult students around Vermont were offered a new course in developing portfolios that would document for credit what they had learned through experience.

"It was in all the state colleges, but mostly CCV was running these courses on portfolio preparation," recalled Tim Donovan, who was a young Iowa native when Miller hired him to coordinate the program's assessment services. "The Office of External Programs was technically part of the [VSC] chancellor's office, though the other colleges wanted nothing to do with either Peter or CCV."

"People wrote portfolios that had all the documentation that yes, they were working at this level and had these skills," Miller explained. "But I set it up to have faculty members from the state colleges serve on the committee that assessed those and assigned credits to them. I knew enough to know how much you had to work inside the system. If those faculty didn't approve, it would all have been seen as gobbledygook.

"The faculty members read the portfolios, came together in a committee to assign credits, and they'd nail it out among themselves," she said. "I'm sure they got tired after a while, having to read all those portfolios — but it worked, because they were recognized as the experts."

Under Miller's demanding supervision, Donovan spent five years traveling all over Vermont, speaking to the portfolio classes and working to make sure they offered consistent content. "After I finished doing that, I had evaluated several thousand students and their portfolios," he said. "I could go anywhere in the state and there would be students who said, 'I remember you. You came to my portfolio class and helped me get credit for what I knew.'"

Transferred to CCV in 1983, the Assessment of Prior Learning (APL) program continues, essentially unchanged from the model Myrna Miller developed. It serves about 200 to 250 students each year, with the Portfolio Development Course offered in ten to twelve sites each semester at CCV sites, the residential state colleges, business locations and other venues around the state.

Some fifteen committees assess the portfolios; each committee still includes two VSC faculty members, plus one non-VSC faculty and one other Vermonter. About one hundred faculty members from colleges around the state participate each year. To date, more than seven thousand students at CCV and the other state colleges have earned college credits with the portfolios they developed.

With Donovan running the APL program in the late 1970s, Miller set about searching for new funding. She secured another FIPSE grant that enabled her, in 1977, to create the External Degree Program, which made it possible for students to use the CCV model of self-designed learning in working toward a bachelor's degree.

"Here was a way," said Donovan, "that people who came out of CCV, or came out of the Assessment of Prior Learning program and wanted to continue something that was more individualized and more flexible — and not have to come to campus all the time — could do that."

The new program was initially offered through Castleton, Lyndon and Johnson state colleges and through the private, now-defunct Windham College, with each college providing mentors whom Miller trained to work with nontraditional students. But in the state colleges, Donovan said, the External Degree Program met with "great resistance from their faculty, who saw it as threatening or cheapening, or something."

"Eventually, Castleton and Lyndon bailed out on it," he said. "But Ed Elmendorf, who was the president of Johnson, said, 'We'll take it.' He embraced it. And by that time, Myrna had moved into her new role at CCV."

The External Degree Program was housed at Johnson State College until 2018, when JSC joined with Lyndon State to become Northern Vermont University. The External Degree Program then ceased to exist in its longtime form; those who had been enrolled in it were "now Northern Vermont University Online students," the university said on its website. In 2023, Northern Vermont University became part of the newly created Vermont State University.

Back in the late '70s, Miller and Donovan became a strong team, after a rocky start learning to work together. "Myrna is a brilliant, brilliant, creative educator, and I'm an operations guy. I like to make things work," Donovan said. "I can't think of a better person to keep me from getting inside the traditional box of higher education. We were just operating outside it, and I thought that was normal! I was thirty years old — what did I know?"

Tim Donovan

In November 1978, Chancellor Bjork assigned Myrna, with me as her sidekick, to "go to the CCV and get the place reaccredited — and you report to me, not the president." This was my first indication that George Bilicic's presidency was doomed, and he didn't know it.

Myrna discovered that the self-study for a March '79 accreditation visit was seriously behind schedule, creating the opportunity to shape its focus. The resulting self-study laid out an academic vision that became the blueprint for the next three years of her leadership — what I describe as a transformation of the institutional mindset from Peace Corps to college.

In the same time period, the Legislature undertook the [March 1979] effort to defund the college. [See chapter 7.] Myrna marshaled students to descend on the State House, and the effort failed.

When the accreditation team came in March, Bjork met them for Sunday night dinner and Bilicic was ignored, only to be relieved of duty shortly after the visit ended. This visit resulted in the three-year accreditation that formalized Myrna's vision for the college and its new mindset. Her work over the next three years largely implemented that vision and, in 1982, resulted in the college securing its first full-term, ten-year accreditation.

'We have to save this place'

In mid-1979, when Chancellor Bjork abruptly fired George Bilicic after just a few months as CCV's president, he made Miller head of the college but not its president. Instead he named her dean of the college, with all of a president's responsibilities.

It has been suggested that this was sexist. Miller sees it differently.

"His reasoning was perfectly in line with higher education," she drily observed, many years later. "He had not conducted a well-advertised blah-de-blah search, and that's the way it's done. So it made perfect sense that he could assign me to do this [run the college], but he couldn't assign me as president or it would have made a big stink.

"I really didn't care what my title was," she said. "I knew it was a huge responsibility. CCV is hard to understand if you don't have a mind already around experiential education and student-centered education. People think of Vermont as a pretty little place with the cute white churches with the spires and the maple trees and so forth — but they don't see the poverty.

"Where Peter and I were alike is, we were thinking about new ways to educate. I identified with the students who'd had no chance to get an education, so part of my desire was to see this thing become a real college that could get accredited. What Peter did was brilliant, in setting things up so that people could get to the centers where there was supportive staff who could help them. That model was wonderful, but I had to impose this accrediting-style traditional stuff. It was the high point of my career."

Moving with Miller from the state colleges' main office to CCV was Rick Hurley, who had been an aide to Bjork and now became the college's director of administration. Even though CCV had survived two attempts in the Legislature to defund it, its status and funding in the state system were still shaky — as was the college's own level of organization.

"The way it operated, with the lack of policies and procedures, accountability was really absent," Hurley said. "So that's where I spent my time, creating a policies-procedures manual and trying to bring order and professionalism to a lot of the chaos.

"We were really struggling on two fronts: one, legislative support for funding, and two, enrollments. Our message was, 'Hey, we've got to save this place, or we won't be employed.' I think people understood that. And we really believed in what we were doing."

As a leader, he said, Miller was "self-confident. I think she really embraced the role, liked the challenge, was enjoying the work. She was big on soliciting others' opinions — because, you know, the Northeast Kingdom is so different from the southern region. There was more variety in the culture of Vermont than people often realize, and you had to kind of work with that."

"In 1979, the college was a loose confederation of site offices, each with a great deal of autonomy," Tim Donovan recalled. "Myrna was clear that this was going to be 'one college.' She charged the Academic Review Board with creating a single catalog of available courses, and insisted that each course have 'essential objectives' that were the same no matter where it was taught or by whom. Going forward, there would be one college-wide course list, published for every semester.

"This legacy lives intact — with much the same terminology."

It was a big and somewhat jarring change to make in the free-wheeling culture of the college. Miller was convinced that without the change, she said, "the thing would have gone right under."

Dona Welch

Dona joined the staff as secretary to the dean shortly after Miller's tenure began. From "CCV Stories," July 19, 2013.

I think some people underestimated Myrna because she was so attractive and sophisticated, but underneath she was warm and incredibly smart and capable....

Here's an early memory that almost ended my CCV career in the first week. One of the duties Myrna told me about was to be secretary to the Administrative Council.... At the end of my first week ... was the first Administrative Council meeting. The members gathered in the big conference room at the front of the building. As far as I can remember, the members were Myrna, chair of course; Peggy Williams, Northern Region director;

Nancy Chard, Southern Region director; maybe Roger Cranse; and Bill Stickney [business manager]....

We took our seats, I took out my shorthand notebook, Myrna introduced me. Nancy Chard said, "First of all, I don't want that ____ woman in the room taking notes." Silence fell. I turned to Myrna and remember thinking whether I spent another day at CCV depended on how she responded. Myrna told Nancy she didn't care what she wanted because she was the dean and she wanted minutes taken at meetings and that was that....

Nancy and I became close friends and mutual supporters and I felt she was one of the best people at CCV, but we certainly had a memorable first meeting.

Nancy Severance

Nancy started at CCV in 1979 as regional director for Central Vermont, and in 1983 became the registrar. From "CCV Stories," July 15, 2013.

Myrna Miller was to be my boss. She had just been appointed dean of the college, part of its legitimacy push, and its major architect, as it turned out. My monthly reports to her were typed on a typewriter, using carbon paper, and the carbon copies were on the backs of old course descriptions, such as "Jogging for Beginners."

Myrna Miller

The real shock was when I had this big staff meeting to get people, beyond just the regional directors, to understand there were going to be these huge changes. I said, "I want CCV's degree to be a *real* degree, and this is how this is going to be a real college."

This woman in the back puts up her hand and says, "You mean my CCV degree isn't a real degree?" I wanted to drop through the floor.

KIND OF A MIRACLE

Roger Cranse

From "CCV Stories," July 15, 2013.

The potential I think Myrna saw in an organization not far from baseline chaos was that a chief executive, with little to hold her back, could make big dramatic decisions all on her own. One came at a college retreat in the early 1980s. In the evening, after dinner, Myrna stood before the entire college and announced — proclaimed — that we would have centrally approved college-wide courses, with course numbers, in a single college-wide course catalog. No more freelance courses at individual sites, no more let's-make-it-up-as-we-go experiments, no more wouldn't-it-be-cool-if offerings.

Roger Cranse

As far as I know, Myrna hadn't shopped this idea around, hadn't consulted important constituencies and "stakeholders" (why does this word always make me see vampire slayers in a forest at midnight?), hadn't worked behind the scenes to disarm opponents. None of that.

I was pretty new and the reaction in the crowd floored me. People leapt from their seats. "No! No!" they hooted. "You can't do that!" People threatened to resign. (Several actually did.) "You're destroying the college!" "Myrna, you should quit!"

Myrna appeared unfazed. She understood, I think, the true nature of power. You don't have to be afraid. You don't have to get angry. You have the power. What you say *will* happen.

And it did. The college swerved onto the road of legitimacy — and convention.

Myrna Miller

The first paragraph below is from "CCV Stories," July 15, 2013. The next two paragraphs are from an interview with the author.

The staff was not thrilled, to say the least! They wanted to keep things responsive to local students' needs. So we had to do some serious soul searching about students' needs in Vermont. I pushed very hard to convince the staff that we had to have courses with traditional credit hours and grades so our graduates could move on to receive advanced degrees.... Classes that were consistent and for credits while delivered close to home was what I saw as the real need. I wasn't sure the staff entirely agreed with this more traditional approach, but at the time our funding was hanging by a thread so they went along.

We literally had a day in which we got everyone together, and we were sitting down by the river, writing the little blurbs that would go into a single catalog. People were cooperating but grumbling. Only one of them told me, face-to-face, "I don't think I can work for you." But I said, "Oh, I think you can. It will be fine."

The new direction was not easy. I was like a dog with a bone because it had to be done. I was trying to make the college something that would last. Other people didn't see it that way.

'There was a huge turnover'

"A whole bunch of people left because of that," said Donovan. "There was a huge turnover among people who were the early believers, many of whom considered that they'd been sold out."

Among those deciding to leave was Karen Saudek, who in the late '70s had become a CIA (coordinator of instruction and advisement) in the Central Vermont office.

In those early days, Saudek said, the college "was decentralized — all kinds of interesting education happening in a decentralized manner — and I really enjoyed it." She became acting director of the Central Vermont site under Miller, and the college began going through changes.

"I never had a real problem with Myrna, but I did have trouble with the changes," Saudek said. "She was working toward standardization of things, and what I had been enjoying was the free-wheeling, we-can-define-education-as-we-go thing and students can define what they want to learn. As the college began to change, it began to be not the place where I wanted to be."

Saudek left to create a new, local education clearinghouse, the Learning Exchange in Montpelier. "I based it on what I had learned at CCV: recruiting teachers from the community, holding classes wherever I could get free space, lots of short courses. We sent trips whale watching. We did beer making in my kitchen, wallpapering. Avram Patt taught Yiddish. It was very, very eclectic. It was great fun." The Learning Exchange continued for several years, and then Saudek went on to become a human resources executive for several large Vermont organizations.

"Another big Myrna decision was to imprint a particular theory of learning on the entire college," said Roger Cranse, who joined CCV in 1980. "Most of our students were adult learners, twenty-five and older. Most were women. Myrna believed the findings and theories of adult development were especially relevant to the work of the college, and she therefore arranged for all the full-time staff to take a three-credit course on the subject. Joanna Noel and Larry Daloz taught the course."

Gabrielle Dietzel

Gabrielle served as a coordinator of instruction and advisement from 1982 to 2004, and then as director of Prior Learning Assessment in the Office of External Programs until 2015. From "CCV Stories," August 28, 2015.

On my second day on the job, I got a call from Nancy Chard, who was at that time the regional director of the southern region. Nancy told me that: a) I was on the Curriculum Committee, b) the meeting was the next day, and c) to bring scissors. Scissors?!? I soon found out. The next day, five or so of my new colleagues gathered around a table, scissors in hand, and we all started cutting up the CCV course lists.

At that time, each CCV site had their own course schedule, and although the course titles were pretty much the same, each site had their own description and version of what, e.g., Applied Math was all about. So here was the curriculum committee, armed with small machetes, cutting out the nine different versions of English Comp, placing them next to one another, comparing, contrasting, and coming up with one blurb that everyone in the college would use. Nowadays, that would be called cut-and-paste. And that's what we did — cutting and pasting the curriculum together. Therefore, on day three of my CCV career, I understood that if something needed to get done, we'd roll up our sleeves and just figure out how to do it, whichever way would work. And that is exactly the way it was, for 33 years. Only the means changed. But the approach was the same.

Gabrielle Dietzel

Gary Moore

Gary began at CCV as a coordinator of instruction and advisement. He went on to become academic dean at Woodbury College and then at the Vermont College of Fine Arts, both in Montpelier. A playwright, poet and performance artist now living and Puerto Rico, he is the author of Abe & Ann *(Torbey, Canada: Komatik Press, 2019), a novel about Abraham Lincoln's first love.*

I saw a sign on Langdon Street [in Montpelier] for "Community College of Vermont," apparently upstairs. I had to take an interest, because I had taught in community colleges in Pennsylvania and Maryland but had never heard of a community college of a whole state. Found my way into enlightening talks with Karen Saudek and Howard Fisher: adult learners, offices in communities around the state, classes mixed with a lot of independent studies to fulfill each student's unique learning plan.

A few months later a job opened up in the Johnson office, coordinator of instruction and advisement. I applied and got the job, and went to work with a feeling of a kind of high adventure in educational democracy. Each coordinator was like a mini-dean for an area of the state: We tried to know our students and prospective students and plan curriculum and hire adjunct faculty accordingly. Most of all, the college as a whole kept alive a vision of education that was not centered on content in academic disciplines, nor around faculty expertise, but on students and what they needed and wanted to know and what they knew as a starting point, and how their learning styles would help them get there.

At that time, learning objectives were custom-developed for each course in a kind of negotiation between students and instructor in the first class or two. This established a sense of student ownership and responsibility for course participation and success. It helped that classes were generally small. We needed seven for a "go," but many courses had ten to fifteen or so in the regional offices where I worked in my two years there: Johnson, Morrisville, then briefly in Barre.

I loved the school's commitment to its educational philosophy. And I loved the kind of people who worked there because they were drawn to such a mission. Myrna Miller, the dean, and Dick Eisele, the chief learning guru, were brilliant at training coordinators and helping us train the faculty we hired, each in our regions. "Student-centered" was the mantra, and we meant it.

I was there in a time of transition, though. I enjoyed college staff meetings very much because I liked the people so much — so smart and positive in their attitudes and so committed to helping learners. And they — we — were real believers in assessment, even before assessment became the dominant drumbeat of higher education. We taught our faculty and students the importance of assessing student progress toward each of the course learning objectives. And if students internalized the process of establishing an objective and then honestly evaluating their progress toward it, they would have a key to open a lifetime of learning.

Adult learning. Lifelong learning. We believed in the philosophy, and we applied the philosophy. But.

Our own honest assessment told us that practicing education in such a student-centered and custom-made and idealistic manner brought challenges of inefficiency, cost and effective interplay with other educational and professional institutions. If the college was to mature and grow, it was going to have to bring its standards reliably closer to those of the higher ed mainstream. Could we do this while at the same time continuing to be dedicated to the needs and learning styles of individual adult learners?

We started a project to install in each course — beginning with the most commonly required ones, like English Composition — a set of required objectives. Other objectives could be added by the class and instructor, but the required objectives would assure that three credits of English Composition meant the presence of about the same required learning in a course of the same name offered across all of CCV's regions.

CCV was in the process of that curricular transition and a growth in numbers that would make it and keep it truly financially viable. How the onetime "storefront college" managed to grow and merge with the wider system while maintaining its devotion to the student-centered idealism of Peter Smith and Myrna Miller and Dick Eisele is a story that I hope others will tell, because it took place after I left in 1982 to become a mentor in the External Degree Program of Johnson State College.

Supporting — and challenging — adult students

In 1980, a proposal written by Eisele brought in a major new grant through the federal TRIO Programs, which had developed out of the Higher Education Act of 1965 to support services for learners from disadvantaged backgrounds. With the funding, CCV created a new group of coordinators of student services, based at the various sites.

KIND OF A MIRACLE

"The important thing for all of us," Miller said, "was keeping people at the local centers to hold each student's hand and walk them through the registration and degree requirements. For many older students, even the idea of attending college is very frightening. In this way we kept the local, student-centered support system in place while we bit off the task of making CCV's teaching and learning more traditional.

"With adults, either their job goes, their carburetor goes, their kids get sick — there's all this stuff in the way of them being able to get a leg up," she added. "That's why it was so wonderful that the sites had these built-in mentors. Find out what the problem is, talk them through it. Whatever it is, help."

The TRIO funding also enabled Miller to task Roger Cranse with creating a new introductory academic program for incoming adult students. Since CCV students typically had been out of the classroom for years, had sometimes struggled in school, and often lacked family role models for college, Miller envisioned a program that would help them build confidence in themselves as college-level learners. It had to be geared toward adults, and it had to be challenging.

"These people want a *real* education. We all do," she said. "We don't want someone to say, 'Oh you poor little thing,' or 'I'll pat you on the head and you can read some easy books.'"

"A month or two later, I went to Myrna to brief her on the development of our new program," Cranse later wrote. "She listened carefully while I told her about a multidimensional learning and support program for disadvantaged students. 'What are you going to call it?' she asked.

"'Not sure yet,' I replied.

"'Dimensions of Learning, that's its name,' she said, her eyebrows arching in a so-shall-it-be-written, so-shall-it-be-done kind of way."

Working with a team that included Joan Kaye, Leonard Foote, Elliot Kaplan and later Bill Callahan, Cranse decided that Dimensions would consist of a sequence of three-credit courses. To build the reading list, he visited Dartmouth College's bookstore in Hanover, New Hampshire, and asked to see the list for first-year English. It included George Orwell's *1984*, the book *Diaries of Women*, and a collection of American short stories. "We added Plato's 'Allegory of the Cave,' and these became

Dimensions' texts," Cranse wrote. But, he added, "if our students read what Dartmouth freshmen read, we would have to teach differently — because, despite our egalitarian sentiments, CCV students were not, by and large, as well prepared for college."

Roger Cranse

From "CCV Stories," July 15, 2013.

In brief, we proceeded very carefully through a text, making sure our students understood what they were reading, how and if the material applied to them and their world, if there were larger metaphoric meanings in the text, and the like. These careful, close reading excursions into challenging materials were designed to achieve several results. First, by learning to understand and interact with college-level materials, students, many of whom told us they were "not that smart" (a heartbreaking phrase we heard often), developed a sense of *academic self-worth*. Second, the study of these materials was also meant to challenge students ... to impel *intellectual growth*.

I was also determined that Dimensions would award college credit — that is, it would not be stigmatized as a remedial "bonehead" course. Myrna agreed and made that decision — again, as far as I know, entirely on her own authority.

The special services team spent the fall of 1980 developing Dimensions, and in the spring launched it statewide. The special services coordinators taught three or four sections each; I taught two. We were also advisors to our students. For each class I prepared a detailed, minute-by-minute lesson plan and mailed copies to the coordinators. I recall Nancy Chard, southern regional director, snorting contemptuously at these plans. Yes, I was a control freak; the point, of course, was that we were teaching in a new way, thus the detailed plans.

As we developed Dimensions in the fall, I visited each site to brief CIAs on the program and to solicit their feedback. A few seemed skeptical but nearly all welcomed the new program. There was almost no resistance to its implementation.

> Again, I attribute this welcoming attitude and lack of resistance to the very fluid state of the college at the time — a third of the way from chaos to consolidation.

'We all became quite close'

"Dimensions of Learning was a grand experiment," noted team member Joan Kaye. "Many ideas were floated, soared, popped and fell, but the finished product worked and worked well. Dimensions still lives" — it's currently called Dimensions of Self and Society — "and being involved in its development was one of the most rewarding experiences I have had."

At the site offices, meanwhile, having new student support coordinators in place meant the coordinators of instruction and advisement could now focus more energy on recruiting, training and supporting faculty — along with advising students on academics and financial aid, selling textbooks, "begging classroom space from anyone willing to have us, and other duties as assigned," recalled Kaye, who was hired as a teacher in 1980 by Pixley Hill, a CIA in St. Albans.

"I was hooked," Kaye said. "Not ever considering myself to be a teacher, I could never have envisioned myself in front of a class — yet there I was, working with the most amazing, engaged and enthusiastic students."

"What stands out to me, besides the intriguing and varied CCV employees, was the range of students," recalled Sherry Blankinship, who was the Springfield office's curriculum coordinator from 1979 to 1983. "Many seemed lost, others were desperate. Some were eager to begin in higher education; others wanted a single course to improve employment possibilities.

"I mostly worked with the high school for space, and local business and arts people for teachers," she said. "I was able to recruit from the Tuck School of Business at Dartmouth — a couple of their graduate students came to Springfield a few nights a week to teach. My favorite part of this job was assisting the teachers with book selection, curriculum development and assessment. The narrative evaluations took time and were difficult for many to write, and quite laborious for us to file."

"Tuition was $65 per three-credit course in spring 1980," said Nancy Severance, who became the Central Vermont regional director in 1979, at an annual salary of $13,500.

"Before registration," she said, "everyone on the staff drove and distributed course lists throughout Washington and Orange counties. We hosted meet-the-instructor and registration nights before our classes began. We gave our first basic skills tests in September 1980. We were all responsible for visiting classes at the beginning and end of each semester. We bought and sold all textbooks and packed and returned unsold books to the publishers at the end of the semester. We laughed a lot."

'Who thought up that jingle?'

The directive Myrna Miller received from Chancellor Bjork at the beginning of her leadership, she said, "was to get enrollment up. That must have been what [Governor Richard] Snelling told him: 'You've got to get enrollment up or we're going to get rid of this thing,' or something like that."

Recalled Rick Hurley: "Bjork said to me — and he said it to Myrna — 'Look, we're in desperate times and people do desperate things, and you guys have just got to get creative, to figure out how you're going to fix this enrollment.' So I dreamed up this wild idea along the lines of, 'Hey folks, if you enroll and you bring a friend to enroll, we'll give you free pizza.' Literally, we were out in the public saying that kind of stuff.

"Next I said, 'Look, we ought to advertise, we ought to market ourselves.' So I worked with a local radio station up there and created a jingle to advertise our registration periods and so on. It had a jingle, then a 'donut' where we would put in the words and then the jingle, 'CCV, Community College of Vermont.' I'll never forget the president of Lyndon [State] saying to me one day, 'Who thought up that jingle? I'm so tired of hearing that on the radio!'

"People starting coming, and really the rest is history. It kind of took off, because everybody was really engaged in this effort to turn the place around and make it successful," said Hurley. (He left in 1982 to become director of administration for the American Association of State Colleges and Universities, and later served as president of Mary Washington University in Virginia).

Neither 'devil' nor 'savior'

By 1982 the college had become "financially stable, as a result of a combination of increased attention to finances and more competent management," said its 1981–1982 annual report. Thanks to a new, $100,000 federal Title III grant, CCV was offering faculty development workshops for its part-time teachers and had developed its first seven standardized degree programs — in business (Accounting, Small Business Management, Secretarial Science, and Management) and human services (Criminal Justice, Early Childhood Development and Human Services Studies).

At the same time, "the College has been refining the individualized degree process," the report said. "Students now enroll for a short (five week) course in which they learn to prepare their plans. A newly constituted Academic Review Board will now review and approve plans prior to implementation. This approach changes the CCV program from an outcomes measurement process to one of advise and consent for a plan of study."

During the first years of the 1980s, enrollment numbers hadn't yet shown the impacts (although they soon would) of the college's new marketing efforts. Total enrollment for the 1980–1981 academic year was 2,049. It was 2,036 in 1981–1982, and 2,045 in 1982–1983.

Breaking down the 1982–1983 numbers:
- 96 percent of students were part-time,
- 73 percent were female,
- 95 percent were Vermont residents,
- 69 percent had applied for financial aid,
- 71 percent were nontraditional age students, and
- 29 percent were seeking an associate degree.

CCV awarded ninety-one associate degrees in spring 1983. By then, the cost per three-credit course was $88.

By then, too, Myrna Miller had moved on. She became president of the former Mohegan Community College in Connecticut, then served in California as president of Marin Community College, renamed during her tenure as the College of Marin. She retired from the College of Marin.

As Miller summed up her relatively brief but quite consequential time at CCV: "Some thought I was the devil who was going to destroy the college, and others thought I was its savior. The truth is that I was very fortunate to have had the opportunity to contribute to a wonderful institution."

Immediately after she departed, the college entered a short spell of interim leadership that was to prove, quite unexpectedly, pivotal in its history.

Tim Donovan

Myrna spent three years as the dean of the college, from the middle of '79 to the middle of '82. She and [Chancellor] Bjork didn't like each other, but I think there was some respect. When Myrna left in the summer of '82, it did not end well between her and Bjork.

Myrna was a very strong feminist, not politically but just in her values and requirements of people; and Bjork was a very traditional, I'm-in-charge-and-you-will-do-what-I-say old-school executive — and a talented one. She just thought, "You don't know enough to tell me what to do," and he would say, "Well, you don't have enough power for me not to." In the end, I think she demanded, "Either make me president or I'm going to leave." And he said, "Okay. Good-bye."

The groundwork had not been laid for a transition. Myrna went off to lead a community college in Connecticut, and Bjork was named as the acting president at CCV. That was August of '82 — so there was a nine-month period where Dick Bjork was the acting president at CCV. I think he came to that thinking: "I don't know what this place is, I don't know what it needs, and maybe I should just kill it. Because it's a bunch of hippies."

But I think he fell in love with the place. His attitude changed dramatically.

KIND OF A MIRACLE

CCV had written a federal grant under Title III of the Higher Education Act, which was for aid to developing institutions. It was mostly a grant program for historically black colleges and universities, but CCV qualified as a developing institution. The grant came through in September, after Myrna left, and it had two activities, both of which are foundational in CCV's history. One of those was to open the western corridor, and the other was to purchase our first computers.

The western corridor: CCV had no presence in Chittenden, Addison or Rutland counties. I think Peter Smith, in order to get support for CCV in the higher education community, had promised institutions in those counties — which is where most of the [higher ed] institutions in Vermont were — that we won't be in your county, we won't compete with you. Not knowing any of that when we were writing that grant, we just thought, "How can we be a statewide community college without a presence in two of the most populous counties in the state, Rutland and Chittenden?" So we wrote in that we were going to open up CCV into those counties.

To this day, there's a phrase you'll see in CCV marketing materials: "We're within 25 miles of 90 percent of the state's population." That came from this grant. We put a five-pound Folger's coffee can on an official Vermont tourism map, drew circles around the major labor market in each of those counties, and guess what? It covered almost every place that anybody lives — and it was exactly equal to a 25-mile radius. I think that got us the grant! And it remains kind of the signature description of the college: We're within 25 miles of 90 percent of the state's population.

It turns out that nobody had really thought about the implications of the grant — because once the Title III program awarded it, the University of Vermont, Trinity College [then in Burlington], St. Michael's College and Champlain College all erupted. "How could you *do* that?"

Bjork was called on the carpet by the higher-ed institutions in Chittenden County, specifically UVM, St. Mike's and Trinity.

He got called to a meeting with them, and he told me, "You're coming with me," partly because I had written the grant.

I'll never forget that meeting. I can tell you the room it was in, who was in the room — and these folks just raked him over the coals. "What makes you think there's a market that's not being served in Chittenden County with all of these institutions?"

This was early '83. At that point in time, the Burlington airport had lost air carriers because of deregulation: There wasn't enough traffic. So the major air carriers had pulled out of Burlington, and a little startup out of New Jersey, called People Express, was offering $25 fares to Newark. They were very popular! So Bjork says to this collection of people, "CCV is the People Express of higher education. They will bring people into this market that you don't even know exist. And if you're smart, you'll do everything you can to get them when CCV's done with them, or they're done with CCV."

Next, Bjork and his finance director worked out a deal with VSAC [Vermont Student Assistance Corporation], which was moving into the Champlain Mill [a large, redeveloped riverside industrial mill in Winooski, next to Burlington] to sublet a third of one floor to CCV. So CCV's in Winooski. That's a huge pivot — and I think it was part of what made Bjork say, "You know, this could be interesting."

And that changed the trajectory of the institution. Within 25 miles of 90 percent: It became aspirational for the college, and it made a political statement in the state.

The other thing that came out of that Title III grant was the ability to buy our first forty-five desktop computers. The IBM PC had just come out, but there was literally a $700 premium for an IBM PC, so we were going to buy what were considered PC-compatible computers, which became a real thing eventually. But in 1984, I would describe it as: They were 90 percent PC compatible. It was that 10 percent that you didn't know about. But it bought us forty-five computers, which we could set up in our locations. Each computer lab I think had six computers.

These were Zenith Z-100s: two floppy drives, 192 K of memory. They cost $2,200 each. Not cheap. Most of them were going into classrooms, and a few were going into administrative offices. They were built like a brick shithouse, a steel frame.

So we bought these computers, and quite frankly we didn't know what to do with them. We created our first real computer course, "Introduction to Microcomputer Applications," and we started using computers administratively. And in February 1983, Ken Kalb was hired as president. He started that April.

'Be it Resolved ...'

Many years later, Donovan, now president of CCV, asked Myrna Miller to join him at a June 1, 2006, meeting of the Vermont State Colleges Board of Trustees.

"I had gone to the chair of the board during the Myrna Miller years, and to Ken Kalb, who followed her as president, and asked if they would support an official rewriting of the college history," Donovan recalled. "They said yes. Marshall Witten, who had been the chair then, said, 'I don't remember why we did it that way but it was a mistake, it was an insult. An insult to the college, and it was an insult to her.' So then I took a resolution to the Board of Trustees."

"He invited me for something else, what it was I don't remember," Miller said. "He drives me off to the board meeting, and I think I'm going to be sitting in the back row listening to the same old stuff that boards do, you know. When this comes up, he practically broke down in tears. It was a very emotional thing because, as he now tells me, he thought he had the votes but he might not have."

Here is the resolution the VSC board adopted that evening:

WHEREAS, Myrna R. Miller was appointed by the VSC Board of Trustees as the chief executive officer of the Community College of Vermont with the title Dean of the College and served in that capacity from July 1979 to August 1982.

A LIFETIME OF LEARNING

WHEREAS, At the time of Ms. Miller's appointment, CCV's academic legitimacy and institution's survival were considered questionable; and

WHEREAS, By the end of her term in 1982, Ms. Miller had envisioned and led a transformation that resulted in ten-year accreditation and had built an academic foundation for the college as we know it today; and

WHEREAS, Since the formation of the Vermont State Colleges, every chief executive officer of a college has served with the title of President with this single exception; there for be it

RESOLVED, That the Vermont State Colleges Board of Trustees acknowledges Myrna R. Miller as the Community College of Vermont's President from July 1979 to August 1982.

Myrna Miller with the 2006 resolution that retroactively named her CCV's president from 1979 to 1982. Applauding is Jim Douglas, Vermont's governor from 2003 to 2011.

Chapter 9

Where Vermonters Go to College

Ken Kalb, 1983-1991

When Ken came into a CCV site, he walked around and spoke to everyone. He didn't just speak to a coordinator, or a dean. He made it absolutely clear that he was involved, he was connected, and he set the tone.

— Bette Matkowski

Ken Kalb had been vice president of operations for American College Testing in Iowa for nine years when, feeling "a little restless," he applied for a job as the Vermont State Colleges' director of personnel. He didn't get it. But in the process he met Chancellor Bjork, and "I kind of liked him," Kalb recalled. A few months later he saw an ad in the *Chronicle of Higher Education* for the president of something called the Community College of Vermont. He applied.

"I got a nice letter back from Bjork, and he was warning me that this was a tough, low-paying job. I wrote back and said, 'Well, that sounds all right to me. I don't need an entourage of support staff, and I don't need this and that.' He wrote back and said he liked that response — and to my amazement, I won out. Tim [Donovan] mentioned once that I probably won out because I wasn't an ideologue about higher education."

A LIFETIME OF LEARNING

Among those who interviewed for the job, "others had had various jobs in higher ed," Kalb recalled, "and they had ideas about what to do, and I was more or less clueless. That may have helped me, because I wasn't pontificating at these meetings. I was asking questions. I think I said something like, 'You guys are swimming in ideas; you probably just need somebody to make the trains run on time, and pull it all together in some way.'"

Over the eight years of his presidency, that's the essence of what Ken Kalb did. He greatly strengthened CCV as an organization, and he did much to knit together a diversity of sites into one college with a unified identity.

Ken Kalb

Kalb oversaw the expansion into Chittenden, Addison and Rutland counties on the western side of the state, giving CCV much more of a statewide presence. He personally interviewed candidates for positions at virtually every level, looking for good people who would complement this unique institution — and he brought in a number of new staff members who would play vital roles in the years of dramatic growth that began under Kalb, and for which he prepared the ground.

"In the '80s, Ken made us a financially sound business," said Joyce Judy, who joined the Springfield staff as a coordinator in 1983, worked there for eleven years and eventually, in 2009, became president herself. "It was really about getting processes in order. We needed to develop some foundational stability."

"I had a lot of respect for Ken. He had such a vision, and he really understood how to hire good people," said Mica DeAngelis, who opened the new Chittenden County site in 1983 as its first coordinator. "And he could be tough when he had to be, because he knew what we were up against. He knew it was going to be a lot of work. I don't know how he knew all this, because he wasn't even a Vermonter — but he knew. He was a very kind man as well, and fun."

'We're going to organize this'

Kalb was fond of pointing out that his presidency began on April Fools' Day, in 1983.

"I remember the first time I went to my office, above the bank in Montpelier," he said. "There really wasn't an office for me — they had to find a room and put a desk in it. I was nervous and apprehensive, on edge and in a lot of doubt. It was a pleasure and a relief to get around and meet people, to visit sites and get a firsthand perspective on what I was supposed to be doing."

The college had site centers then in St. Albans, Springfield, Brattleboro, Barre, Newport, Morrisville, St. Johnsbury and White River Junction, that last one a single room in the aged Hotel Coolidge. When the college set up its first cramped Chittenden County site at the Chase Mill in Winooski, it was "under loud protest by the other area colleges, who believed CCV would take students away from their institutions," noted Gabrielle Dietzel, who had become an academic coordinator in '82.

As Kalb drove from site to site and had conversations with everyone on staff, "I tried to be concerned with the culture of the place — the way people were treated, related to each other," he said. "I got my fingers fairly deeply into the recruiting process, for all positions. I was looking for a certain compatibility."

"He brought a really strong sense of the value of effective organization," said Tim Donovan, who joined the CCV staff under Kalb when the college absorbed the Office of External Programs, home to the Assessment of Prior Learning project. "Some would say hierarchy, because he was kind of traditional in that regard. Ken really strengthened the regional director's role, and he moved the college beyond a loose confederation of twelve sites.

"He moved people around based on what he perceived were the needs," Donovan added. "He wanted meetings scheduled, minutes taken, reports — and all of those things were kind of new. But it's hard to imagine the college succeeding in the way that it has, had that transition not taken place. He was the guy who said, 'We're going to organize this.' At that moment in time, that had to happen."

'He wanted to know you'

Kalb never forgot the first meeting of state college presidents that he attended. It was at Johnson State, and "they were dissing us," he said. "Our best courses were on Elvis Presley or making pickles or whatever. That was part of my initiation."

If CCV was to build respect and credibility, Kalb saw that it needed to develop more internal cohesion and consistency. "Any time you're trying to unify various entities into a single system, there will be some backlash, or people who think it's done in an inappropriate way," he later reflected. "But I think there was a general perception that we needed to be more organized, or consolidated. And most people I think were glad to see the coherence that resulted from that."

"The best way to get a dispersed organization to think of itself as a single organization is to *do* things as a single organization," noted Donovan. "Ken started Convocation, a whole-staff gathering and one-day retreat at the beginning of the academic year. Otherwise you're only talking to the people at your site.

"Ken was the first to say, 'Let's agree on what our next logo's going to look like, let's get agreement on what our marketing slogans are going to be, what our catalogs are going to look like.' Those things really came together under Ken. He created the environment in which people saw that those things have value."

"When he interviewed me, he did not ask the usual questions," said Bette Matkowski, hired to open the Middlebury site in 1984. "I went into his office and he said, 'Tell me about yourself.' And he didn't say another word! I think he used that strategy on almost everybody he hired. He said the most important thing a president can do is hire good people. He believed that, and he worked it. It didn't matter what position it was for. He wanted to know you.

"At that time there were one hundred staff members at CCV; at one point there were five men and ninety-five women," she recalled. "Ken set the tone, but those values I would say were feminist values. He didn't resist that. He probably encouraged it. He was wickedly funny, too — probably one of the funniest people I ever met."

"This is my favorite Ken Kalb story," said Megan Tucker, who joined the staff in Springfield in 1987. "When I came to be interviewed, Joyce had said, 'You're going to meet with Ken Kalb.' So we sat down and talked, and I said to Ken, 'So what is it that you do at CCV?' And he said, 'Well, you know, I hire people, and I keep track of the programs,' and then we talked about Montpelier because I grew up in Montpelier, and I had no idea who he was. Later, somebody said, 'Well, he's the president.' I said, 'Oh!'"

Around the state:
Surging enrollment and skeleton crews

Mica DeAngelis opened the Winooski site in February 1983. "We started in the Chase Mill, and within a year we moved to the [nearby, larger] Champlain Mill, because we had this huge surge in numbers right away," she said. "I had to start hiring teachers and finding students.

"The first semester we had thirty-something students, and the tuition was $88 for a three-credit course. I'll never forget that. And we were doing everything — all the coordinators were. If we had a meeting with food, you had to buy the food. If you wanted to get the course list out in the community, you drove around and left it in laundromats and libraries."

The other higher-ed institutions in Chittenden County, she said, "didn't want us. Trinity College thought we were going to take their students; they had a very successful, active adult program. Burlington College too. We were all going after the same students, only our tuition was a third of what theirs was at the time. And the mission of CCV, you can't argue with it: You're trying to get people into college that wouldn't normally go. Most at that time were adults who needed flexibility, so we offered classes once a week, mostly in the evening then, and at an affordable rate. And we hired people right from the community.

"In Chittenden County we had a lot of possibilities for great instructors," she said. "It just took off. It wasn't rocket science; we just had all the pieces."

Barbara Murphy soon joined DeAngelis as Winooski's second CIA.

A LIFETIME OF LEARNING

Barbara Murphy

There was a call for qualified community members to teach in that first year or two [in Winooski] — so I applied to teach an English Composition course and got hired. I taught my first class in the VFW hall, right in Winooski. Had six people at a little square table, under one light bulb. Someone was there selling the textbooks, and it was kind of love at first encounter. I just thought, "This is learning reduced to its most essential parts." So I was hooked, and I wanted to be there — and when a position opened up as coordinator of academic services, I applied and got hired. That was my first full-time work in higher ed. That was '83.

What made CCV different and remarkable was its access, that pretty much anyone who could show a high school diploma could enroll in a class. And the costs were as low as they could be anywhere. There was one point where Mica and I went to the South Burlington mall and had a table, and we were selling courses for $99. I remember signing up a guy to take a course, and he said, "Well, we don't have the money." It was spring semester, so dead of winter. He said, "Let me go out and shovel a few driveways, and I'll be back with the money."

There was a sense of openness and possibility, education without all the hoops to get in — I think that was the most exciting part of it. The idea that you could access higher education without a process designed to weed people out. The door was really swinging in, at that point. And as long as you complement that with qualified people teaching courses, it's a great recipe.

The college also opened an office in the center of downtown Middlebury in 1984, with Bette Matkowski hired as its first coordinator of instruction and advisement. That site began with some twenty-seven courses and more than 125 students (see Bette's story on pages 152-154).

David Buchdahl had moved to Vermont after failing to win tenure at Brown University ("luckiest thing that ever happened to me, I realize in retrospect"). He joined CCV as a coordinator in St. Albans at the start of 1983, and in '87 became the third director of the college's Western Region, after Michael Sawdey and Tim Donovan. The college counted its enrollment both by individual students and by course placements: One student taking three courses would count as three course placements. Within that first year in Winooski, total course placements in that site went from about ninety to more than five hundred.

"David Buchdahl kept saying, 'We're going to get to eight hundred course placements,'" recalled Dee Steffan, who was coordinator of assessment services with the Assessment of Prior Learning program, stationed then in Winooski. "Our eyes got as big as saucers — 'Are you crazy?' But he kept saying, 'We're going to get to eight hundred course placements; we're going to outgrow this.' So we moved in anticipation of growing, and we really quickly passed that goal."

By the time Murphy, now a coordinator, taught her second English Comp class, the Winooski site had moved to the Champlain Mill, where she had a proper classroom and more than twenty students in her class.

"The argument from UVM and Trinity and Champlain [colleges] was, 'We have colleges here, you don't need to come,'" she said. "Our argument was, 'Well, you don't have *this* college. You don't have a college that's welcoming everybody and has a different price point.' Of course, that's what people were scared of. It was the cheapest game in town."

'We were all jacks of all trades'

The college's overall enrollment numbers grew steadily during the first half of the 1980s:

- In 1982–1983, average enrollment was 2,178 for the spring and fall semesters, an increase of 7 percent over the previous year.
- In 1983–1984, average enrollment was 2,495, an increase of 15 percent. By now the college had eleven site centers, with enrollment distributed this way:
    - Barre, 21 percent
    - Winooski, 15 percent

- St. Albans, 15 percent
- Brattleboro, Springfield, St. Johnsbury, 8 percent
- Bennington, Morrisville, Newport, 6 percent
- White River Junction, Rutland, 3 percent.

- In 1984–1985, average enrollment was 2,570 — and by spring 1986, it had risen to 2,906.

The sites were reorganized in 1986, with the Western Region now including St. Albans, Winooski, Morrisville, Middlebury, Rutland and Bennington, and the East including Newport, St. Johnsbury, Springfield, Montpelier, White River Junction and Brattleboro. But staffing was still bare-bones, with people pitching in at whatever needed to be done.

"In the '80s, a CCV center would have anywhere from two to four or five coordinators," said Eric Sakai, a coordinator and then regional director who would become the college's director of learning technologies in the 1990s. "Some of them would be student service coordinators; they were funded under a TRIO grant, and they were more student support specialists than instructor specialists. But we were all pretty much jacks of all trades, no matter which role we had. We had an office manager and a receptionist, and that was pretty much a CCV office staff at the time."

"The centers were small, the staff was small, you knew everybody," recalled Megan Tucker, who joined the Springfield center as a receptionist/clerk/typist in 1987. "We had the Western Region and the whole Eastern Region; they rearranged it at different times, but the whole Eastern region, Newport to Brattleboro — all the staff for that — could fit in a classroom."

There was always, she added, a struggle for respect.

"You always came into any kind of meeting with the attitude that we have to work twice as hard with less, because we're not thought of as real. I grew up in Montpelier, and I remember when CCV started it was always, 'Oh, you're going to go to CCV and take underwater basketweaving.' That was the standard line. So it was always a chip on our shoulder: 'You don't know how good we are.'

"We ran the Springfield academic center, there were three of us there. We didn't have financial aid counselors yet — those came in the next couple of years. We used to drive to students' houses and take them paperwork to get signed. Those are the things I remember, the struggle to feel like you were respected. Obviously, we are there now."

"You could see that CCV was very different," said Dee Steffan. "It had the ability to draw on really good thinkers, creative thinkers, problem solvers, people who were absolutely fine with going on the fly and responding quickly to changing landscapes. I think the reason we were so successful is because students were always central to what we did. Our own concerns or needs were always secondary or tertiary.

"We tried really hard to make it a good experience for faculty, too — but if they didn't get it about students being the center, they didn't get to teach there twice. We tried really hard to find people who were teaching for the right reasons."

Here are more voices, and stories, from regional centers in the '80s:

Bill Callahan, Brattleboro

Bill joined the Brattleboro site in 1982 as a coordinator of instruction and advisement. From "CCV Stories," July 15, 2013.

My resume listing Bentley College, the U.S. Army and the United States Post Office, then traditionally exclusive male bastions, did little to prepare me for the very different universe I was about to enter. I joined a staff of 90 women directors, coordinators and advisors — I was one of five men tooling along with them. Eighty percent of our students were determined women in their 30s and 40s, many of whom were seeking to re-enter an interrupted education.... The place was abuzz with student learning, staff development and preparation for the five year accreditation review by the Association of New England Schools and Colleges. To my delight, my new colleagues swiftly introduced and helpfully guided me into CCV's supportive and collaborative world dedicated to excellence and learning.

Michael R. Sawdey, St. Albans

With a Ph.D. in English, Michael was recruited in 1980 to teach two courses in St. Albans, Modern British Literature and Develop-

mental Composition. He joined Pixley Tyler Hill as a CIA in the St. Albans center from 1980 to 1983, then served as director of the Western Region until 1985. From "CCV Stories," July 15, 2013.

The Modern British course was one I had taught before at other schools, and was even related to my doctoral specialty; one might remark, however, that it might be the first and last time that *Lady Chatterley's Lover* received an in-depth treatment in St. Albans, Vermont. The Developmental Composition class was a bit more of a challenge. I had never taken a composition course in my life, since I placed out of it as an undergraduate, and I had only taught it a couple of times before, in a very different institution. When I showed up at the VFW hall, I found a group of ten tough-looking women and one very scared male veteran. Before I could introduce myself, one woman asked, "You married?" "Yes." "Shit. Just my luck." It was more or less uphill from there....

At the time, the St. Albans CCV office was in space shared with the Agricultural Extension Service. The downside was that we had only two tiny cubicles and some shared space to meet students, provided our schedule didn't conflict with a session on re-using canning jars. If there was an upside, it was that government offices shut down at 4:00 p.m., so we had an excuse for a comfortably short work day. But business was booming, and the first order of business that fall was to find larger quarters.... We finally settled for a one-story building on Main Street, an 1860s feed store that had undergone a number of transmogrifications, most recently as the home of the local telephone company. Once it became the home of CCV, we (almost affectionately) dubbed it Hungerford Hall, in honor of the landlord, who, it was rumored, had won it in a poker game. We moved in time for the Spring 1981 semester, luxuriating in our own private offices, a large front lobby, secretarial space and a couple of sort-of classrooms, thus slightly reducing our dependence on rented space in the community.

In the friendly confines of Hungerford Hall, Pixley and I were joined by the newly hired special services coordinator, Joan Kaye, and secretary Suzy Campbell (her day job: She and her husband were also the official keepers of the Swanton swans, a present from Queen Elizabeth II). Special Services was a federally funded program to meet the needs of underserved college populations and those with multiple obstacles to success in college — a definition that pretty much fit every CCV student.... Joan reported that, when she explained to one student that the goal of the program was to help remove the obstacles to getting a college education, the student asked whether it would pay for fixing the brakes on her car, since that was the main thing that was keeping her from getting to class.

... In that era CIAs did everything — it could be a steep learning curve. What does that stuff on a DD214 [military records request form] mean for a degree-seeking student? What's transferable from an out-of-state school you've never heard of? When should a student be encouraged to fill out financial aid forms? The answer to the last one was easy: 100% of CCV students were poor enough to qualify; in fact, 100% of the forms came back for verification because the computer in faraway Iowa couldn't believe that anyone could live on so little income. Little did they know Vermont.

Then, of course, there were all the "other duties as assigned." Setting up the curriculum each semester — what we offered was determined not only by what we thought students might need, but also by who was available to teach. On more than one occasion, Pixley and I went to one or more restaurants in town and went from table to table finding out who had a master's degree and might like to teach something. The upside was that there were a lot of people in Vermont who had advanced degrees, even teaching experience in higher education, but were hiding out in the boonies doing something else. Once we'd screened and hired some folks, there was also the matter of instructing them in the "CCV way" of doing things. At that point, it was almost better to have people who hadn't taught in college before, since they were less likely to balk at having to write learning outcomes for the course or design assignments that actually spoke to those outcomes. Those who were "experienced" college teachers tended to come with their own syllabi and their own presuppositions about how to teach. For these we took on an "unlearning" task in some cases.... Pay was low. At one point, when faced by a prospective teacher who appeared to be trying to make a living from this, I recall paraphrasing Groucho Marx to the effect that I wouldn't want any instructor who wanted to teach for our wages. In fact, almost all CCV instructors did it because they enjoyed it — what an opportunity to work with a class of 10 or 12 highly motivated adults, sharing with them something that you did in your real life.

David Buchdahl, St. Albans and Winooski

After serving as a CIA in St. Albans and as Western Region director, David became the college's academic dean, and then its director of institutional research and planning. He retired in 2012. From "CCV Stories," August 7, 2013.

It was 1983, and I was starting a new job as a coordinator of instruction and advisement in St. Albans.... We had ... two other coordinators who taught me everything I needed to know about my new job — Pixley Tyler Hill, who was the first coordinator hired in St. Albans, and Joan Kaye, one of five student service coordinators hired to teach the first Dimensions of Learning classes, which had been created just a couple of years earlier as a special course for CCV's adult students, then about 90% of our student population. Plato's *Republic* [its "Allegory of the Cave"] was already part of the standard reading in Dimensions, and Joan's classroom, a dark-paneled windowless room in the back of our site, was aptly called "the cave." It was one of two classrooms in the site — the other an open space, also with no windows, was where we taught Degree Planning Seminar, a one-credit course where students were asked to demonstrate how their CCV learning contributed to competence in ten different areas, including self-awareness, mechanical competence, and moral reasoning. Ah, those were the days!

The site itself had most recently been a women's clothing store, so the only windows were in the large lobby, formerly the "showroom." My office, separated from Pixley's by pieces of particle board nailed to 2-by-4s, had been a changing room. It was there that I began to learn how much students needed and desired what CCV had to offer — local, affordable, accessible higher education. We take it for granted now, then it still seemed like a miracle.

It was a simpler organization in those days.... Sites had a secretary and one, two or three coordinators, and there were about a dozen other people who worked in the central office on the second floor of a bank building in Montpelier before we moved to Wasson Hall in Waterbury where we stayed for nearly 30 years. When we registered someone, we filled in the information on those old multipage carbon forms: a white one for the student's file, a green one for the business office, a yellow for financial aid, orange for the registrar and pink for the student. If you could remember which color went where, you were qualified to be a coordinator!

David Buchdahl

We coordinators wrote down the cost of all the courses — about $90 per course, added the $10 registration fee and told the student to go pay at the front desk. I'm sure there was financial aid available, but I have no recollection of how students went about getting it. Seemed to me most students scraped together the $50–$100 they needed for the semester, but no doubt my memory is faulty.

My first week on the job ... I got caught in a snow bank delivering course lists to stores up and down Route 7 from Milton to Swanton and back to St. Albans. I don't think we mailed course lists in those days — it seemed easier to have new employees who didn't know how to do anything else go and deliver them. And I got to sell books, too. I drove down to Milton High School, where we offered some of our classes. (There were almost no classrooms in CCV buildings in those days. We thought it was a virtue to save taxpayers and the state of Vermont money by utilizing public school classrooms in the evening when they were not in use. It severely limited our ability to offer daytime classes, but that didn't seem like a problem at the time....) So I sat in the lobby of Milton HS with boxes of books that I lugged in from my car, and as students came in looking for their class I intercepted them, told them I could sell them the books they needed and where their classroom was. It all seemed to work fine, except when I couldn't make change. Then I'd arrange to meet the students during their first break, having run in the meantime to the closest convenience store to get the change I needed.

Among my most enjoyable memories from my earliest days at CCV were regional coordinator meetings, when coordinators from the northern region or the southern region would get together to discuss a variety of issues.... The atmosphere of those regional meetings when the college was still young and restless was an odd mixture of encounter sessions, laugh-ins and deep seriousness. Most of us coordinators were relatively new to our jobs (the longest-serving was Kathi Rousselle who had started the CCV site in Newport in 1975) and we all had a very real sense that we were making everything up as we went along. So we argued about everything, laughed constantly, trusted that we couldn't fail, and had a sense of ourselves as continuing the revolution of the Sixties in the hills of Vermont. We were the rebels tunneling under the walls and into the halls of the higher education establishment — out of the caves of illusion into the light of knowledge. Ah, what a glorious mission we shared! And if we had to drive through blizzards to attend these regional meetings, well, all the better to prove ourselves worthy of our great and noble cause. We'd stumble into the back rooms of local restaurants, shake off the snow, pull off our boots, and take up the business of creating a college that could change the world.

KIND OF A MIRACLE

Bette Matkowski, Middlebury and Rutland

Bette worked for sixteen years on the CCV staff. She later became president of Lamar Community College in Colorado from 2000 to 2005, and then Denver campus president of Johnson & Wales University until her retirement in 2012. From "CCV Stories," April 22, 2013.

In 1984 I was out of work and just happened to see a help wanted ad in the *Burlington Free Press* for someone to teach English Comp; as it turned out, it was one of the first two classes ever offered in the Middlebury area.... From there Michael Sawdey, the regional director, asked me to visit local high schools to talk about CCV, and I did some of that work as well.

In the summer CCV was awarded a big federal grant, part of which was to open a site in Middlebury.... I was officially hired as the CIA in Middlebury on my 37th birthday in October of 1984. Our plan was to be ready to go for spring 1985. We had no office, no textbooks, no schedule, no instructors, nothing. But by spring we had 167 course placements, 27 classes, and an office in the historic Battell Block (where CCV is still housed). Because Middlebury has so many highly educated citizens, it was easy to find instructors — many of whom believed fiercely in what we were doing.

The college was wide open with opportunity. If you were eager and willing to try something, there was room for you to grow. The tolerance for mistakes was high. There was a "missionary zeal" to the work, and staff and instructors worked extraordinarily long hours because they believed in the mission of CCV. We were paying instructors about $385 per course, and my first contract as a 10-month employee was for about $12,000.

In the summer of 1986 Ken Kalb, the president, and Tim Donovan, the regional director, asked me to go to Rutland for two years to resuscitate that site. Rutland was down to about 70 students; the office was in the basement of the old city jail, and the whole site was on its last legs. I'll never forget that I asked Ken Kalb what would happen if I couldn't resuscitate the site, and he was, as always, forthright — that I'd be job hunting! This was a tough job, and Rutland was a tough nut to crack. But after two years our enrollment had tripled, and we were on the verge of moving into the old Howe Scale building [on Scale Avenue].

In the summer of 1988 David Buchdahl, who had been the western regional director for two years, took another position at CCV, and Tim and Ken asked me to take on the regional director's role for six sites — Morrisville, St. Albans, South Burlington, Middlebury, Rutland and Bennington. I drove every day up and down the western part of Vermont. As CCV was maturing from its infancy to its adolescence, sites kept moving around to accommodate their growth. In one year I oversaw moves in Burlington, Rutland, Bennington and Morrisville. In Morrisville the owner of the hardware store with an adjacent space we were moving into "signed" a ten-year lease with renovations with a handshake — he was a wonderful landlord, a person whose values aligned perfectly with the work of CCV....

Bette Matkowski

At that time, the other VSC colleges were not required to accept CCV credits, and that was always a challenge.... We had many of the hallmarks of a "fly by night" college — no fulltime faculty, constant moves from one space to another, a student enrollment that was unpredictable, very little marketing money. There was always the desire to prove ourselves, but not at the expense of the creativity and imagination that made CCV work....

I loved the way we worked together. The spirit and the mood of the college were so pervasive, so personal, so aspirational that you wanted to do your best work. The idealism of Peter Smith, the founding president, set the course, but there were so many more folks who believed in his vision and carried forth his dream. Ken Kalb was a master at setting tone, and this was before email, so we had to rely on snail mail, occasional all-staff meetings, and a ton of driving around the state.

For example, I hired Mike Kolesnik in 1985 to teach an evening computer course in Rochester at the high school. He got there one night and realized that the building was locked up tight, so he crawled through a window, opened the front door and taught the class anyway. When we needed a coordinator in Rutland, who better than an instructor who was willing to crawl through a window to teach!

One of my saddest memories of CCV is the death of Nancy Winfield, the head coordinator of the Burlington site. Nancy was one of the kindest people I ever met; she used to see problems and solutions as "a piece of the puzzle." Her death shook the Burlington site to the core. I went to see her the week before she died, and she told me then that she would do anything to be back at CCV — she was a good woman doing good work, and she has been an inspiration to me for 20 years.

… [I took on] CCV's advancement functions, including alumni affairs, marketing, publications, and fundraising, and by 1998 I was the dean of advancement, although I still oversaw three CCV sites. With Barbara Murphy's and Tim Donovan's encouragement, I began looking at community college presidencies for myself, and by 2000 I accepted the presidency of a small rural Colorado college on the high plains.

Allison Kirk, Middlebury

Allison served as a coordinator at the Middlebury site from 1986 to 1988, and then later from 2006 to 2009. From "CCV Stories," July 15, 2003.

The Middlebury site was starting only its fourth semester of existence in 1986 when I came in. In a small new site, it felt to some extent like we were creating something completely new each semester, guessing at a good balance of courses, recruiting instructors ($500 per course, which was still a big advance over the volunteer force when the college started), trying to round up students, trying to persuade students to take an alternative course instead of just getting a refund if the one they'd signed up for was canceled.

In the manner of the saucy, upstart college we were, CCV's promotional literature included a "campus map," which was simply a map of the state of Vermont with the twelve sites and Waterbury pinpointed. We were proud of owning no buildings and investing what resources we had into the students.

The Middlebury site, then as now, was a few rooms on the second floor of the Battell Block, the

CCV's learning center in Middlebury is still in the historic Battell Block, in the center of town.

wonderful old Victorian brick structure at the corner of Main Street and Merchants Row. Our first site office consisted of two very dark adjacent rooms. In spring of 1987, Tim Donovan, then director of the Western Region, negotiated to move the office to the magnificent large corner room — magnificent because part of it was in the round tower of the building, projecting out over Middlebury's main intersection.

The space, I thought, could make the point that the students are the center of the college. Gail Knapp, our wonderful site office manager, and I had the books for a resource room [with] bookcases around the perimeter of the circle and a round table with chairs on a round rug in the center. This, literally and figuratively, was our student center, a place for students to hang around or study. The rest of the large room was open, warm, airy and light, thanks to the large windows.

We had an open house to inaugurate the new space. Toward the end of the event, Tim said to me, glancing around the space, "Now all we have to do is get enough students to pay for it." He could see from the look on my face the pall that remark had cast over the occasion. The pressure to build enrollment felt extreme.

Gabrielle Dietzel, Barre

Gabrielle started as a CIA in Barre in 1982. From 2004 to 2015 she was director of the Office of External Programs. From "CCV Stories," August 28, 2015.

In 1982 ... the Central Vermont site was in Barre above the old Lash Furniture store. (Every time Lash turned its carpet rolling machine on, all conversation had to cease since we wouldn't be able to understand our students', teachers' or our own words.) ...

It was exciting, challenging, fun, and required huge commitments from staff. We all worked hard. We did the most amazing things — they are hard to imagine now.

When the new course list came from the printer, CCV staff would drive around in their area and hand-deliver the list in person, to stores, laundromats, community agencies, companies, local libraries and so on. This gave CCV staff the opportunity to interact with the community in person, answer questions, entice potential students to take a course, and sometimes receive requests for new courses....

We drove the new technology — VCRs! — to CCV classrooms, which were all over the place. We took the leftover soup from one teacher night (the dinner before the semester started) to the next teacher night at another CCV site. Staff often prepared the food. Sometimes, teachers (at that time our instructors were still called *teachers*, not *faculty*) prepared food. Materials were transported from site to site or class to class — such as sharing three art history slide sets between everyone in the college. The joke was that when a new academic coordinator was interviewed: "Yes, she's nice, but does she have a station wagon?"

Ray Lambert, Bennington

Ray became the first coordinator in Bennington in 1983. From "CCV Stories," October 8, 2013.

CCV in Bennington ... began at 324 Silver Street, my residence, and the phone number was my home phone number. As I recall, Tim Donovan from the CCV offices in Montpelier called me to ask if I would be willing to be the Bennington CCV coordinator. It was the last week in August.

Fall courses were to begin within two weeks. What were the courses to be? We decided that introductory computer courses might be appropriate. Within a week there were ... 40 students enrolled, so it was necessary to create two course sections. Who was the instructor to be? That had not really occurred to us. So I contacted Danny Kane, the computer instructor at Mount Anthony Union high school, who willingly agreed to teach the two course sections. That was the beginning of CCV in Bennington.

Connie Yandow, Newport

Connie was a coordinator of student support services in Newport from 1989 to 1996. From "CCV Stories," September 24, 2013.

When I was hired, I was the first full-time CSSS (coordinator of student support services) the Newport site had had. At that time, the pay for the coordinators was under discussion, CSSS being on a step lower than the CIA. I am not sure why the distinction existed, except that there was a teaching component required of all CSSSs — teaching Dimensions of Learning every semester. At the end of my first fiscal year with the college, the pay changed, and both coordinators were placed on the same pay step. The focus of the position was on basic skills courses (scheduling and hiring instructors as well as supervising them), academic support in the form of tutoring, and new students who needed to be placed in those courses as well as working closely with Reach Up [a state program that helps parents of limited means to gain job skills]. In addition, all basic skills testing, scoring and placement was done by the CSSS.

In the beginning, no testing or enrollment in basic skills was mandatory for students, just highly suggested. When I began, my mandate was to try to get every new student tested and placed correctly, so my mantra became "take the tests and then we will talk about course selection" and basic skills testing became mandatory in our site. As a result, I became known by our current CSSS director as the "queen of basic skills." As enrollment in the college as a whole grew, so did the CSSS job, encompassing supervision of other curricular areas and advising a more varied group of students. As a result of that, teaching no longer was a required part of the job.

In the Newport office at the time was a very large women's bathroom, whose walls were marble, just off the front of the site and the hall that held the coordinators' offices. One such wall was the largest, clearest space easily accessed by all staff, so the site office manager and secretary posted every course on its own sheet of paper, and during registration, students names were entered on those sheets. The principle behind the wall was that the courses were easily viewed, so the coordinators could see how courses were growing or not and have a solid handle on what needed to be bolstered or canceled. I attended many "bathroom meetings" with the other coordinator (and sometimes other site staff and regional directors) to discuss course enrollments.

The Newport site was housed on the third floor of the state courthouse building — on the first floor was Probation and Parole and Motor Vehicles; second floor was the actual courtroom…. There were times when staff and students got to ride in the elevator with prisoners in shackles and later, when security tightened, all were wanded and searched before being allowed to enter the upper floors, including the president of the college on her first visit to Newport's site. In addition, when the court was short jurors, our students were stopped on their way in and preempted, sometimes on the first day of classes.

A LIFETIME OF LEARNING

Mary Ellen Lowe

Mary Ellen began a thirty-year career at CCV as the office manager at the St. Albans site. She later served as assistant registrar. From "CCV Stories," May 12, 2014.

I can remember one time in the early days when I was in the center late, just before classes began. One of the students came into my office just to talk. Then another one joined us, then another, and another and another. Pretty soon it was like an impromptu family party with laughing and everyone sharing how their classes and lives were going. At the end there were about twenty-five students: young and old, science and English students, Vermonters and movers in, male and female, and any other diversity in existence all in my office which was twelve by twelve feet.

Academics: Degree planning and pressures for change

In a talk he gave to a gathering of high school guidance counselors at the end of 1983, Roger Cranse, lead developer of Dimensions of Learning, compared some common perceptions of CCV with its growing reality. He began by listing some "things you may have heard":

- "CCV was started by hippies and Peace Corps types that are social workers, not educators."
- "We're big on courses in herbal tea and astrology … all for college credit."
- "CCV is a M*A*S*H* unit, as portrayed on TV … a rag-tag outfit somewhere in the boondocks clowning around while patching up the lame and the wounded of higher education with makeshift quarters."
- "CCV is a college for adults — parents, not young people."

Next, he said, "let's move on to the facts":

- CCV had recently earned a ten-year accreditation, "the max given anyone."

- Its enrollment of over 3,600 made CCV one of the largest colleges in Vermont.
- The college had begun attracting more traditional-age students. The average age was now thirty-three, but seventeen percent of students were under twenty-two.
- The college's CIAs, who both advise students and recruit and support teachers, are "a learning agent going between both sides. This is a rare role in higher education; it's very supportive to student learning, especially in the first two years of college."
- As 1984 began, the college had more full-time students, site offices had more classroom space, and students could learn to use computers — the heavy-duty Zenith Z-100s.

"We have high rates of students transferring to senior colleges," Cranse concluded. "We send an average of seventy-five transcripts per month, more at graduation time. We are for real."

The college's academics had been founded on a commitment to learning that was self-designed and personally assessed, and that required a process that, for all its dynamic value, was cumbersome, complex and often confusing. As more and more students set their sights on earning a bachelor's degree after CCV, many of them pressed the college for an approach to degree planning that was at least a bit more traditional, and could make CCV transcripts more readily transferrable to other institutions.

Michael Sawdey

From "CCV Stories," July 15, 2013.

Sometime after Ken Kalb arrived as president, we spent an ungodly number of months assembling the first more-or-less uniform curriculum, to be ensconced in an honest-to-gosh printed catalog. We read existing syllabi until we were cross-eyed, begged-borrowed-stole catalogs from other schools (sometimes by getting our students to write letters requesting copies, as though they wanted to apply for admission!), argued in endless meetings, sometimes after spreading out dozens of variants of "the same" course on the floor to attempt comparison and collation. There were a few screaming matches with disgruntled instructors who threatened never to teach for us again if we so much as hinted what should be in their courses. In the end, having a catalog and some uniformity to courses probably demystified things a bit for students, perhaps even for the ever-scrambling CIAs.

Gabrielle Dietzel

From "CCV Stories," August 28, 2015.

Degree Planning Seminar (DPS), a one-credit course each degree student had to take, required students to design their own programs by meeting nine competencies. Students were often frustrated by this task — they wanted to know what exactly they had to take and which class would fulfill what requirement. Consequently, the first "Red Book" was created, laying out the degree programs (about ten) and specifying required courses. The development of the Red Book was huge and consequential. Advisors exhaled a common sigh of relief, and students were screaming for their copy. Slowly, the nine competencies were adapted and changed. President Ken Kalb secretly enrolled in the Degree Planning Seminar and created a degree plan for the fictitious "Thelma Spieler" so he could understand the process better — and Thelma's plan was sent through the Academic Review Board (ARB). During those days, all student degree plans were reviewed in a two-day marathon meeting of the ARB at the Waterbury Central CCV office. They were chaired by Nancy Chard, clutching her famous coffee mug that said *"I'd rather be having a beer!"* All students received direct feedback from the ARB. It was a cumbersome but thorough process that is unthinkable today — student numbers were so much lower than today.

The grading system in the 1980s was pass/fail. Students received a written, narrative evaluation of their learning, based on common "essential" objectives that were slowly designed by the curriculum committee with the help of teachers…. This was a huge undertaking but very successful as it clearly delineated student learning expectations/outcomes common for all CCV courses. CCV academic staff believed strongly in the usefulness of these narrative evaluations. Students, however, felt differently. They wanted grades.

David Buchdahl

This is from David's essay "The ARB Chronicles: 1983 to the early '90s," published in "CCV Stories," September 5, 2013.

I had been at CCV two years in 1985 when I was invited to be one of two coordinators of advising and instruction who sat on the Academic Review Board, the precursor to the present-day Academic Council. There were just seven members: two regional directors, the director of student services, the registrar, a clerk and two coordinators who rotated on and off with two-year terms.

We had two primary responsibilities: (1) to review and develop all needed academic policies and degree program requirements, and (2) to review students' degree plans. The ARB met on the first Thursday of each month to handle its first assignment, and the third Thursday of each month to review degree plans. We had what we called degree plan review marathons, which could last twelve hours a day with pizzas delivered to keep us all going.

In those years, Nancy Chard, director of the old Southern Region, was chair of the ARB and ruled meetings mostly with an iron fist. If you disagreed strongly with Nancy, you did so at your own peril — yet everyone respected Nancy's bedrock dedication to the mission of the college, and coordinators, at least, were cowed enough by her to not even think about disagreeing. Roger Cranse, on the other hand, the man who gave the college Dimensions of Learning and the ARB an air of erudition, loved to disagree with Nancy at every opportunity so that ARB meetings often became an amusing test of will between these two titans.

A LIFETIME OF LEARNING

Before there was an ARB, degree plans were reviewed by *local* degree plan review boards, so it was a big deal when this critical function was centralized and the ARB came into being. In those days, all degree plans were "individualized," which meant that students could take pretty much any courses they wanted to, as long as they could show how their learning provided competence in ten different areas — which included such things as aesthetic awareness, interpersonal relationships, manual and physical competence, self-awareness, communications, cultural awareness, community relationships, creative competence, relationship with the environment, and analytical competence.

Of course, there were many standard choices that students employed to demonstrate competence in the different areas. One of my personal favorites was the use of Introduction to Computers to satisfy mechanical competence — presumably because you could insert and eject five-and-a-quarter-inch floppy discs into the old desktops, or, later, prove your skill with a mouse.

A key job of the coordinators in those days was to teach the Degree Planning Seminar, where students learned about the competence areas and how various courses could be employed to demonstrate learning in each one. Students would then develop a preliminary degree plan that would be reviewed by the ARB. Plans were reviewed by a pair of ARB members prior to meetings, delivered before computers by "pony express" in large manila envelopes, then presented with evaluative comments to the whole ARB at the meetings. Stacks of degree plans were piled everywhere around the room — you could actually hide behind a stack of them if you wanted — and we dutifully proceeded to review each one and pass judgment. Oh, the horror!

By far the most intriguing or ridiculous thing about degree plans, depending on your perspective, was what we called linking statements. Linking statements were short two- or three-sentence paragraphs intended to explain how a student understood the connection — the link — between the courses in their plan and a particular competence area. Every degree plan began with a goal statement, followed by ten pages, each one with a linking statement at the top and a list of the courses selected by the student to develop competence in that area.

I wish someone had a tape of ARB reviewing degree plans and debating how, or if, or to what degree a linking statement actually demonstrated a link between courses and competence areas. Mind you, many of these linking statements had already been rewritten and improved by coordinators who understood the hurdles that students faced in getting plans approved by the ARB. They knew all too well that it was not usually the courses listed on the page that made the difference between approval or rejection, but the quality of these trifling linking statements. Sometimes, in desperation, ARB members would edit a statement right there in a meeting, then return it to student and coordinator with a note that said, effectively, "Here, write it this way."

I served on the ARB continually from 1985 until 2007, when I transitioned from an eleven-year stint as academic dean. I can't remember exactly when during those intervening years we did away with degree plans and their cursed linking statements, but I can assure you no one was the least bit sorry to see them go.

A LIFETIME OF LEARNING

'A town meeting in print': Vermont Affairs, 1986–1990

In winter 1986 the college launched *Vermont Affairs*, a twice-yearly publication that David Buchdahl, its editor, said would "bring you the views of well-known Vermonters and others who have an in-depth understanding of today's events.

"*Vermont Affairs* is a journal of public issues and ideas," the editor wrote as he introduced the inaugural issue. "It is not meant to entertain but to inform, to help you think about our state and its future. As the issues we face grow in complexity, the need for more and more accurate information grows also."

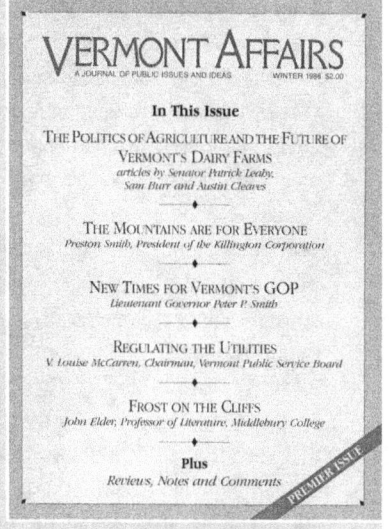

That first issue lived up to its billing: It featured a package of three articles on "The Politics of Agriculture and the Future of Vermont's Dairy Farms," including a piece on farm policy by U.S. Senator Patrick Leahy. Peter Smith, who now was lieutenant governor, contributed an essay on the state's Republican Party. The president of the Killington Corporation, Preston Smith, wrote on behalf of the ski industry about the controversy over whether Killington should make snow from treated wastewater, and whether continued development on ski mountains should be permitted. Louise McCarren, chair of the Vermont Public Service Board, explained utility regulation — and John Elder, author and literature professor at Middlebury College, added "Frost on the Cliffs," his thoughts on the Robert Frost poem "Directive," which reflects on a climb up a mountainside.

"The pared down branches and rock that remain in early winter are reminders that human agendas for Vermont flourish and subside too," Elder mused.

▶

Vermont Affairs would quickly flourish, and then subside. Its final issue in spring 1990 was just eight pages long, and contained Buchdahl's "Retrospective Look at the Life of a Journal."

"A bare-bones venture from the outset," his essay recalled, "its arrival in January 1986 was unheralded, lacking the expensive publicity and promotion that often accompany new publications. We started small, with only 400 paid subscribers. Two years later that number had nearly tripled. However, at the same time we were attracting readers, we were discovering the full cost of supporting a journal like *Vermont Affairs* within the framework of a small, decentralized community college, which is always stretching a tight budget to accommodate remarkable growth."

By the journal's second issue, which focused on water quality and how best to protect it, "we had begun to demonstrate our notion of being a town meeting in print, a place where a wide spectrum of viewpoints could be found," Buchdahl wrote. "*Vermont Affairs,* like the Community College of Vermont, was not going to be easily typed. It would be open to anyone . . . with important and intelligent things to say."

Five more issues covered state aid to education, Vermont's efforts to build business and cultural connections with Japan, "Cleaning Up Solid Waste," "Can We Manage Growth?" and, in winter-spring 1989, reflections on the arts in Vermont. By then subscriber numbers were dropping — as they tend to do, Buchdahl wrote, after an initial surge of interest. Ads were costing as much to attract as they were contributing in revenue, and much "time and expense would be needed to seek special funding," some of which had already been contributed by the Vermont-based Windham and Lintilhac foundations.

"After much soul-searching, we have decided to discontinue the publication of *Vermont Affairs,*" the editor wrote. Among those he thanked were Charles Bunting, in 1989 the chancellor of the Vermont State Colleges, who "took an active interest in the publication"; staff member Brent Sargent, "a tenacious copy editor"; and editorial assistant Mary Ellen Lowe, the office manager in St. Albans who later became assistant registrar.

"One of the things that I enjoyed the most was working on *Vermont Affairs,*" Lowe later wrote. "I only wish that the journal had endured for a longer period of time. It was an ornament in CCV's crown."

•••

A LIFETIME OF LEARNING

The spirit of teaching and learning: Debby Stewart's career of giving back

Debby Stewart

When she began taking classes as a young parent in the mid-1980s, Deborah Stewart was the first in her family to attend college. What she did with her CCV education has influenced a generation of community college teachers, in Vermont and all over the United States.

After taking a course in creative writing through the Springfield center in 1984, Stewart, then recently married, became pregnant with her first son. When her boy was a few months old and Stewart was working in Springfield as a waitress, she re-enrolled at CCV.

"I had always intended to go on to college after high school. I just was not sure how to make the transition from high school to college," she said. "I had every intention of it, but no one in my family knew how to help make that happen. As a result, it was a huge goal for me. I was really excited to dive in; I quickly shifted to three, sometimes four classes a semester, because I wanted to complete my associate degree as quickly as possible.

"When I began at CCV, I really felt at home. I loved that these were small class sizes, designed to be like graduate school seminars. CCV is built, in so many ways, for adult students, but the thing we discovered is how much every student can contribute. We had a fourteen-year-old and a seventy-five-year-old in one class. We really believe that students have as much to learn from each other as they do from the faculty. I think that is a really important model, and I felt like I flourished within that."

Her graduating class in 1989 was the first to wear caps and gowns. Stewart was the commencement speaker.

"I probably can't emphasize enough how important it was — how pivotal the experience I had at CCV was — to me personally, but also to my own trajectory and the trajectory of my family," she said years later. "When I went on for my bachelor's degree, I began to think about how I could give back to the CCV community, to other students, to give them what I had had."

▶

Learning to teach, then passing it on

Over the next four years, Stewart earned a bachelor's degree in literature, taking weekend classes at what was then Vermont College's Adult Degree Program in Brattleboro, and then a master's in fine arts from the same college in poetry.

Stewart's advisor at CCV in Springfield had been Joyce Judy, then that site's lone coordinator. When she was close to finishing her master's, Stewart went back to interview with Judy, who hired her to teach a CCV class the next fall.

"On so many levels, it was so gratifying," she said. "I was not trained as a teacher, so there was a great deal of learning around pedagogy and all that. There was a real recognition that faculty who came to start at CCV did not necessarily have a degree in teaching, but they were steeped in the fields they wanted to teach. Part of what CCV did was to say, 'How can we help them be successful in the classroom?'"

Stewart began teaching in 1993 and became a coordinator herself in '97. In 2004, a book she had written, *Effective Teaching: A Guide for Community College Instructors*, was published by the Community College Press, of the American Association of Community Colleges.

"In 1992, CCV developed its first 'teaching for development' handbook," her introduction to the book said. That first handbook, titled *Teaching for Development: A Handbook for Instructors*, was written by Dick Eisele. Contributors to two subsequent editions included Academic Dean David Buchdahl, Dee Steffan, Dianne Maccario, Gabrielle Dietzel, Natalie Searle, Mel Donovan, Ann Newsmith, Ann Schroeder, Amy Stuart, K. D. Maynard, Rebecca Werner and Penne Ciaraldi.

"At the 2003 annual conference of the American Association of Community Colleges," Stewart wrote, "we introduced a major revision of the handbook as part of a presentation titled 'Supporting Adjunct Faculty and Instructors as if Your Life Depended on It.' As a result of the overwhelming response to that presentation and the handbook, we embarked on a project to rewrite the handbook for a wider audience," resulting in *Effective Teaching*.

"As the use of part-time faculty has increased throughout higher education," Stewart wrote in her introduction, "other colleges have approached CCV in order to learn from our experience how to ensure quality instruction with part-time faculty.... Throughout this guide, you will find specific strategies for teaching — the kind of practical advice that circulates among veteran teachers whenever they gather together — but you will also find an emphasis on the spirit of teaching and learning, the reflective aspects that deepen our understanding of and appreciation for the tremendous work that happens regularly in the community college classroom."

For a time, *Effective Teaching* reportedly became one of the Community College Press's nationally bestselling titles.

'The heart of what we do'

Stewart became associate academic dean at CCV in 2001; she was named dean of students in 2010, then dean of academic affairs in 2014. In a 2020 interview, she reflected on more than three decades with the community college — as student, teacher and administrator:

"In my time of working at CCV, in almost every role I've had, I have felt there was a lot of trust provided to me and to other people who worked there. You have a sense of autonomy over your own work. There isn't a lot of micro-managing; there is a lot of freedom to explore what you can do and become better at it.

"A good idea can come from anywhere. So no matter what role you had, what center you worked at, what little corner of the state, somebody would have an idea, and that idea would take off, sprout forward, and it would change something really big at CCV — because somebody said, in a meeting somewhere or to a colleague, 'You know, I wonder if we did this, that might be good.' And that would pass forward, and before you know it people would be calling that person and saying, 'Could you tell me more about that idea you had?' And we would just implement it.

There weren't a lot of things that got in the way of the college thinking, 'What do we need to do to be the best we can for students?' Really the student is the heart of what we do."

•••

Computers and networked information: An era begins

Ken Kalb became president shortly after the federal Title III grant had enabled CCV to purchase its first set of microcomputers. This was the onset of a new era — and he was among those who had to learn how to adjust.

"Ken was an IBM Selectric guy," said Tim Donovan, speaking of the heavy-duty electric typewriter, with its distinctive typeball, that had until now been all but ubiquitous in office settings. "He typed everything at a Selectric; he loved the feel and sound of it."

Confronted with a big, blocky new Zenith 100 on his desk, Donovan said, "he was really not happy. But he said, 'I'll do it for the college.'"

A student with a Z-100

As much because Donovan had written the Title III grant as for any other reason, "and because no one knew anything about computers, or wanted to know anything," he said, "I was either told or decided, I will run this project. So I said 'I know. I'll buy one.'"

> **Tim Donovan**
>
> This is 1984. I have a two-year-old child at home, I'm two years into a mortgage on a house, I'm probably making $13,000 a year — and I buy a $2,200 computer. My spouse just looked at me in befuddlement. "You did *what*?" But I think my mind-set was, "If I put money into this, I'm going to make sure I get my money out of it." So I learned how to use it. It came with WordStar, MultiPlan, DOS, all that stuff. Green screen.
>
> We set up some computer labs. Two students shared a computer. And we created our first real computer course,

which was called Introduction to Microcomputer Applications. I would describe it as the Whitman's Sampler: a little bit of word processing, a little bit of spreadsheet, a little bit of data management. It's probably still one of the largest enrolled courses; it's become a really good starting point for people who would come in and say, "My boss told me I have to start using a computer, and I don't want to tell him I don't know how."

In 1984, Megan Tucker, a recent UVM grad who was then pregnant with her first child, took an early course in computer programming through the Springfield site. After her son was born, coordinator Joyce Judy asked her to come back and teach the scourse in microcomputer data processing.

Megan Tucker

"We used machines that had five-and-a-quarter-inch floppies," Tucker said. "You had to put the operating system in, then the application in; then you took the operating system disk out and put in another disk. I think we had five computers and ten people in the class, so each person shared. I was twenty-five, twenty-six years old. The class was so popular that they added a second section — so I did that, too."

Cathy Frank

Cathy began teaching at the Winooski site in 1983, and continued for sixteen years. From "CCV Stories," July 19, 2013.

My first memory of CCV was of the large high-ceiling classrooms in the Champlain Mill in Winooski, second floor, northeast corner. Mica DeAngelis had asked me if I was interested in teaching a computer class. My total computer experience had been on our family Apple II. CCV was using PCs. I had never used a PC before but I cavalierly said "Yes." That first semester I spent more time in the computer lab than my students! Talk about a learning experience.

Tim Donovan was then the Northwest Region coordinator and the person most knowledgeable about computers on the entire CCV staff. I learned a lot from Tim while trying not to let on how much I did not know. Tim claims we were only a few steps ahead of our students back then, but from my vantage point and skill level, that was being generous. On some days I was only a day or two ahead of my students.

In 1983 windows were still things that allowed light into rooms. DOS was the operating system of the day and it had not been designed with humans in mind. Computers were not yet networked and the World Wide Web (www) was nonexistent. Viruses, worms, Trojan horses and spam were unheard of. The lab had one computer for every two, sometimes three students, and the software was loaded onto each computer from 3.5 [inch] disks, one disk at a time. It took ... forever when it worked and even longer when it did not. What kept us going was the excitement of the potential these computers held for learning. That and a great little coffee shop on the first floor of the Mill, a small Vermont company called Green Mountain Coffee Roasters that roasted its own coffee beans right in the building....

In time CCV outgrew that space and moved to Dorset Street in South Burlington. The staff was excited that there was now an art studio and science lab.... The little kitchen area ... was right outside the computer room door. No food or drinks were allowed in the computer lab but that did not stop the inevitable and irresistible smell of freshly popped popcorn from wafting into the computer room during class. I never succeeded in convincing the staff that this was cruel and unusual punishment....

Meanwhile it felt like technology and software were evolving and changing by the day. We instructors debated which software we should use to teach — Microsoft Works or Word or WordPerfect and how much of the operating system our students needed to know. We each had our own strongly held opinion.... And, bless him, Tim, the maker of all software decisions, accommodated all of us.... Meanwhile every semester brought software upgrades to all the software, changes we had to adjust to. I envied the people teaching English literature. My lesson plans were never good for more than one semester....

Because we were operating a student lab and the computers were not yet networked, there were no passwords required to use a computer.... One day when no one was looking, a mischievous student set a password for each of the lab computers. The first class to arrive the next morning, my class, was totally locked out of the computers as we had no idea what the password might be....

CCV moved to Pearl Street in Burlington [in 1994] to accommodate its continually growing enrollment. By now our computer lab had a computer for each student, but we were still loading the software one disk at a time, as many as 30 disks per computer, one computer at a time. It took all day if all went well, which it still never did of course. Each student saved their work on a floppy disk, but their floppy disk went home with them to be used in multiple unknown computers. One day one of those floppy disks came back to the CCV lab infected, and in no time the entire complement of individual computers was infected.... Classes had to be canceled for a day and the cleanup and reinstallation process done all over again. Thereafter anti-virus software, then in its infancy, became a mainstay of our software load....

While the courses I taught were called such sterile names as "Microcomputer Applications" and "Spreadsheets," I often thought that whatever specific skills I taught, about how to use a particular software at a particular point in time as a tool in learning and in life, were not nearly as important as the problem-solving skills we all learned in dealing with such wonderful but problematic machines called computers.

Over the course of the sixteen years I had the honor of teaching at CCV, there is no doubt in my mind that I learned far more from my students than they from me. Perhaps that is what has made and continues to make CCV so special.

A new kind of college library

A good college needs a good library — but with no central campus and a very tight budget, there was no way CCV could create a serious collection and reference system at each of its growing number of sites around the state. For continued accreditation, that was a big weakness; and to librarian Eileen Chalfoun, it was also a major reason why the rest of Vermont's higher education community was often dismissive of the community college.

When she accepted a new position as the college's first coordinator of information services in 1982, Chalfoun set out to change all that. It was a steep challenge.

"Instructional sites were far from each other," she later wrote, "and during a typical Vermont winter it was virtually impossible to share information resources in a timely manner." What to do?

Chalfoun had been a librarian for private international schools in Japan, Greece and Lebanon before she and her husband settled in Vermont in the late 1970s. Working as a CCV coordinator in Brattleboro from 1976 to '79, she saw how urgent this problem was.

"We were saying to our students, 'Go use the public library,'" she recalled. "Then the head of the state library got up in arms because we were using libraries in small communities because we didn't have a library of our own. I was breaking into a very very traditional environment in Vermont. We remained that ugly stepsister until we got some actual support, both financial and moral."

That support began to develop the year Chalfoun took on her new job. In 1982 the VSC chancellor's office organized a group, including Chalfoun and representatives from the four residential state colleges, to make a close assessment of library and information services throughout the state college system.

"How to provide library services to CCV was one of the driving forces in this joint planning project," she wrote. "The challenge: get it together, get people to talk and plan, just get going. Build a state library network."

The report that the group issued in mid-1983, after almost a year of work, concluded that all the state college libraries were weak in light of the professional standards of the Association of College and Research

Libraries. It recommended that the VSC System develop "a single, joint on-line catalog" in an interlinked network that would also include UVM, Middlebury College and the State Department of Libraries. It also called for a "five-year coordinated collection catch-up program to add 15,000 volumes per year to system holdings, including small reference collections for CCV offices," at a total cost of $2.6 million.

For the community college, that investment would make possible the key first stage in the development of an uncommon college library system: a combination of online, physical and in-person resources that before long would provide access to a wide and growing range of information and research services at every CCV site, all around Vermont.

Eileen Chalfoun at right, with a student.

'The plunge was imminent'

By the early '80s, electronic library cataloging wasn't new. But the capacity to link and combine different library catalogs online was.

In 1967, a group of colleges and universities in Ohio, and another in New England that included Vermont, each formed a collaborative whose aim was to make possible the electronic cataloging of library holdings. Ohio University switched on the world's first digital system in 1971. By the late '70s, automated catalogs, newly efficient and speedily searchable, were in widespread use by academic libraries in New England and elsewhere.

The next step was to link multiple libraries and their collections online, and by the early '80s that had become possible. Standards had been developed for exchanging digitized catalog data in consistent, computer-readable form. That enabled different libraries within a region, a state or a system, such as the Vermont State Colleges, to connect and combine their catalogs, offering access to users at terminals within libraries and at computers outside them, at first via dial-up phone connections.

Acting on the recommendations of its library assessment project, the VSC System invested in library automation software developed by Data Research Associates, one of the pioneers in this emerging field. VSC's working group on the project also engaged the University of Vermont, Middlebury College and the Vermont Department of Libraries — and that developed "the capability to look at each other's library collections," Eileen Chalfoun said.

"The turning point was to get everybody's collection online. That was a massive, massive undertaking," she said. "The chancellor's office monitored and orchestrated that." Dennis Lindbergh of the chancellor's office staff played a lead role, chairing both the original library assessment and then the VSC working group

In a December 1986 ceremony, Gov. Madeleine Kunin opened access to the state's new Automated Library System, which offered an online catalog and automated circulation services that linked together the collections of the state colleges, UVM, Middlebury and the state library system.

"When the Governor cut the computer ribbon," Chalfoun wrote, "many librarians' hearts beat just a little faster, knowing that the plunge into the world of 'electronic libraries' was imminent."

"The thing that made it so wonderful for CCV," she explained, "is that our students and instructors could borrow stuff from academic libraries in the state for the first time. Our patrons could sit at a computer, put in a password, bring up the shared catalog, order books, and have them delivered to site offices. We contributed money for a delivery system. Eventually, we were able to invest in some visual materials to share."

'An unusual variety of library services'

While the state's automated system was being developed from 1983 to 1986, Chalfoun led CCV in developing a new, distributed library system — one that combined physical materials, the new online access, and building students' research skills for this new networked era. By 1987, the college was offering "an unusual variety of library services to its patrons," Chalfoun reported in an article that year for *C&RL News*, the journal of the Association of College & Research Libraries.

Those new services came in three linked areas:

- *Collections:* The college set up reference collections at all twelve sites, each of which by 1987 contained about six hundred volumes and was staffed by a part-time reference librarian. "The collections were never designed to be mini-libraries to fill all the research needs of students," Chalfoun wrote. "Instead, they could be described as laboratories for learning library/research skills." Each site now had a small card catalog, and hosted classes in research and writing skills. Suzanne Gallagher served as CCV's library coordinator and cataloger as the college bought books and media for its distributed collections. Chalfoun built a circulating collection of VCR tapes and other materials that teachers could use in their classrooms.

- *Reference:* All the sites were now connected by a toll-free phone line to Chalfoun's library coordinator office. Four sites were also linked by fax to the four VSC campus libraries, so that CCV students could request journal articles they had found in online indexes.

- *Online searches:* CCV provided each site with an application called IRIS (Instructional Research and Information System), which could help instructors find and share "successful and exciting teaching techniques, classroom materials, exercises, books, videos, films, filmstrips, journal articles, bibliographies" and more, Chalfoun wrote. "Each site office library was equipped with a microcomputer, printer, and software."

In the years that followed, Chalfoun and Dennis Lindbergh presented together at several library conferences around the country, describing how the Vermont collaboration had finally made it possible for this college-without-a-campus to develop a new, distributed library system.

When she shared that story in *C&RL News*, Chalfoun titled her article "With a Little Help from Our Friends."

'The sooner we learn this, the better'

In 1987, Chalfoun and several CCV colleagues compiled and published a sophisticated sixty-five-page guide to student research skills that they titled *Biblio-Tech: Survival Skills for the Information Age.*

In harmony with CCV's aim of producing self-reliant learners, the new manual "was addressed to students, and allowed them to follow the steps to doing careful research without the strict guidance of an instructor," she later wrote.

The authors noted on *Biblio-Tech*'s first page that students will spend far more time in the rest of their lives than they will in college, and "we must take responsibility for our own lives by being willing to dig for information, open to what we find, and capable of managing it wisely.

"The sooner we learn how to do this, the better," they continued. "It puts us in control of our lives, affords us protection, and opens the way to achievement of our goals — in college, in our careers, and in our personal lives."

In the late '80s and early '90s at CCV, "I also chaired a committee called Emerging Technologies," Chalfoun said. "Tim [Donovan] and I both worked on this committee. He really is a technologist; I was not. Tim understood the technologies from the beginning and was willing to experiment with me — and teach me at the same time."

"Eileen was a huge proponent in the VSC and at CCV for extending this resource outside the sole realm of libraries," Donovan said. "At first it was pretty limited and all text-based. Eileen was the fountainhead for the notion of the value to CCV of access to networked information."

Late in the 1990s, the internet would blossom into what would quickly become a universal, world-altering resource. But even before it did, in the early and mid-1990s CCV would take pioneering new strides in its own venture into this new, interconnected world.

"In our 1992 regional accreditation," Donovan said, "the college was heavily criticized for not meeting any of the standards for college libraries — number of books, books per student etc. A reaction could have been to change course and buy a lot of books and shelves in each CCV site. But Eileen was a stalwart, and stayed the course toward an electronic future that most could not yet see. At our 2002 regional accreditation, the college was lauded as an exemplary college library of the future."

A LIFETIME OF LEARNING

End of the 1980s: 'Where Vermonters Go to College'

The college's enrollment surge continued through the late 1980s, as total headcount passed 3,000 in spring 1987, then 3,500 in spring '89. "In full-time equivalent terms, the figure is now over 1,300," CCV's annual report said at the end of the 1988–1989 year. "In the course of a full year … we serve over 6,000 Vermonters, giving some credence to our new tagline, 'Where Vermonters Go to College.'"

"About 650 courses run each semester," said that end-of-decade report. "The average class size has risen slightly in recent years, but is still around ten, which fits our philosophy of attention to the individual and the opportunity for active participation."

That spring, 123 graduates were awarded associate degrees. For the first time in the college's history, commencement was held on a traditional college campus, at Vermont Technical College in Randolph Center.

For the first time, too, the graduating class marched into the ceremony in caps and gowns.

Staff members had debated and struggled over whether to adopt the traditional commencement attire, Mica DeAngelis recalled. "Then someone suggested, 'We should ask the students.' Did they want to wear caps and gowns? Well, they did!"

> ### Michael Sawdey
>
> *From "CCV Stories," July 13, 2013.*
>
> Commencement at CCV was a peculiar institution in itself: Students traveling from all over the state, accompanied by huge numbers of family members, since they were usually the first in their extended families to graduate from college, and CCV put no limits on the number of guests they could bring. And there was the custom of giving each graduate a single rose — which the graduate was, in turn, to present to the person who had been most responsible for the student managing to complete a degree.
>
> Not unexpectedly, the rose often went to a parent, spouse, best friend, but sometimes to a child who had helped take up

> the slack during the years of part-time study. And at times to a CIA: One year, I took home six.
>
> Many students were overcome by the emotion of graduating, but I remember in particular one big, strapping state police sergeant who nearly fainted out of sheer nervousness at having to walk across a stage "in front of all those people," as he put it afterwards.

The growing enrollment helped spur several moves in the late 1980s to larger facilities. The Chittenden County site left Winooski's Champlain Mill for Dorset Street in South Burlington, upstairs in the small mall that now faces Barnes & Noble. Central Vermont left its noisy perch above Barre's Lash Furniture in 1986 for 118 Main Street in Montpelier. Brattleboro had moved in 1984 from 67 Main to 15 Green Street.

By 1985, Springfield was on Front Street, and Bennington found quarters on South Street in '87. St. Albans went in '85 to 1 North Main Street in that city, and Newport moved to its Court House quarters at 81 Main St. in '86.

Though a number of the new sites offered dedicated classroom spaces for the first time, all were still rentals. Early in the next decade, CCV would begin shifting to a new approach to its facilities — using spaces that, while still rented, were configured and set up specifically for the community college's use.

Nancy Chard: Fierce, opinionated and 'an enormous influence'

"She was an amazing force," Joyce Judy said of Nancy Chard, CCV's first academic dean. "She was passionate about what she believed, and she believed so much in the value and power of education."

Chard joined the Brattleboro staff as a coordinator in 1975, became Southern Region director in '78, and served as academic dean from '85 to '88. Few others, if any, in the college's first decades had more impact than she did on CCV's quest to claim full credibility in higher education while staying true to its core values of open access and student-centered learning.

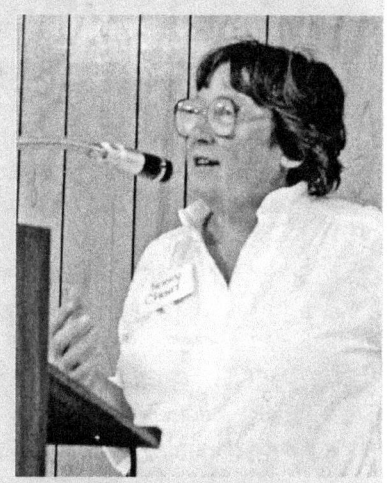

Nancy Chard

"She was a huge supporter of self-reliant learners, of our whole mission of helping people access education and then have it be really meaningful to them," said Judy, CCV's current president, whom Chard hired to be a Springfield coordinator in 1983. "She was very willing to take education to Vermonters. We held classes in lots and lots of small towns and villages under Nancy's watch. If someone could find a group of people and they wanted a class, we'd figure out how to deliver it."

"Nancy was full of energy and kept us laughing in the best and worst of times," said Sherry Blankinship, curriculum coordinator in Springfield in the early '80s. "She worked hard to get the appropriate support for the Southeast."

"That was her personality," said Judy. "She was lively and entertaining, but she was also a very strategic thinker. She had very

▶

strong beliefs; some would call her incredibly opinionated. If she liked you, she was amazingly loyal, and she would go to the mat for you. She was fierce."

"Nancy Chard was an enormous influence on the college," said Eileen Chalfoun, the college's first librarian and a close friend. "It was Nancy who understood the need to develop research capability for CCV students and instructors. She was a U.S. history scholar who was a brilliant teacher and lecturer, and she played a huge role in getting the [VSC] chancellor and Board of Trustees to support the college."

"Nancy has played a key role in the development of the college," agreed Ken Kalb, in a tribute he wrote when Chard left in 1988 to direct the VSC's Southern Vermont Education Program. Chard, wrote Kalb, "has shown creativity and perseverance in working through the ranks, chairing the academic governing body for the college, and being the college's liaison with the New England Association of Schools and Colleges. Her imagination and problem-solving skills have served as a model to all of us."

In 1990, Chard won election at age fifty-six to the Vermont House, where she represented her Brattleboro district until 1994, when she was elected to the State Senate. She chaired the Education and Health and Welfare committees in the Senate, where she served until 2002. She also chaired the New England Board of Higher Education, and was a trustee for a number of statewide and Windham County nonprofit organizations.

"She set high standards for herself and liked to see others reach high," longtime friend Sarah Carter told the *Brattleboro Reformer* after Chard died in 2010. "She wanted each person to be the best they could be, and she led the way."

"She was a character," said Judy. "And she was really fun to be around."

•••

The Kalb era concludes

When Ken Kalb retired from CCV's presidency in mid-1991, he left a college much grown in regional sites and student numbers — also better organized, more cohesive and unified, stronger in central leadership, and substantially more highly regarded across Vermont.

Within CCV, "people were more conscious of being a part of a bigger institution," Kalb reflected in an interview during his retirement. "We were gaining some respect and recognition. We had a good base for expansion. And I think we started to see ourselves as a bigger college, with more sites, more outreach, a growing student population. We were growing pretty rapidly during that time, and gaining recognition as we did that."

Eric Sakai, who was a CIA in Montpelier in the late 1980s before moving on to other college positions, reflected later on "the people that came to CCV in the early to mid-'80s: Barbara Murphy, who became president of CCV [and later Johnson State College]. Bette Matkowski, who became president of a community college in Colorado, and of a Johnson and Wales campus in Denver. David Buchdahl became the academic dean at CCV. Tim Donovan went on to become president and [VSC] chancellor.

"It was a crop of coordinators in the early and mid-'80s who really helped the college grow, he said, "and grew themselves into leadership positions in higher education, in Vermont and elsewhere."

In retirement, Kalb pursued a long-held interest in writing. His novel *The Wounds of Winter* (Santa Verbera, CA: Nebbadoon Press) was published in 1998, and he had several poems published as well.

"During his tenure, enrollment at the two-year non-traditional institution ... grew by 50 percent," the online news service *VTDigger* wrote after Kalb passed away in May 2020 at eighty-six. "He expanded the college's footprint to all regions of the state, putting CCV within 25 miles of 90 percent of Vermont's population. An operating deficit was eliminated and several long-range programs were developed and implemented.

"To those who knew him personally and professionally," the obituary added, "Mr. Kalb was a gentle man with an enormous capacity for humor and intellect."

People who worked with him often tell stories about Kalb's lively sense of humor. Possibly the best one comes from a recollection by Tim Donovan.

"Around April 1, 1988, there was a lunch in Waterbury celebrating Ken's fifth anniversary as CCV president," Donovan wrote. "I was sitting at the head table next to Ken. At some point, I made a comment that no one should go through life without being 'pie'd' at least once. A woman who worked in our business office went back into the kitchen, got them to fill a plate with whipped cream, walked up behind me and planted it in my face. Ken was laughing so hard I turned and 'served' him the leftovers."

"I figured any president of a college who could take a pie in the face had to be okay," Donovan said years later to Kalb, in an interview.

"Well, I took it, and I was glad I did," Kalb replied. "It worked out."

"Three years later," Donovan wrote, "there was a birthday lunch for Eric Sakai and me in the Montpelier site. A gorilla in a tutu showed up and pie'd me good. It was Ken, two months away from his retirement."

The two remained good friends for the rest of Kalb's life. "In fact," Donovan wrote, "when I sat with him on the day before he died, I told him he had to get better because I still owed him a pie — getting one final laugh from him."

A just-pied Tim Donovan, with the president of the Community College of Vermont in a gorilla suit. (And a tutu.)

Chapter 10

To Produce Profound Change

Mike Holland, 1991-1994

Tim Donovan

When Mike Holland became president in July 1991, CCV's headquarters were in Waterbury on the grounds of what had been the Vermont State Hospital, a nineteenth-century-vintage mental institution, now mostly home to state offices.

On Mike's first day as president, we had just retired the last of our Z-100 computers. They were now eight years old, and these things were built like tanks — they weighed about forty pounds.

So I walk down a third-floor hall in Wasson Hall with a Z-100, push it out on the fire escape and throw it off, at the very moment Mike is driving into the parking lot for his very first day.

He sees this. It's probably the first thing that got his attention.

Of that last Z-100, Donovan said, "We then plugged it in. It worked just fine."

KIND OF A MIRACLE

In 1993, after he had been CCV's president for about two years, Mike Holland submitted a striking annual report to the Vermont State Colleges Board of Trustees. The community college, he told them, had changed so much lately that it "must now confront the fact that it is reinventing itself."

"CCV began nearly twenty-five years ago as a highly decentralized, community-based institution offering instruction to place-bound adult Vermonters," he wrote. "Operating without a campus or a permanent faculty, the college was viewed as a low-cost, infinitely flexible organism that could easily grow and contract to meet educational needs.

Mike Holland

"For many years, these founding assumptions served CCV well, and came close to defining the college's actual operating style. Recently, however, growth and the complexity of a much larger social organization have conspired to produce profound change."

Student numbers were exploding. Between autumn 1982 and fall 1992, the college's enrollment had more than doubled, from 2,045 to 4,727. CCV was now Vermont's largest state college, with 45 percent of the total enrollment in the system.

The steep growth had created serious pressures for rethinking the college's approach in three key areas, Holland told the trustees. First was facilities: "CCV simply exceeds the capacity of most communities to provide convenient, accessible space." Second was academics: Coordinators could no longer keep up with the demands of guiding so many students through designing their own individualized degree programs. Third was the college staff's deeply prized, highly democratic way of reaching decisions and talking through challenges together.

"CCV has always been a flat, highly participatory organization," the president wrote — but that tradition was now at risk. The college, he declared, "must find a way to do its work efficiently and fairly without destroying a culture that encourages dialogue and opportunity for each interested voice to be heard."

A LIFETIME OF LEARNING

Mike Holland's tenure as president wasn't long, just three years, but it had a lasting impact. He wasn't there long enough to see this process of self-invention all the way through; but he, together with others on the college staff, saw the need for it, saw the importance of preserving CCV's core values, and set in motion several projects whose impacts look visionary today.

"Mike came here from Oregon, where he was the commissioner of a system of sixteen community colleges, and in Oregon those are traditional, very well-established community colleges," Tim Donovan observed. "I think until Mike got here, we didn't have a sense of what it meant to be a community college in a national sense. We weren't built on the prevailing model, and Mike came out of that prevailing model."

"I was surprised by most of what I discovered at CCV," Holland recalled. "I marveled at how the prior presidents, and the wonderful staff, had created a vibrant college with pure energy and determination alone. CCV received almost no money from the Vermont State Colleges, yet served almost half of the entire system's head-count enrollment. It paid all employees starvation wages, operated out of derelict facilities, and was almost totally without modern technology (e.g., information technology). Facing those challenges, the former presidents had delivered a college that somehow worked — and was actually hungry for an even larger role in Vermont's higher education community."

Holland guided the college in expanding that role. During his tenure, CCV created a "virtual campus" that electronically connected all its far-flung staff and regional sites, setting the stage for the college's pioneering, soon-to-come venture into online education. It also made determined strides into a new generation of facilities. These were classroom, lab and office spaces that had been deliberately set up for the college, to accommodate its expanding needs — and that looked, for the first time, like authentic college settings.

Holland and his academic dean, Barbara Murphy, who would succeed him as president in 1994, set in motion a move to a simpler, more structured yet still flexible approach to degree planning. They greatly expanded CCV's work in workforce development, developing new skill-building courses, job training programs, and partnerships with Vermont businesses.

To CCV's own operations, Holland introduced a team-based management approach. Based in the regions, the teaming sought "to achieve more focused decision-making," he said, "while avoiding spirit-deadening control mechanisms." Looking outward, he created CCV's first unified public-relations effort, with a new staff position devoted to the work and driven by the conviction that CCV deserved the respect and recognition it had earned.

"Mike was a big one on branding," Donovan noted. "He said, 'We're not going to be bigger and more important if we don't *act* bigger and more important. If we act it, then we become it.'"

Tim Donovan

Let me give you an example. We had to find a different place to be in Chittenden County in the second year of Mike's presidency. We started putting out RFPs [requests for proposals] for locations in Burlington that would allow us to continue to grow. At that time, the state was putting up a new building in downtown Burlington for the Department of Health — a huge building, and they weren't going to need all of it. It was a full block deep; the Health Department's front door was on Cherry Street, and the back door was on Pearl Street. So the state rented CCV the back, not even a quarter, on two floors.

Mike had asked me to work on facilities. So he and I are looking at this building. It's just been built, and we're going to go into it. We're standing by the post office on Pearl Street, and he looks across the street and says to me, "Sign that sucker like we own it."

So we put enormous bronze CCV logos on either side of the back-door entry, and big bronze letters across the top: "Community College of Vermont." On the front of the building, there was this little sign about "Department of Health." Not long after it opened, I was sitting with the guy who ran the building project for the state, and he said, "Let me tell you a story about that building. When we had just finished and everybody was about to move in, my wife was going up to Burlington, and I said, 'Honey, take a look at the new building I just finished running the project for.' She said, 'Okay,' and when she came home, I said, 'What did you think of my building?' She said, 'I looked and looked for your building, and I couldn't find it — but you ought to see the magnificent place CCV built!'"

'We're going to have real college facilities'

"The very first thing I wanted to improve was the physical spaces our staff and students were using," Holland later wrote. "With the exception of our site in Brattleboro, every other [CCV] teaching site in Vermont was impossibly inadequate."

After years of borrowing free spaces wherever it could — in high schools, church basements, the back rooms and neglected upper floors of downtown buildings — the college had gradually shifted to signing short-term leases. Yet there were myriad problems still: cramped staff offices in dilapidated buildings, expanding classes wedged into too-small rooms, inadequate ventilation in crowded spaces that could grow smelly, upstairs spaces without handicapped accessibility, and unsuitable spaces or none at all to meet the growing need for science and computer labs.

"We were in third-floor walk-ups that were dirty," Donovan said. "Mike was the one who started saying, 'No, you have to be in places that people aspire their lives to be like, not in the places that remind them of their lives now.' He really brought that perspective, and so we turned a corner."

Before Holland arrived, CCV had begun under President Kalb to select better spaces, and to configure them as best it could. "They needed to do some planning, to be a little more thoughtful," said Tom O'Brien, a young Burlington architect whom the college recruited to help with that planning.

Tom O'Brien

Tim Donovan had become the director of wearing many hats. He was the dean of administration, and he would call me up and say, "Listen, can you come to Brattleboro tomorrow?" We would meet at the park-and-ride in Berlin at six in the morning. We'd drive down to Brattleboro, and in the back seat and the trunk of his car he would have computers, printers, whatever he was bringing, because he was the IT department as well. And we would go look at two or three spots that they had identified for us.

Tom O'Brien

I would do some really quick sketches, and we would meet at lunch. We'd get some pizza, I'd hand out the sketches I'd done that morning, we would evaluate the sites, and usually by the time we were ready to leave, we would have narrowed down three or four sites to maybe one or two. Whatever it was, it was done on a shoestring budget, and it was done quick.

We went from renting space from a church or borrowing space from a local organization to having a landlord. The landlords gradually got better, because we gradually needed more space. CCV never hired contractors; we never executed contracts. Tim would sign a lease, and the lease would say that the landlord will do the setup.

As the sites got bigger and a little more complicated, the costs began to grow a little bit more. But at the same time, the college was now getting credibility. They had references. They could tell a prospective landlord, "Here's three other landlords we're working with — contact them and find out what we're like." And what they'd find out was, the college paid their bills, they paid on time, they never stiffed you, they did what they said they were going to do. So in many ways, the college quickly became a fairly sophisticated tenant. The college understood what they needed to do, to provide a suitable environment for the students.

One of the things Tim and his folks needed to pay attention to was that most of their students were the first college student in their families, and these students needed to feel like they were going to a real college. So a lot of the things we did were guided by the principle that this needed to feel not like a high school, not a bunch of lockers in a hallway; it needed to feel like what these folks were hoping for themselves and their families for the future. So our aesthetic became white-painted sheetrock walls, with some color. Simple carpet, clean, doors that worked, windows that operated, lighting that worked. Nothing elaborate, just clean and neat, the corporate office of your typical little successful Vermont business.

Every time we moved CCV, we left behind those early, first-generation spaces — across from the X-rated bookstore, the front door with no window, the rooms with no windows, the building with the lighting where the fluorescent tubes were four different colors. Whatever it might be, we left that and went to a space that was a nice, clean, simple, professional environment. It wasn't flashy, but it was what students aspired to in their vision.

A chance to build

When Holland began his term, he saw the chance to build on what his predecessor had begun.

"One of the first things Mike said to me was, 'I've read through some of the facilities planning documents Ken Kalb did with Tom O'Brien, and I think it's a good start,'" Donovan recalled. "'I want you to develop a facilities development plan for the college. We're going to have real college facilities, and I want you to figure out how to make that happen.'"

As enrollment grew, students needed more daytime classes, and it grew harder and harder to find affordable downtown spaces that could accommodate day classes and had adequate parking nearby. Immensely boosting the college's motivation had been the 1990 passage of the Americans with Disabilities Act, requiring that people with disabilities be able to use all public accommodations, including education facilities.

"We needed to have facilities that were accessible," Holland recalled. Also, "we needed to have actual labs where you could teach regular science classes. Computer labs were beginning to emerge at that time; we didn't have any. There was just a whole series of things that could not be accomplished with the facilities we had, and we needed to put ourselves on a path to getting better."

"So we began to evolve toward having slightly bigger facilities," said architect O'Brien — "and we had landlords that began to say, 'We'll build a building for you. We'll custom-build it, we'll own it, and we'll rent it to you.'

"There was a building with a whole lot of heavy renovation done for us in Morrisville, a strip mall that was largely empty where we became the anchor tenant. In Bennington, we went into the old Bennington Motors building that the state was renovating. We kind of backed our way into bigger facilities, because the sites were growing and they needed that."

The first building designed and developed specifically for CCV as its sole tenant was opened in 1992, at 142 South Main Street in St. Albans. That project was another turning point in the college's history.

> ### Carol Vallett
>
> *From "CCV Stories," September 10, 2013.*
>
> I ... was hired as a coordinator of instruction and advisement with CCV St. Albans in August 1991. At the time, the site was located at 81 North Main St., the current home of Howard's Flower Shop. The building was similar to many other CCV sites in use in that era — downtown location, very limited parking, cramped for space and in our case, few windows which made for a dark interior with an environment that was cold in the winter and really hot in the summer.
>
> There was a tiny reception area where the secretary-receptionist worked, a small office for the office manager and two crowded classrooms on the first floor, along with a minuscule room with a few computers (aka — the computer lab). A steep and enclosed staircase led to the upstairs, where there was a maze-like corridor that eventually revealed six irregularly sized offices for the remaining staff....
>
> The lack of interior space meant that we were limited in what functions could occur at the building (none really), what equipment could be in the classrooms (not much), and how many students could be in the classrooms. (I think 12 was the maximum for one room and maybe eight for the other?) I don't recall much being accessible via our current ADA [Americans

with Disabilities Act] standards, but I do remember staff moving a small wooden ramp in and out of the front door area when we expected a visitor who might not have been able to make the step into the building.

I didn't realize at the time I joined CCV, but I had the incredible good fortune to be part of a new era for the college. Within a year or so … a new building was being planned! This wasn't a move to another storefront along the downtown row, but rather a new building, built by James Warner, a local developer, specifically as an educational site for CCV.

Mary Ellen Lowe

Jim [Warner] and David Buchdahl, one of CCV's academic coordinators who later became a regional director, our academic dean, then director of institutional research and planning, started to talk about CCV's space. David recognized the overwhelming need for new space…. Jim began to develop a property on South Main Street a few blocks from downtown with CCV in mind as tenant. Andy Dufault, a local builder, was chosen. Soon a foundation was laid and a building began to take shape. Consultations between college staff, Jim and Andy led to a space that was ideally suited to the college's needs.

Excitement reigned as the building progressed. It was one of the best days for the academic center, staff and students when the new building was occupied. This was an innovation for CCV. No academic center had ever had space which was specifically tailored to its needs.

The building was lovely; it gave the St. Albans Academic Center a true identity. There was green space, lawn and trees surrounding the building, giving it a campus ambience. One phrase finally disappeared from students' lexicon. Before, it was not unknown for a student to come and tell us, "I'm here to take a few classes, then go on to a real college." With the new building that phrase disappeared. We took on the ambience of the real college that we were.

"I believe the new building did much to contribute to the site's growth," Carol Vallett agreed. "We could offer more daytime courses, we were fully accessible to students, and we became much more visible in the community. Most importantly, our new and up-to-date space sent the message that CCV was a growing and thriving institution, and our students deserved to learn in a modern and technically connected environment. The site became a showplace for a few years; we even hosted a Vermont State Colleges Board of Trustees meeting."

"If you put yourself in the center of the community, then you can grow," said Emerson Lynn, longtime owner and publisher of the *St. Albans Messenger*. "That's the whole thing.... They developed a pretty serious reputation pretty quickly here."

The St. Albans project "was followed by another new building in Springfield," Mike Holland said. "Soon after Springfield, CCV was fortunate enough to partner with the State of Vermont and relocate its Burlington operations to a new state office building in downtown Burlington. During my three years we also relocated our Rutland site, White River Junction site, Montpelier site, and were close to relocating the Bennington site.

"With these improved sites came appropriate signage announcing our presence and presenting our brand in a way that was much more visible," Holland said. (The current maple leaf logo made its earliest appearance at this time.) "It is very important to note that none of these improvements would've happened without the leadership of Tim Donovan. When I first arrived I immediately became aware of Tim's talents and energy, and brought him into the central office to fully engage him in transformational projects, including these buildings."

The three-day revolution: Advent of the Virtual Campus

The autumn before Holland became president, CCV had submitted an application for a new federal Title III grant. The idea was David Buchdahl's: Why not put a new computer — one that was networking-capable — on every staff person's desk, then connect them all together?

The grant proposal did not succeed, but among the documents the new president reviewed was the executive summary of the application. Not long after, he called in the staff member he'd seen pitch a Zenith computer off a balcony.

"He says, 'I have a job for you,'" recalled Donovan, who was then director of the Eastern Region. "'I want you to leave what you're doing now and come to work on some special projects.'" One project was developing the facilities plan; the other, inspired by the Title III application, was to create a staff computer network.

"He said, 'This is brilliant — I want this done in a year,'" Donovan recalled. "'I'll find the money, but you make it happen.'"

"It was necessary for CCV to enter the electronic age," Holland later said. "When I first arrived, sites communicated with each other by telephone or courier. Desktop computing was rapidly being deployed throughout America, and networked sites were transforming the workplace. CCV needed to join this movement, and when a cash surplus appeared in the spring of 1992, we decided to take the plunge."

The state college system recommended that CCV adopt Macintosh computers, because Apple had built networking capability into those machines. So the college invested in Macs as its second generation of computers, to be placed on every staff member's desk.

That part was simple enough. Now Donovan had to figure out how to link all those computers together.

Tim Donovan

This was early '92. There was no internet. The notion of networking within a building was brand new; the notion of networking across a state was unheard-of. The infrastructure did not exist. There was no obvious way to do this.

There was a network guy in the chancellor's office, Tom Maguire, who started talking with some of his telecom vendors. One of them said, "Oh, we have a new product that will take a number of telephone lines and combine them, then use it so that it'll take little tiny cocktail straws of data, and combine them into regular-size straws — and that will create enough capacity."

So we probably were one of the first implementers. We bought a product that was able to create a network connection of 384K. Today, slow internet in Vermont, a DSL line, is maybe 1.5 MB. So this was a trickle — and it was expensive.

One of the things we did was to carve off one little corner of that straw and pipe our internal telephone calls through it. We had been spending an enormous amount of money every year on long-distance telephone calls between CCV locations, because everything was a long-distance call at that time. You were paying eleven, twelve cents a minute for long distance within the state. We said, "If we can eliminate all of the telephone calls within the college, that will pay for this pipeline."

The phones we had at the time had a row of buttons along the bottom, line 2, line 3, line 4. We made lines 4 and 5, the two furthest right buttons on everybody's phone, what we referred to as "the tin line." That's what we called it. If I wanted to talk to somebody in Brattleboro, I would pick up my tin line and dial four digits, which would get answered in Brattleboro and put through to their line 4.

Tin lines were highly compressed, and they had a bit of delay and echo, like two tin cans strung together. We just embraced it: "I'll call you on the tin line." I don't know how long that lasted, three or four years, until the telecommunications infrastructure in Vermont allowed for something different.

By the first of November, we had all the computers in place, we had all the networks in place, it had all been tested. We had done a round of training with people, and it's at the point when we're getting ready to throw the switch. Mike Holland says, "What can I do to help?" I said, "Don't send anything out by the U.S. Postal Service to anybody in the college for one month."

In three days, the revolution was over.

We threw the switch, and everybody had it at the same time — because the value only came when everybody had it. At that point in time, if you didn't have all the same stuff, it just didn't work. So we were strict: "You're going to have WordPerfect; you're going to have it on a Mac. There are no choices. But we will guarantee that if you send something to somebody else and send an attachment, they will see the attachment as you saw it."

That's why Mike's leadership in that regard was really important. He basically said, "This is how I'm going to communicate with you. If you want me to read what you're sending me, this is how it's going to be done."

The difference between us and any other college was, most colleges are sending things between buildings that are thirty feet apart; we were sending things between buildings that were thirty miles apart. It took what was a liability for the college and simply eliminated it. Gone! Time and distance disappeared, and that laid the groundwork for everything that happened in the college over the next twenty years.

In 1992, we had the audacity to call it the Virtual Campus. That sounds pretentious now, but at the time it was radical — and it planted in the mind-set of the institution that geography was not a barrier. Within three years we did our first online course. So this was a mind-set shift that was so perfect for this institution.

Academics: New approach, new partnerships

"We also began to rethink our degree attainment model," Holland said. Begun but not completed under his presidency, this rethinking centered on whether surging enrollment had made CCV's uncommon core approach to academics too unwieldy.

All students seeking the associate degree had until now been expected, Holland discovered, to "engage in a deeply introspective, but staff-guided, process to design an individualized degree plan." This "required students to sit down with a staff member multiple times, and go through this intricate process: 'What are your goals? What are your values? Where do you want to head with your life?'

"They would sort of negotiate a degree path for the student, and any deviation from that path would require additional negotiations," he said. "Well, when you have a small staff and you want to increase your student body and get more degrees awarded, we had a degree-attainment model that was at war with that."

In a project led by Barbara Murphy, the academic dean, the college developed a five-year academic plan, first implemented in 1992–1993, that set in motion the process of change.

"A Dean's task force on degree restructuring will likely propose that the college become much more explicit about course requirements for CCV's most commonly awarded degrees," Holland reported in his 1993 letter to the VSC trustees. "Students who want an individually designed degree will still be able to pursue that option in consultation with an advisor, but for most students, carefully articulated concentration areas encouraging broad choice will be the norm. If a student is interested in a business concentration, CCV would publish a list of courses that would satisfy this concentration.

"With this redesign," he explained, "CCV's overworked academic advisors will need to worry less about the mechanics of student course selection. More time should be available for student advising that is focused on problems, planning and academic progress."

The academic redesign also called for an introductory workshop for new students on the degree-attainment process, and a new, integrative "capstone" course that would become a graduation requirement.

A fresh 'flood' of workforce training

CCV's growth also affected other aspects of academics — most notably in a successful effort under Holland to greatly expand its program and partnerships in workforce development and job-related training.

"When I came to CCV I was struck by how modest our efforts were to serve employers in Vermont," Holland said. "Our price structure and flexibility were advantages that, to my mind, ought to be attractive to businesses that needed customized training." But he quickly learned that the state college system was "not terribly excited about CCV becoming ambitious in its outreach to employers."

"The response out of Vermont Technical College was 'No — that's what *we* do,'" Donovan said. "There was resistance externally, there was resistance internally. But Mike thought in terms of, 'What's the rest of the world hoping to get from community colleges that we're not doing?'"

Holland and his core staff forged ahead.

"With additional staff and increased college interest," he wrote in his letter to the VSC trustees, "workforce training and developmental activity is at a flood stage.... With strong leadership from Brent Sargent, CCV's associate dean of academic services, the college has established a workforce task force, to evaluate training opportunities and coordinate the college's response.... It is clear that CCV's workforce agenda is more visible and prominent than it has ever been."

"From a few clients in 1986, TOP [Training Opportunities Program] has expanded its customer base to over a hundred businesses today," Holland wrote in a May 1992 president's report. "A TOP training begins with a collaboration between a TOP coordinator and a business. From there an extensive needs assessment is developed with the customer, and a proposal for training is developed.... The trainings themselves are carefully designed by the trainers and TOP staff, according to specifications and outcomes identified by the customer. Then the program is delivered with close monitoring by TOP staff. Evaluation and followup are the next components.

"... Like all CCV efforts," the president continued, "the focus is on the teaching/learning process and integrating the learning into the lives of the students. And, like all our efforts, the process is hands-on and labor intensive," with "public offerings to Vermont professionals, our in-house trainings for business and industry employees, our special offerings in management and quality sciences, and our for-credit programming to industry."

"Over 3,000 individuals participate every year in some CCV-directed training program," Holland reported to the trustees in '93. "Partnerships with business and industry for customized training programs continue to grow at a breathtaking pace. CCV's expertise in quality science programs is particularly sought out by business and industry."

In autumn '93, for example, the Training Opportunities Program was running courses on conflict management for BioTek, a scientific instruments manufacturer in Winooski; in computer training for Pagesetters, a Brattleboro typesetting company; in effective written communications for the pharmaceutical firm Wyeth; in team-based quality improvement for the Swiss technology firm Karl Suss in

Waterbury; in management and team skills training for Blodgett Ovens in Essex Junction; and in business and professional writing and technical proposal writing for Simmonds Precision in Vergennes.

"The Simmonds effort represents great coordination and cooperation between many players from Brent's office as well as Bette [Matkowski] and Middlebury staff," Murphy reported to the president. "I think we will get even better at coordinating these projects."

David Buchdahl

After serving as Western Region director in the early 1990s, David succeeded Barbara Murphy as academic dean in 1994.

The other thing, during the '80s and '90s, is that we started articulation agreements with the secondary technical programs. In the beginning it was, "Let's create a pathway from the technical schools to the CCV degree." We didn't have a lot of technical degrees, but we began creating them. This was a very big national movement. There were national conferences, and we took a group of people down to Rhode Island to meet with the people at the Community College of Rhode Island and the University of Rhode Island, who had these in place. We created a lot of good networks with the technical schools around the state. We worked with all of them.

Some of the new degrees that we created for this were associate of applied science degrees. One was in manufacturing sciences. We involved people from industry, we involved the newly created Workforce Investment Board — I was co-chair of that first board. So this was all in a rather new direction. We were in the position that the four-year colleges had been with us: "Oh, we don't want to deal with the technical centers." Even though those students were the most likely to come to community college. So we worked through that.

As tech prep gained footing around the country, there was a set-aside in Perkins grants specifically for tech prep programs. We began to apply for that money. And this was a big deal: At first, all the tech centers were applying for the money individually, but we convinced them that we should apply jointly for all of the money available to Vermont. We did, and we were successful in getting that.

Changing perceptions: CCV in the Vermont community

By spring 1993, CCV's headcount had grown to just under five thousand students, of whom 75 percent were women and 56 percent were seeking an associate degree. Yet CCV still struggled with the perception that it was something less than a "real" college — or that, even as its student numbers grew, it should stick to its first focus on serving low-income adults who couldn't attend a conventional program.

"This was a particular problem in the state college system," Holland recalled. "When CCV started, it was okay to serve students that nobody else wanted to serve, or no one else knew how to serve: the struggling, place-bound adult who wasn't going to look at a four-year college anyway. But if CCV had ambitions to serve traditional high-school-age populations, that was a real problem. There was real trouble if CCV wanted to develop an ambitious agenda around workforce training and employed individuals. So there was a lot of stuff going on about CCV and its role. Part of what I was telling the other colleges is that if you increase college-going at the community college level, that is going to have a downstream positive effect for the four-year colleges.

"That has certainly been the experience in Oregon," he said. "When community colleges first got started in Oregon in the early '60s, there was huge resistance from the four-year colleges. But over time, they realized that having more people connected to a college experience ultimately benefited four-year schools, too."

Holland pushed CCV's people to expand their sense of what the college could do and be. "There was a growing realization that there was a bigger, more ambitious role for CCV to play," he said, "and a willingness I think on the part of the college to look at some of those options."

He also set in motion the first unified, coordinated effort to change the Vermont community's perceptions of the college, through a new commitment of staff and budget to promotion and external relations.

"We have consolidated the responsibility of publications, advertising, public relations and development activities into one Director of Community Relations," Holland noted in a September 1993 memo to Donovan, whose post was now dean of college services. "We have staffed that position with a full-time Program Assistant and some work-study assistance and dedicated budget."

Named to the new director's post was Ann Newsmith, until then a CIA in Brattleboro who had taken on the PR work part-time, with Liz Patch as her capable assistant.

Ann Newsmith

I started as a CIA in Brattleboro in Christmas week, 1986. It was a great job. I was hiring teachers and advising students; I did a lot of PR and marketing, but back then each location did their own thing locally. Then one day I was in Waterbury, walking down the hall, and Mike Holland said, "Ann, I think it's time for CCV to have a statewide [public relations] initiative. Would you be willing to work on it?"

Ann Newsmith

I started doing it a day a week, while I was still a coordinator. We had kind of a chip on our shoulder, a sense of being second rate because we were different. We didn't have a campus, we weren't on the [highway] signs, we weren't on people's radars as a real college. There was no budget at that point; I was just being paid as a coordinator. Sometime in '93, we changed that. They hired another coordinator, and I became director of public relations.

We got some money together. We started with the publications, trying to create an image to project that was consistent across the college, in the course schedule and brochures. Fairly early on, Tim created a website that I was involved in. This was back when things were so, so basic: The background was neon pink, and the letters were white. It was quite not-aesthetic! We were just switching into the computer age. Quality improved, and we hired designers.

We went through a bunch of different slogans. At one point I strung them all together, and it was very funny. We came up with "Ask Someone You Know" — because everyone knows someone in Vermont who'll tell you how great CCV is.

The first CCV logo was a tree, but it was kind of scrawny and unhealthy looking. Then they went to what they called Egyptian type, really big, blocky letters — and the V was a map of Vermont. One of the first projects I worked on was hiring a designer to streamline that lettering and replace it. When I did focus groups around the college, people said, "It doesn't matter what it looks like, as long as you keep the map in the V." Because that was the identity: We are Vermont. But guess what? There are very few fonts that will hold the state of Vermont inside a V. So we ended up putting a maple leaf over the V, as a symbol of Vermont; and later on, the maple leaf got moved again. That was a big step, to have this new logo.

There wasn't a master plan. Tim Donovan used to say, about CCV, "We're building the airplane as we fly," and that's kind of what we did with the marketing campaign. As the web became a thing, we got to the next-level website. We kept growing it, and enrollments were really going well. So people felt like the marketing was a good investment.

"None were better"

"I got a lot more out of CCV than CCV got out of me," Mike Holland said years later.

That may be overly modest. His three-year presidency set in motion processes of pivotal change in the college's academics, its facilities, its public relations, and its own sense of how it could contribute to Vermont.

By mid-1994, though, the college's fourth president was ready to move back home.

"My wife just never really made the transition. She had gone back to Oregon a year earlier, so I knew I needed to follow her pretty soon," he said. "At the same time, the chancellor was getting tired of my act, and I was getting tired of the chancellor's act. It was just time to leave."

Returning to his home state, Holland became vice president for finance and administration at Linn-Benton Community College in Albany, Oregon. He stayed there fourteen years, then retired.

"I've worked at a lot of colleges, with a lot of staff and faculties — and none were better than the CCV staff," Holland said in a 2020 interview. "None were better. I'm talking about the commitment that people had to the college, and to the students. It wasn't phony, it was real.

"These guys had no sense of turf. It was not like, 'This is my money and you can't have it,' or 'I've got my own priorities.' It was, 'We have a common college and we're going to spend our money in absolutely the best way that we can to make a difference.'

"And it was so refreshing to see these folks all putting their heads together, trying to make the best decisions possible for the students at CCV. A lot of times it was just, 'Get out of the way and let these folks do what they do best, and they'll come to a great solution.' That was at the leadership level, and also at the lower staff levels.

"It was just amazing to watch."

Chapter 11

What Are We Growing Into?

Barbara Murphy, 1994-2001

> *She's the daughter of a secretary and a construction worker, she was the first in her family to pursue a college degree, [and] she returned to school as an adult. While that fits the profile of the typical CCV student, it's actually a description of CCV President Barbara Murphy, and it goes a long way in explaining her commitment to the college.... She was the first president to have risen from "within the ranks" of the college.*
> — profile of Barbara Murphy, *CCV Alumni News,* 1998

Nancy Winfield, a much-loved coordinator and women's studies instructor at the Chittenden County site, died in 1995 after a brief, brave battle with cancer. "I think that was the first death that our college experienced," Bette Matkowski recalled. "It was really fast, and it was really tough on the Burlington staff."

By then, Barbara Murphy had become the college's fifth president (counting Myrna Miller, but not the very short-tenured George Bilicic). She served as interim president for about a year after Mike Holland's autumn 1994 departure, then accepted the full position. Murphy had started her work with CCV on the Chittenden staff, and she knew Nancy Winfield well.

Murphy is a published poet, and she completed a master's degree in poetry while working for the college. She developed a scholarship in tribute to Winfield; she also wrote a poem dedicated to her friend, later collected in her book *Almost Too Much* (Somerville, MA: Cervená Barva Press, 2015):

Loss

After a while,
she is not there. The difference between
alive and dead is not the monosyllabic slam
of a wooden door, but the same sweater
on the same hook, until one day,
after long enough, someone sighs,
holds it close, breathes in deeply
to remember her scent,
folds it, puts it gently
in the box to go
to Good Will.

"We all listened when Barbara spoke," said Mica DeAngelis. "She could write about education, students, budgets in a way that was not only instructive but always considered her audience. Her words set a positive tone that helped strengthen CCV as the college was becoming a key player in Vermont higher ed.

"I was on Barbara's first interview for a coordinator position in 1983," she continued, "and since then I watched her move to academic dean [in 1989] and president. In every position she excelled at her job and brought a unique style to higher-ed

Barbara Murphy

leadership. As academic dean of a college that was nearly 70 percent female, it was a plus that she was female, at least in my view. Barbara reached out to this population, many single mothers, in a few ways. She always wanted to hear about our students, and she put their concerns at the center of her mission."

Dee Steffan

Dee joined CCV in 1985 to direct the Assessment of Prior Learning Program, then served as an academic coordinator at the Chittenden site until becoming director of the Western Region in the late 1990s.

Having served as academic dean, Barbara modeled someone who took academic quality to heart. She understood that access was central to our mission, but she also knew that our survival in an increasingly competitive higher education environment depended on our ability to prepare our students for whatever came next: jobs, transfer or graduation as a launchpad to both. Therefore, she was attentive to the quality of the classroom (and online) experience from the vantage point of good teaching.

Dee Steffan

Under her leadership, CCV got very serious about faculty development. As academic advisors who hired and supervised faculty, we were encouraged to support growth in teaching and learning, and to hold folks, instructors and students alike, to high standards in the classroom. She was a staunch defender of our students' right to a quality experience at CCV.

As a poet, and a very good one at that, Barbara was our most articulate president. She was also our classiest dresser. That may seem trite, but I truly believe that her ability to impress through words and image was important for CCV at this particular time in our development. CCV was entering a period of maturation. We were a college working hard to be taken seriously by our peers, and Barbara's leadership was very much about that.

She was a joy to work with. She knew how to bring out the best in her staff. Her leadership style was honest, supportive, collaborative and inclusive. Like most leaders at CCV, she understood that good ideas can come from anyone, so she hired well and then let folks do their best work unfettered by micromanagement or second guessing. She took pride in our faculty, staff and students' accomplishments, and she fully embraced the critical role that CCV played *(plays)* in Vermont.

Starting the second quarter-century

As the college passed its twenty-fifth anniversary in 1995, it observed in a publication that "CCV now serves nearly 5,000 students each semester in communities throughout the state, and more than 80,000 Vermonters have taken classes at CCV during our first 25 years."

It was now offering some 668 credit courses, with an average class size of 12.6 students and a tuition of $91 per credit for Vermont residents. About three-quarters of its students were female, 96 percent were Vermonters, and almost two-thirds, by this point, were working toward the associate degree.

With an annual budget of $11.3 million, CCV still had twelve site offices — in Bennington, Brattleboro, Burlington, Middlebury, Montpelier, Morrisville, Newport, Rutland, St. Albans, St. Johnsbury, Springfield and White River Junction — with a total staff of 188. Courses were taught by 497 instructors; all were still officially part-time, though a growing number were teaching multiple courses.

In a message noting the college's anniversary, former president Ken Kalb reflected that "CCV makes three significant, interrelated contributions to Vermont higher education. First and foremost, it provides relatively affordable, accessible means for Vermonters to learn, grow and prepare for jobs. In a small, rugged, rural state that's a tall order.

"A second contribution lies in developing and refining non-traditional education, tailoring it to meet the needs of adult students in a rural state without the benefit of a campus. CCV has advanced the state of the art on several fronts — Assessment of Prior Learning and Dimensions of Learning, to name just two.

"The third contribution grows out of the second one: helping validate nontraditional education in Vermont, as evidenced in the recruiting and acceptance of CCV students and their credits among senior institutions. Happily, these broader contributions have also fueled the growth, and thus enhanced the fulfilling of the founding mission of the college. May the tradition of access and opportunity, so crucial to that mission, carry on for all Vermonters."

'Here's a radical idea'

As well-established as it was by now, CCV was still different — and it was still often viewed as "less than" a mainstream college. For a September 1997 issue of *Vermont Times*, a weekly newspaper in Shelburne, instructor Deborah Straw contributed an essay about her experience teaching at the Burlington site and her frustration with how the college was often viewed from outside.

Deborah Straw

For ten years, I have been an adjunct instructor at CCV. And for ten years, I have received little respect from my professional friends for this work. Whenever one of them asks where I am teaching this semester, she doesn't want to hear about community college. Instead, she asks about my work at other local colleges where I've taught, all with campuses, more facilities, and more money.

I'm sick of this. Having now taught at five area colleges, I believe that some of my most rewarding work is at community college. I like all my teaching and appreciate the variety of classes and students. But I find my students at community college particularly fascinating. They work hard, and they know the value of an education.

Community college warrants respect for several reasons. First, for its students, who, throughout Vermont, are 75 percent female with a median age of 32. Most are parents, many single, and most [are] committed to their education, seldom passing in late work and almost never absent, unless her/his child is sick or out of school. I've had students of more nationalities than I can remember, a deaf student who works with tag team interpreters, military personnel, and a mother of six. Fundamentalists and atheists share opinions in the same class. Two spirited sisters from Zaire educated us about their culture.

Yes, I've seen students whose low self-esteem holds them back, who watch too much TV and never read for pleasure. They may have never been to a museum or outside the state on a vacation. But it's a challenge to work with them. The work is never boring.

Three semesters ago, in my English Composition class at Community College of Vermont, I had a somewhat typical group of students — two single moms, an ex-con, a Chinese professional, a 30ish hippie headed for a nursing career, a Russian woman biologist, an Army recruiter and four traditional-age students undecided on their majors. All loved Raymond Carver's short story, "Cathedral," all had trouble dealing with commas, and all learned to do research and revise, revise, revise.

Classes are small — between ten and 20 students who range from 18 to 68 years old. Course offerings are substantial. For example, we have a solid core of science, math, and business courses plus many literature, writing, art, and language options. There are no "gut" courses. Research projects are required in the majority of them, as are oral presentations and interviews. Returning students tell me that our classes are as demanding, if not more so, than those of other Vermont colleges. Sometimes they come back for one or two at CCV because of the class size and the attention they receive.

Aside from the advantages of great classes, support services, and dedicated teachers, students benefit from affordable tuition. The cost per credit is only $103, and financial aid is available. Several of the workshops are free for our students, as are the labs.

Of course, frustrations do exist for instructors at a community college. The pay is not high, a result of low tuition costs and not enough state support. The college has no budget for professional development nor for membership dues in academic associations. These factors can be demoralizing, but the administration is honest about its financial constraints and praises its instructors often. Praise does help when the money's inadequate.

Just last week, another acquaintance asked if I were still teaching at my other college. I said, "No, but I'm still at community college." Ten years is a long time. Hundreds of my students have graduated (I hate to admit it, but I'm starting to see second generations), and many go on successfully to four-year colleges like Middlebury and Smith. I believe it's time that community colleges start receiving the respect they deserve.

Here's a radical idea. Maybe community colleges could serve as models for attention to individual students, affordable classes, fine teaching, and belief in their faculty at larger and more expensive colleges and universities. After all, shouldn't those be the priorities at any educational institution?

An essayist and author of The Healthy Pet Manual *(Rochester, Vt.: Healing Arts Press, 2000), Deborah was CCV's 1998 nominee for the Carnegie Foundation's U.S. Teacher of the Year.*

Academics: Coming of age

The 1990s decade was the time when, as CCV's leadership phrased it, the college's associate degree came of age.

While Murphy was academic dean in the early '90s, she led an effort that took a close, careful look at the degree: its goals, its components and the process of attaining it, set in the context of student and employer needs plus the college's burgeoning student population. That examination led to some lasting changes.

"Starting this spring, CCV's expectations for learning and concentrations are more clearly stated," *CCViews*, the alumni newsletter, reported in spring '94.

From the college's early years, it had offered a single associate degree — but the process of pursuing that degree had been mapped out in a complex, highly individualized process between student and advisor through the Degree Planning Seminar. Each plan was closely examined, often sent back for revision, and ultimately approved by a review board: at first a locally recruited panel, then in succeeding years by a central Academic Review Board.

Now CCV would offer seventeen associate degrees, each with a specified concentration. It would dispense with the Degree Planning Seminar and would introduce a capstone course, the Seminar in Educational Inquiry, which most students would take during their final CCV year. The college also trimmed its general education areas from five to three: communication; math, science and technical applications; and human inquiry.

"Because the college's growth in the last ten years now ensures a more predictable curriculum in the sites," the alumni newsletter explained, "students can be sure that the courses for which they enroll will advance them toward their goal of an associate degree.... In most cases, review of a student's plan can take place with an advisor, rather than the Academic Review Board."

Before these changes were introduced in the 1994–1995 academic year, "every degree was essentially a self-designed degree," Murphy recalled. "You could identify your courses and your learning and put it all together and present it, work that out with your advisor. Along the way, we just said, 'You know what, this is a little too homespun.' We really had to position students so they were able to transfer to a four-year program, and they were not going to be able to do that if they just said, 'Well, I took this course and I did an independent study in that, because there wasn't a course offered in that.'

"So we laid it out for students. A lot of the motivation came from students themselves — they said, 'I want to be able to use this as currency.' It was very dramatic, and a lot of these things are kind of heart-wrenching — because every system has its good reasons for coming into being, and has its fans who said [in this case], 'If we give up independent, self-designed majors, we're giving up the heart of the college.' We just said, 'No, we have to speak the same language as our students. And have courses with recognizable names.'"

"The big conflict was that we wrote degree requirements: Here were all the courses you needed to take," added David Buchdahl, who became academic dean in '94. "Some people in the old guard thought that was terrible, taking away choice and independence. And we went from a college that did not give grades to a position where students could ask for pass/fail. I think that option may still be there, but nobody asks for it any more."

"Letter grades became the default," agreed Eric Sakai, who had been teaching the introductory Dimensions of Learning course and would soon become CCV's director of learning technologies. "I remember at a meeting of the Academic Council, we had a panel of students, and we asked them: 'Do you guys prefer letter grades or pass/not pass?' And to a person they said, 'We want letter grades. We need them to transfer to four-year colleges, and we need them for reimbursement from employers sometimes. And,' said the students, 'that's the way the world works.' That was the most influential input we got about making letter grades the default."

"In order to play on the broader higher ed landscape," Murphy reflected, "CCV did have to make some changes, make some decisions about who qualifies for what — and they were all made at a table where people would argue passionately. About transcripts: Do we want to have letter grades? Do we want to have the kind of transcript that has a life beyond this college?

"After a while those questions just kind of resolved themselves, because we felt like we owed it to students to have an education that was not confined to the college, wonderful as it was. You should have a record that could be taken anywhere, that could open students to transfer possibilities, travel possibilities, graduate school possibilities."

A new capstone, and a focus on rigor

During the 1994–1995 year, 222 students became the first to take the college's new "interdisciplinary 'super-course'" — the Seminar in Educational Inquiry, or capstone course, that all students would now have to complete before graduating.

Piloted that year, the capstone "focuses on the knowledge and skills that underlie all educational experiences — the processes that lead to an inquiring mind," said a CCV publication. "It is the only course that graduating students — no matter what their concentration — enroll in together, and it is a requirement that affords a diverse mix of student interests."

KIND OF A MIRACLE

A group of CCV staff members with experience in teaching and curriculum design had developed the course, pairing "essential learning outcomes" with a syllabus that included readings of essays in the sciences, humanities and social sciences. "The course was designed," the college reported, "to break down some of the artificial barriers among disciplines, emphasize the interconnections among subjects, and help students derive and articulate personal meaning from their total college experience.... Students are expected to reflect on their own development as learners, and to apply skills to a major, culminating research or creative project."

From the first semester's delivery of the capstone course, the college highlighted these examples of student projects:

- "One student, a native of Panama, researched the historical background of a poem from the Panamanian oral tradition and subsequently adapted the poem, first into a short story and then into a play. As part of her oral presentation, she handed out scripts and asked other students to 'play' the parts."

- "Another student wrote a complete handbook on how to select the right college after CCV. She talked to CCV students, interviewed staff members, and reviewed the pertinent literature. The resulting handbook will be distributed to the 12 CCV sites."

- "A seminar student who works with international students at VTC [Vermont Technical College] interviewed her VTC students, searched the literature for information about other programs, and synthesized her own experiences to design a comprehensive orientation and support program for international students that could be used by any U.S. college with a diverse student body."

"This was the hardest course I have taken at CCV in the past two and a half years," one student reported. "I feel very proud that I was able to be one of the first to experience it."

"A lot of the other things we did in the '90s," Murphy said, "were to keep hammering away at making sure our courses were rigorous, demanding — so that if you took U.S. History After 1850 at CCV, it was going to be as demanding and rich as at another college. We just kept pushing ourselves to make sure that we had rich deep curriculum, that we had the right people teaching courses."

"Barbara really focused on expanding the liberal arts, sciences, the science labs, libraries, improving teacher evaluation and training, improving faculty salaries, paying attention to quality," agreed Susan Henry, an academic coordinator at the Chittenden County site in the '90s. "She was really about quality and thoughtfulness, and doing the broad liberal arts with excellence. I think that era of her presidency was marked by that. She was also taking a leadership role, as Mica [DeAngelis]was, working with UVM to get our courses to transfer."

The effort to work out an articulation agreement with the University of Vermont, allowing CCV graduates to seamlessly enter UVM, turned out to be a fairly epic struggle. In the end, it was an immense step forward in the college's push for acceptance and recognition in the higher education community.

By the mid-1990s, there was increasing pressure from CCV students to have their credits accepted at institutions to which they could transfer, especially Vermont's public colleges. An articulation or credit-transfer agreement was reached early on with prestigious Smith College in Massachusetts.

Barbara Murphy

That was an inspiration. If a college as highly selective as Smith recognizes what community college students can do, why can't our own state university? We started saying, "We should be able to send our students to the university. We're one community college in this state; there's one land grant university. This should work."

We hoped it would alert the university to the power of community colleges and of this community college. And it's kind of a class breakdown issue. This was truer then than it is now, but the students who began at community colleges often didn't have a whole lot of options. So it was a place where you could start; and then, if you believe in the power of education to cause change at the interpersonal and personal levels, students open up. They become aware of their own capacity and confidence because they've achieved and because they've been in the company of people who've said, "You can go on from here. This is just the beginning."

So we wanted the world, starting with UVM, to know that you can begin in one place and grow, and keep growing. We wanted students to know this. We wanted them to understand that they were beginning a learning adventure that was going to open up wider and deeper than they could imagine right now. We wanted potential as well as current students to know the possibilities; we wanted the university to know it. And we were probably signaling broadly, to the state, that if UVM's going to do it, you all should take note.

The UVM negotiation: Frustration and breakthrough

Making this work turned out to be a formidable challenge.

"I knew our students could succeed there," said Mica DeAngelis, the first Chittenden County coordinator — but at UVM, she added, faculty and leaders "didn't think they could, in the beginning. They said, 'Your students won't be able to handle it.'

"Well, that was baloney, and we all knew it.

"It took years. We went to a bunch of meetings; I was finding syllabi for every course we had, so they could scrutinize it. We had meetings that were tense. The problem was the registrar, and some faculty members who were just kind of snobby, I think.

"Our syllabi were different from what they wanted to see. They wanted to see how many pages a student in Psych 101 would read in a week, and ours had learning objectives that were measurable. We actually had pretty amazing documentation on our courses from the very start. So I just started pulling stuff together and would send them over there. I became just adamant that this was going to happen, somehow."

One meeting at the university — an especially memorable one — led to a turning point in the negotiations.

"It was with the UVM registrar in his basement office in Waterman Hall to iron out what courses could transfer and what their UVM equivalents were," DeAngelis said. "He said our graduates wouldn't be prepared for UVM's upper-level courses. He was discouraging and dismissive. As I remember, Barbara closed her notebook, picked up her pencil, and said, 'We are done here.'

"After that meeting," DeAngelis said, "Barbara started talking to Joan Smith and Judith Ramaley."

That was the turning point.

"UVM's dean of the College of Arts and Sciences, Joan Smith, was a community college believer," Murphy said. "She was a very accomplished woman in higher education, and she began her education as a single mother in Chicago, at a community college. She knew where it could take you; she knew what going in that one door could do. So she was an early champion."

Judith Ramaley had served as a professor and president at Portland State University in Oregon before she became UVM's first woman president in 1997. Oregon had a well-established, statewide system of community colleges.

"Around the rest of the country, by the late '90s, community colleges were very big and had become very powerful as educational institutions," noted Buchdahl, CCV's academic dean. Ramaley, he said, "got here and couldn't understand why there were no relationships [with CCV], with the university or the state colleges. She was the one who wanted to create the articulation, as a way of getting more Vermont students into the university. The idea of competition, which was the whole issue with the rest of the Vermont State Colleges, never occurred to her."

David Buchdahl

The incident that broke the logjam was when we had a meeting at the Burlington CCV office with UVM department heads. In most universities, the department heads set the rules for transfer, what's accepted as a course, and all that. It all happens at the department level, and Joan [Smith] knew there was going to be plenty of resistance to accepting CCV courses for transfer: English Comp, Chemistry 1, any of the freshman courses. So she said, "We're going to have to have a meeting with them and some of your people." I think it was Joan who suggested, "Why don't we go to CCV downtown? I'm sure they've never been there."

In those days we were in the Department of Health building. So about twenty or twenty-five department heads showed up for the meeting that afternoon, squeezed into a little classroom with our portable tables and chairs, and we began.

It was awkward because a lot of them didn't want to be there and didn't want to have anything to discuss. The first few people who spoke said, "I don't see how this could work. Your faculty doesn't even have Ph.D.s, a lot of them." That was a big issue. On it went for about twenty minutes, and I was thinking, "This is bad." Finally, there was a guy — I'm almost certain it was the chair of the math department — he said, "I want to begin by saying that CCV saved my son's life."

There was a collective *"Whoo."*

The guy's son was a student who was having a lot of academic trouble. I think he started twice at UVM and failed out both times, and someone suggested, "Why don't you go to CCV and take a couple of courses there?" So he did, and he got his footing there, established himself as a student, went back to UVM, and graduated. He turned himself around.

That changed the entire outcome of the meeting. From there, everybody was ready to discuss, "Okay, what do we need to do to work on the thorny issue of transfers?" In the course of the next six months we worked out the details.

The start of a partnership

"UVM did a study, around the time of the articulation battles," Dee Steffan remembered. "They acknowledged that CCV transfer students were their most successful cohort at UVM. That was huge for us."

"They started looking to see how those students had performed and were performing at UVM," Barbara Murphy said, "and their own research showed that the CCV to UVM students did at least as well as the native UVM students who'd begun as first years. So they couldn't deny that."

On October 20, 1998, the University of Vermont and CCV announced that they "have entered into a new partnership in which CCV graduates who have completed specific courses may transfer more easily into certain academic programs at UVM," reported the *UVM Record*, which carried a photo of presidents Murphy and Ramaley shaking hands over the signed memorandum of understanding.

"The general purpose of this agreement is to encourage and facilitate transfer from the Community College of Vermont to the University of Vermont for students seeking to complete a four-year degree," the memorandum said.

"Officials from both institutions praised the new program for the increased access to affordable education it will give Vermonters," reported the university's newsletter. "… A number of UVM students began their academic careers at CCV, and they have done very well, according to Dr. Joan Smith, dean of the College of Arts and Sciences, which is making this formal agreement with CCV. Working with CCV academic dean Dr. David Buchdahl, Smith and her faculty approved 169 CCV courses.

"Smith, who began her academic career as a community college student with two young children, praised the language of the agreement," the newsletter said. "… A CCV student who has completed 60 credits that meet the specific requirements of UVM's College of Arts and Sciences and who has a grade-point average of at least 2.5 will be able to transfer into UVM as a junior."

"It was a change in thinking all along the way," Murphy said. "Even for CCV staff and faculty: 'Oh, I'm teaching in a place where I could be preparing university graduates.'

"I remember the celebration," she said. "When UVM was convinced and excited about it, they wanted a big public deal. They wanted a signing ceremony; they wanted media there. They wanted this agreement executed in public."

After that, she said, "Everything exploded. Everybody wanted us as their partner."

It took a steady, patient series of negotiations with the Vermont State Colleges to reach articulation agreements there. But Buchdahl persisted, and succeeded.

"That's why the UVM articulation agreement was such a big deal," Murphy said. "It opened the way to further agreement. So there was a lot of stereotype busting that happened."

'She is living proof': The first CCV-to-UVM grad

In many ways, Debbie Stevens Fletcher was the typical CCV student. A divorced single parent raising two children without any help or support, she had worked a series of low-paying jobs after high school before resolving to earn a college degree. But Fletcher is also unique — she was the first CCV graduate to enroll at the University of Vermont after the two schools signed an articulation agreement in 1998.

Susan Henry, an academic coordinator at the Burlington site when Fletcher studied there, remembers well the UVM award ceremony just before the university's commencement in 2001. That was when Fletcher, a summa cum laude graduate in anthropology who went by Debbie Stevens-Tuttle then, accepted the William A. Haviland Medal for excellence in her major.

"Debbie was a work-study student, and we were all big fans of hers," Henry recalled. "She said, 'Would you guys like to come,' and we were thrilled. We took up a collection so Debbie could go downtown and get a beautiful suit from Filene's to wear.

"Here's where I start crying when I tell this story, because I'll never forget. At that ceremony, the UVM faculty were all up on stage in their regalia. When Debbie was called, the chair of anthropology said, 'This student is the first to come to UVM under the transfer agreement with the community college — and she is living proof of the wisdom of that agreement.'"

'This was what I wanted to do'

Fletcher couldn't afford a babysitter when she first visited CCV's Burlington site to ask about enrolling, so she brought along her second-grade son and fourth-grade daughter. "I didn't have a plan," she said. "The only thing I know was that I had told myself, 'If I'm going to do this, I'm going to do it all the way. I want a 4.0 grade average. I want to be the best I can be.'

"I wasn't sure I was smart enough," she said, "but I knew I was willing to work hard enough. That was the difference."

Work hard she did. "I had to schedule my classes while the kids were in school. I babysat the kids next door, so I had to make sure I was there to get everybody off to school, then home when everybody came back. I went full-time some semesters, sometimes half- or three-quarters time. I had to work around my time constraints with the kids."

She earned a 4.0 average her first term and achieved at that level all the way through CCV and UVM. Between the two schools, she said, the community college professors were actually more demanding.

"They make you work a lot harder, because they are preparing you. They are geared toward helping every student become the best student they can be. If you don't hand your assignment in, they want to talk to you.

Debbie Stevens Fletcher

"The only time I ever got called into a professor's office at UVM, I thought I was going to die. It was art history. I had a major in anthro and a minor in art, and I was taking this class with probably the toughest art professor they had. So I sat down, and I was shaking like a leaf. He said, 'You know why I called you in here?' I said no. He brought my research paper out and he said, 'This is a master's thesis.'"

Fletcher's parenting responsibilities kept her from enrolling in grad school after UVM. Instead, she went to work as a research assistant to an anthropology professor, and then as a research specialist in neurology at the university, where she assisted in teaching several courses and co-authored several published research papers. She had, she said, learned to write academic papers in her first-year Dimensions of Learning class with Rebecca Werner at CCV.

"Part of that class is learning how to write a research paper," Fletcher said. "I knew what good writing looked like, but I didn't know any of that stuff — so Rebecca taught me the mechanics. And she's an anthropologist. It was anthropology that stirred my interest in people, that made my eyes light up. This was what I wanted to do."

•••

Going live: The first online courses

Eric Sakai

Eric became CCV's first director of learning technologies in 2000. This is from "CCV Stories," July 17, 2013.

It was around 1995 that CCV's President's Council found itself glumly acknowledging that we could not deliver all of our academic programs to students at all twelve of our academic centers (then called site offices). Access has been the cornerstone of CCV's mission since our founding in 1970 and the primary reason why we chose to bring the college to communities around the state rather than requiring students to travel to a central campus. But the reality was that several of our academic centers lacked student populations large enough to support course offer-

Eric Sakai

ings in all programs. It appeared that we would have to warn students of the need to limit their aspirations to certain degree studies or plan on driving long distances to a larger center.

Fortunately, at about the same time, CCV's Emerging Technologies Committee (ETC) was exploring a new approach to course delivery. Emboldened by the success of the 1992 Virtual Campus project, which brought the transformative communication medium of email to our far-flung college, the ETC decided that it was time to test the waters in the new field of distance education. Honestly, we had little expertise in academic technology, but at the urging of then-Dean of Administration Tim Donovan, the ETC decided to venture a single online course for the spring 1996 semester.

At the time, there were few models to emulate. Blackboard and Moodle didn't exist as what are now known as learning management systems, and only a handful of colleges and universities had begun to deliver course materials and instruction online. We ended up cobbling together an online course using electronic bulletin board software and a Web page hand-built by a tech-savvy CCV office manager, Megan Tucker.

CCV's first online course was Introduction to Political Science, taught by the late Bill MacLeay. Because we were launching an untried delivery system, we decided to offer the course free to twenty-five pioneering CCV students, supported by CCV academic coordinator and ETC member Dianne Maccario. We were pleasantly surprised by the success of the course, which included a rather daring experiment with a guest "speaker," Senator Patrick Leahy, who participated in an online chat session with students.

We took the summer of 1996 to evaluate our experiment and plan three new online courses for the fall semester. In addition to a second offering of MacLeay's Introduction to Political Science, we added an online section of The Constitution, taught by Anne Buttimer, and a section of Science Fiction Literature, taught by CCV academic coordinator John Christensen. Both Anne and John have been teaching CCV online courses ever since — Anne in criminal justice and John in history. In partnership with Megan Tucker, John has been the guiding light of online learning, growing the program from those three initial offerings to what is now the largest provider of undergraduate online courses in the state of Vermont. From that first online course in '96, the growth in our online delivery was just explosive.

"I taught online beginning in '98," Megan Tucker recalled. "We offered one course the first semester we did it, then we offered three, and I think we did eight the first semester I taught. We got to a place where there were about thirty, but all we gave students was a website and Webex, a chat service. That was threaded discussion, a discussion board, and it wasn't for higher education at all; it was for companies. But it was the only one that was available to us at the time.

"We very early on did online learning workshops. Anybody who was going to take an online course would come to the academic center, and not only would we show them the technology, we would also talk to them about the pedagogy of taking a course online. It was about what to expect. John Christiansen did all the professional development, worked with the faculty, and I did the technology to back it up. Eventually, we had an IT department, but John and I were the start of that."

"A lot of colleges saw online as a way to get a lot more people in classes and cut costs," said Tim Donovan, who would serve as CCV's president from 2001 to 2009. "We always viewed the money we needed to put into online classes, for infrastructure and support and those kinds of things, as not much different than if we had to find facilities for those same students. What this allowed us to do was to make more classes available for more people in more places. We put people into it — because it's not free."

"It was all about access," observed Joyce Judy, who became president in 2009. "Many schools have turned to online because it's more lucrative; there are all kinds of reasons. For us, it started being about access, and to this day it continues to be. We've always maintained that it's not better or worse than another format. It's just different.

"We have kept our online classes small, no bigger than twenty. They're highly interactive; we continue to take attendance. Even though things have changed dramatically, the seeds that were planted in 1996, some of those core values, we have carried forward."

Learning in community: Skills and 'miracles'

CCV continued to challenge most incoming students with its Dimensions of Learning humanities course, but it was finding that a large portion of new enrollees needed to build basic skills before they could succeed in a course that demanding. In September '98, Buchdahl devoted the first page of his *CCV Dean's Newsletter* to both those aspects of building what he called "CCV learning communities."

Those are communities "that recognize learning as a collective enterprise," he explained, "one which is always unfinished, exciting, and transforming. At CCV, our challenge is to create these communities in our classrooms, knowing that sometimes they will extend beyond those boundaries.

"... As we explore how students experience these learning communities and become active participants in them, we are taking a fresh look at the role of Dimensions of Learning as a place where many students begin at CCV." In the course, he wrote, "students read an eclectic mix of materials, from diaries of women's lives to Holocaust literature to Plato's *Republic* (the Allegory of the Cave). They learn to reflect and write about matters of deep human significance, and they learn to see learning and themselves in new ways."

Buchdahl quoted three veteran Dimensions instructors on their experiences with Dimensions. "The metaphor of the *quest* describes for me how Dimensions of Learning is transformative for both students and instructors alike," said Rebecca Werner, a coordinator in Burlington. "Within this quest, learning connects and occurs between course 'content' and very real human contexts — intuition, imagination, logic and analysis."

In Newport, "my students tell me that it is a great course because they find out they know a lot they didn't think they did," said coordinator Connie Yandow. "They learn skills that will help them 'survive' college, and they see themselves as successful learners, often for the very first time in their lives."

A revelation like that is "kind of a miracle," said longtime instructor K. D. Maynard, director of CCV's TRIO programs for students from disadvantaged backgrounds. "How do we know — and measure — that these miracles are happening? We use the standard classroom techniques, but more poignant to me are the students who register to vote or submit a letter to the editor for the first time; the students who shyly announce that the kitchen table clears off for homework each night, the TV is shut off, and kids and parent(s) share tidbits of what they are working on; the students who literally sit up in their chairs, meet the gaze of another, and offer — with substantiation — their own opinion."

But not all new students were entering CCV with the basic skills that would make those learning strides possible.

"A few years ago," Buchdahl's newsletter noted, "we made an increased commitment to assessing the academic skills of first-time CCV students in writing, reading and math, and making sure that students with low skills in these areas begin with the remedial courses they need.... So this is another dimension of learning at CCV — the remediation that nearly one-fourth of our students require as they begin college.

"We are like other colleges around the nation in this regard. So we are working this year, beginning this fall in the Burlington site where there are nineteen basic skills courses being held, to invent ways to make these classrooms as dynamic and transformative as [Dimensions of Learning] classrooms. It is a daunting task, but we are going to try."

Dual enrollment: 'Lighting a fire' in high schoolers

During the 1990s, administrators at Champlain Valley Union High School in Hinesburg were looking to "give kids as many choices as possible, coming out of high school," said Val Gardner, who was CVU's principal then.

Serving a region close to Burlington that is both suburban and rural, the high school had "a very high number of students who were from families that knew the college routine, knew it well," she said — but "how do we help kids who have no experience with college? What are the opportunities that these kids will never choose to do on their own, because of their family history or their background knowledge?"

Volunteering at CVU then to promote service learning was Gail Albert, a Shelburne resident whose two daughters attended the high school. A former longtime staff member at UVM's Center for Service Learning, Albert went to work in 1997 for Linking Learning to Life, a new youth-serving partnership between Burlington High School and the Lake Champlain Chamber of Commerce. As a CVU parent, she collaborated with Helen Neidermeier, director of guidance, to create a project that could offer students who might not consider themselves college material — or had simply disengaged from the high school classroom — a chance to experience college-level learning for themselves.

"It was the development of an entire program to take kids to college campuses," said Gardner. "Our interest at that point was to take a group of kids who would never aspire to go to college and get them through the door so they could say, 'Wow. I could do this.'"

"I taught high school for ten years and thought it was awful for some students," said Bette Matkowski, who by the late '90s had become CCV's

Western Region director. "At one point I read that half the dropouts were the smartest kids in school. That defied common wisdom at the time."

Matkowski was serving on a task force in Burlington, led by the director of Linking Learning to Life, that was "looking for ideas to help with dropouts," she said. "My twist was that even smart kids can hate high school, so let's create a program for any student who might benefit from challenge and a fresh start."

There was, of course, the perfect place for a program like that: the Community College of Vermont.

Matkowski wanted to get something started at CCV, but "I was drowning in workload," she said. So she hired someone who seemed perfect, she said: "the amazing Gail Albert."

Albert joined the CCV staff in October '98 as a part-time coordinator of a new dual-enrollment program for high school students. Offering dual enrollment first through Burlington High School, CCV was startled to find that the first group of BHS students who signed up for college courses were highly motivated first-generation new Americans, most of them from Vietnamese families. Since 1980, the urban centers of Chittenden County, Burlington and Winooski had been welcoming newcomers to the United States, primarily from regions of conflict in southeastern Europe, Africa and Southeast Asia, including Vietnam. (See pages 266-270 for more.)

The demographics of the dual enrollment quickly broadened as its student enrollment grew and spread to more schools. "In the first year," Albert said, "I worked with a group of teachers and support people who came together at South Burlington High School, at Burlington High School, and at CVU. I would come to the schools and introduce students to what the program was. As it evolved, we developed a really strong relationship with the tech center [the Center for Technology, Chittenden County's technical high school, in Essex Junction] as well. The program began to develop fairly quickly."

When the national media discovered this effort in 2000, it became the focus of profiles in the *Christian Science Monitor and* the *Chronicle of Higher Education,* and on the *Oprah Winfrey Show.* CCV's dual enrollment program appeared to be the first in the country to be offering its particular mix: a chance for high schoolers who did not think they were college-bound to experience the college classroom, with funding developed through collaborations between the college and the participating high schools.

'A powerful way to get kids involved'

"When High School Isn't Working" was the headline on the January 11, 2000, full-page article in the *Christian Science Monitor*. "Bette Matkowski's epiphany about reaching disengaged high schoolers," it began, "grew out of her experience with her daughter Anne — a bright girl who nonetheless found herself bored, restless, and failing high school. 'She had this active intellectual life but it just wasn't in school,' says Ms. Matkowski."

After her daughter transferred to a different school and was inspired by its more challenging curriculum, the *Monitor* said, "it hit Matkowski... Why not put bright but struggling high-schoolers into community college classes?" There they would encounter "tougher work, a better student-teacher ratio, a more motivated student body.

"... Today, CCV has 90 students under the age of 18. That's only 2 percent of its 4,700-student enrollment, but the college is developing programs with several local high schools and would like to see the figure rise to several hundred."

The article continued: "Traditional high school is an overly structured, age-segregated experience that just doesn't work for some students, say its critics, and it shouldn't be the only alternative available to adolescents.... 'Community colleges are flexible and are really designed to meet individual needs,' says George Salembier, associate professor of education at the University of Vermont. 'It's a powerful way to get kids involved in higher education.'"

Although "about 21 states today have bridge programs that allow high school students to take college courses," wrote the *Monitor*'s Marjorie Coeyman, "... for now, the CCV experience remains somewhat unique," in that the college has provided funding support for dual enrollment and has also "worked actively with local high schools to find other funding and access opportunities.

"... At Burlington High School, a program called College Connections allows 24 students to attend CCV classes through funding supplied by a private foundation. At Vergennes High School, another private grant allows the school to offer one CCV class, tuition-free, on-site every semester."

To make dual enrollment accessible to more students, CCV came up with an idea: "Let's sell coupon books for high schools, for ten CCV courses," said Tim Donovan. "We discounted it by 20 percent, on the theory that 20 percent of them would never get used." Each coupon would allow a student to attend one CCV course tuition-free.

"If a student was interested in doing something different," Donovan said, "the guidance counselor could open their drawer, pull out the certificate, and give it to them." The coupons, he added, "would already have been paid for — schools could buy them at the end of their academic year if they had a little money left over and use them into the future.

"It started very small," he added. "Then it just grew."

"The professor talked to me like an adult"

After the *Monitor* article appeared, staff from the *Oprah Winfrey Show* "came to CCV and Burlington to find out more," said Matkowski. "One of our students was flown to Chicago to appear on her show."

The *Chronicle of Higher Education* followed up with an article in June that quoted Christina Aiken, a Vergennes High School student who had "daydreamed, doodled and ignored some of her teachers" at school, wrote the *Chronicle*'s Erik Lords, until taking a CCV English class "lit a fire under Ms. Aiken. She earned an A.

"In the college class, the professor talked to me like an adult, and there was more one-on-one interaction," Aiken told the *Chronicle*. "College students were there because they wanted to learn, and there weren't cliques or people sitting in the back of the class goofing off, like in high school."

To help high schoolers succeed, first in dual enrollment and later in college, Albert developed Introduction to College Studies, a free, twelve-week noncredit CCV course. "It was a little bit of study skills, a little bit of getting used to the college environment," she said. "We called the dual enrollment program 'College Connections,' because students would earn both high school and college credit for their work with us."

By 2000, the program was drawing high schoolers from Danville up north to Bennington in the far south. "Every school wants a customized relationship with CCV, so what we're doing in Chittenden County isn't exactly what we're doing in Bennington County," said Matkowski in a *Sunday Rutland Herald/Times Argus* story by Heather Stephenson that April.

At CCV, high schoolers are "in an environment where they're expected to be adult [and] take responsibility for their learning, and are an equal member in a classroom," Jeannie Jenkins, CCV's coordinator for the program at Mt. Anthony Union High School in Bennington, told the *Herald*. "... The difference it makes in students' self-esteem is wonderful to watch."

"You have to be committed to stay in it, not just sit there and do nothing," said Staci Crawford, a sixteen-year-old student in Mt. Anthony's program. "Over here, you're responsible for yourself."

CCV's Dual Enrollment Program continues: During 2019–2020, it served 1,785 Vermont high school students. It offers eleventh and twelfth graders the chance to earn up to six college credits while they're still working toward high school graduation, and it still offers the free course that's now called Introduction to College and Careers. CCV's model was adopted statewide with the 2013 passage of Act 77, providing free dual enrollment for all high school students and greater access to free early college, which combines the senior year of high school with a first year of college. (See pages 312-317 for more.)

A new century, and a changing college

The first year of the twenty-first century was CCV's thirtieth anniversary. It was also Barbara Murphy's last full year as president; in mid-2001 she would take on the presidency of Johnson State College in the VSC System. By now, CCV serving nearly five thousand students each semester — and its challenges, always steep, were changing.

The entry into online education had been a big success, and the fast-growing demand for online courses created the possibility that virtually any CCV course could be made accessible to students in all parts of Vermont, even the most rural. At the same time, the college's mix of students was changing. It was becoming somewhat less predominantly female, and significantly younger as well.

Back in 1989–1990, when enrollment had reached almost 4,000 per semester, just over 20 percent of CCV students were male. In fall 1999, with enrollment at 4,812, almost 30 percent were male.

The surge in younger students was even more impactful for the college. Here is the portion of students 22 years old and younger from 1990 to 1999, compared to CCV's total student population:

- Fall 1990: 15% (same as fall 1985)
- Fall 1995: 18%
- Fall 1999: 27%

Focus groups had shown that "young students like CCV's small classes (13 students per class on average)," said a 1999–2000 fact sheet. "They like the adult expectations and environment of CCV classes; they like the academic support and developmental classes. In general they see CCV as a starting place or stepping stone for their college education."

The college completed its first strategic plan in 1999, setting goals for the years 2000 to 2004. Among the goals were to find more diverse funding streams, to "establish staff salaries commensurate with similar education organizations in Vermont," to grow CCV's online course offerings, and to become more entrepreneurial in recruiting and retaining students.

And as the college entered the first decade of the new century, pressues for new positive change were coming from all of its member communities: students, instructors, leadership and staff.

"I think the UVM [articulation] agreement forced the college to up its game," Tim Donovan reflected. "The pressure then was on everywhere in the college, not just in Chittenden County, to be able to fulfill the promise that that agreement had in terms of consistency and quality."

As part of Murphy's push for improved academics, the college had begun a major effort to develop and support the skills of its teachers, with leadership from Academic Dean Buchdahl and Assistant Dean Debby Stewart. "By 2000," said Donovan, "we were doing more teacher development of our faculty than [traditional] colleges do for their full-time faculty, let alone their part-time faculty.

"If we were going to have an entirely part-time faculty, then we needed to be sure they were able to teach."

Taking action on teacher pay

Not everyone in the faculty believed that CCV's system of having part-time instructors teach all its courses was sustainable, or fair to the instructors.

"CCV is no longer the small, storefront school it was twenty-five years ago," instructors Barry Trachtenberg and Patrick Standen had observed in a 1996 essay in CCV's *Burlington Instructor Newsletter*. "... If we are going to continue our commitment to providing a high level of instruction to Vermonters, it is time that CCV begins hiring full-time faculty."

Instructor pay had been low ever since the college began paying its teachers. But now, for "an educational institution serving a large and broad sector of the community," the two argued, "many faculty depend on CCV for their primary means of employment. In failing to recognize this, the institution is failing both teacher and student.... CCV's refusal to deal with the lack of job security and its decision that wages should not increase with experience are issues that are not going to go away as more and more students look to Community College for their education."

In 2000, a long-sought change made it possible for CCV to at last raise teacher pay in a significant way. After much advocacy by CCV leaders, the Vermont State Colleges System remade the way it divided state funding among its member institutions.

By now, about half of all the students in the VSC System were enrolled at the community college — yet "CCV had been getting pennies for years," Joyce Judy said. "This was to try to bring some parity, as CCV was serving more students than anybody else."

In 2000 Robert Clarke became the VSC chancellor, and among his first major projects was to negotiate a new formula for parceling out the state's annual appropriation to the state college system.

"We had become the five-hundred-pound gorilla, and no money had ever followed that," Donovan said. "I had been involved in raising this issue, and there were a number of formulas looked at, all of which would have been closer to parity. They would have all been based on something having to do with enrollment — but all of them would shift too much money away" from the four residential state colleges.

The final compromise was to split the annual funding five equal ways. This brought CCV's share up from 11 to 20 percent. "We still weren't anything close to parity based on enrollment," Donovan said, "but it was a huge thing. And the question became, 'What do we do with that? Do we lower tuition? Increase staff?'

"We knew our pay for faculty was problematic. Not because it was going to create a union situation; it just wasn't enough. That was the biggest hole. So the last budget Barbara created was the first year of a three-year transition to the new VSC funding model and, not coincidentally, the first year of a three-year plan to increase teacher pay to parity with the part-time faculty at the other colleges. We knew we had to do that — so we put every dollar of that change in our appropriation into teacher pay."

Before the change in VSC funding, from fall 1996 to fall '99, CCV's instructor pay increased by an average of 4.2 percent each year, or 18 percent in all. Then, from fall 1999 to fall 2002, instructor pay rose by 53 percent, an average of 15.2 percent each year — from $487 to $745 per credit (the great majority of CCV courses were three-credit).

"By fall '02, CCV teacher pay was slightly higher than VSC part-time faculty starting pay," Donovan said.

In total, over the seven years from fall '99 to fall '06, CCV's instructor pay increased by 86.9 percent, reaching $910 per credit in 2006. In contrast, tuition increased by 45.5 percent those same years, from $117.50 per credit in fall '99 to $171 per credit in fall '06.

Instructors could, and did, argue that pay for part-time teachers at CCV was still too low, just as it was for part-time adjuncts at the other state colleges. CCV instructors would also push for a larger say in shaping courses and other college decision-making as they began a serious bid to unionize in the coming decade. But for now at least, CCV had achieved parity within the VSC System for paying its part-time teachers — who would remain part-time, as they still are, and still largely drawn from Vermont communities.

'A library for the 21st century'

Spurred by the impossibility of developing a traditional physical college library that all its students could easily access, CCV in the mid-1980s helped lead the creation of an innovative automated library system that linked together the collections and circulation services of the state colleges, UVM, Middlebury College and Vermont Department of Libraries. The college also created its own distributed library system, with "mini-library" reference collections at all twelve CCV sites; a toll-free phone line connecting each site with the library coordinator and the four VSC campus libraries; and an online service at each site through which instructors could search out classroom materials, teaching techniques and other resources.

Then in July 2000, a partnership that CCV's first librarian, Eileen Chalfoun, had sought to nurture in the early '90s finally came together. The college and Vermont Technical College (VTC) announced that they were creating a new, consolidated library.

Over the coming three years, the newly named Vermont Community & Technical Colleges (VCTC) facility would become "a library for the 21st century that blends both 'high tech' and 'high touch,'" said the autumn 2000 issue of the *CCV Instructor Newsletter*.

"Accomplished through the good work and collaboration of the library staffs during the past academic year," the library would, the newsletter said, include "a central repository of print, media and microform collections at the Hartness Library on the VTC campus [in Randolph Center], access to an expanded collection of academic information and services online," and "increased availability of instruction in library and information literacy skills."

At CCV's twelve regional site centers, "small physical collections of basic reference books and instructor-selected reserve collections will be supplemented by access to online interlibrary loan and full-text services such as netLibrary, an electronic collection of thousands of current books," the newsletter said. The VCTC library card would allow students, instructors and staff at both colleges "to make use of cutting-edge technology that will bring library services and material to the desktop, 24 hours a day, seven days per week. The card will also enable online request and delivery of borrowed material directly to home or site and access to more than 80 hours per week of reference assistance."

"For me, one of the most important developments" of this period "was the creation of the library partnership with VTC," said Buchdahl, then the academic dean. "Eileen was the real pioneer in that; she created the first link. She left, and I spent a lot of time with both Steve Ingram, who was academic dean at VTC, and the librarian there, Jane Bartlett. It required a lot of work, in terms of budgets and responsibilities — the joint budget had to be developed each year. We really had to up our annual library budget, to match what VTC thought was going to be sufficient."

Under the agreement signed by Murphy and VTC President Allan Rodgers, CCV committed to raising its annual budget for library collections from $10,000 to at least $100,000.

Directing the new library was Jane Bartlett, who had been VTC's library director. She retired in mid-2003 and was replaced by Tom Raffensberger, who had directed a library in the United Arab Emirates.

"Tom did the legwork, including all the electronic, digital databases that became the backbone" of the new library, Buchdahl said. "It was very satisfying work, and Tom was a fantastic guy. We were very fortunate to find very good people to direct this project over its first five or ten years, when it was developing. It has made such a difference."

Rethinking registration for the online age

CCV also set about reconceiving its registration process during the final phase of Murphy's presidency.

"CCV had gotten much bigger," said Donovan, "and the work load associated with our time- and labor-intensive registration process simply hadn't, and wouldn't, scale for that. It was all too hard for students to navigate."

"Present registration process has us compressing in-person advising, financial aid applications, assessments, and registration into a month of mayhem three times a year," said a report produced by Rethinking Registration, a college task force. "Registration has been conducted in largely the same way as when the college was half its present size," and when each site center operated much more independently.

"With students taking courses in multiple locations, particularly online, and our faculty being more mobile, we no longer could operate as twelve independent entities," Joyce Judy observed. "As an example, we had twelve registration forms. So if you took a course at CCV in Montpelier and you took one in Winooski, you had to fill out two different registration forms — and in the same way, a lot of our policies were implemented differently. And students really drove that: 'Look, I don't want to be playing by two different sets of rules, so you guys get your act together!'"

Computers and communication technology had made streamlining the process much more feasible. The registration task force envisioned a process, adapted somewhat to the differences between the regions, that would allow students to access needed forms, take needed assessments, and apply for financial aid online, with help as needed via email from their advisor. Students could view course offerings and then register on the college website, and order books online through the CCV bookstore, all with in-person alternatives available for those who lacked computers or web access.

"A few of us at CCV and elsewhere were pressing the VSC hard for a major investment in new computing systems — which the board agreed to in 1998," said Tim Donovan, who would succeed Murphy as president in 2001. "Registration was still something that could be done manually at the other colleges, but CCV had to automate. The Rethinking Registration task force was part of an effort to get positioned for that challenging opportunity, which would occupy that last year of Barbara's presidency and the first several years of mine."

'Lives can change in unimagined ways'

In spring 2001, CCV announced that Barbara Murphy would be departing the college in July to assume the presidency of Johnson State. "In her tenure as president," said the college's alumni newsletter, "CCV's enrollment and budget have grown, and academic offerings have become richer and more varied. The College is a statewide leader in online education, and many partnerships have been formed with businesses and agencies throughout the state to provide greater access to education and training. She leaves the College a stronger place for teaching and learning."

Having been the first CCV president to have come from within the college's own staff, Murphy sought, in a 1998 talk at Convocation, to share the values and convictions that shaped her tenure, and to put into words the heart and soul of this still-uncommon college:

Barbara Murphy

Convocation, autumn 1998.

What are we growing into? What do we not want to grow away from?

I don't want us to grow away from being a community-based college with expertise located all over the state.... Brattleboro and St. Johnsbury have a lot in common, but are each who they are, reflecting the talents and humors of staff, the passions of local instructors, the curriculum insisted on by students.

... I don't want us to grow away from our modest beginnings. That doesn't mean that I long for the overcrowded storefronts that were too cold in the winter and too hot in the summer. But it seems good to remember that our college began as a place where the price of admission was a student's willingness to learn something new. Such institutional simplicity can remind us that it is still an enormous act of trust for a student to enter a college classroom, that lives can change in unimagined ways through something as simple as an encouraging advisor, a good teacher, a smile from the person at the front desk, a $50 voucher to buy a textbook.

I heard community colleges described lately as "four walls and an opportunity." It's probably that which I don't want us to forget.

I want our definition of access to grow with us. For a while, it meant that any student could take any course he wanted. I think we have come to a more inclusive definition of what access means. As Vermont and the world are changing, we have become much better at accommodating the needs of students with disabilities, and while we have done it with better architecture and up-to-date technology, we have done it as much with our students, with the willingness of instructors, and — a favorite CCV strategy — through lugging equipment from site to site.

Nancy Severance tells me we have 20 international students this semester; in past years, we have had two or three. This does not include the 25 immigrants and refugees who are receiving aid through new scholarships, and those students who don't fit those categories and are just here, quietly changing how we look and learn.

If we take our lead from our students in thinking about change and growth, we hear that they feel more confident and that this confidence extends beyond the classroom; that they erase earlier beliefs about themselves as stupid; that they consider themselves better citizens and family members; that they no longer live "in just a little part of the world," that they came to CCV for a specific purpose to learn a particular thing and those original reasons have changed and grown with them.

They talk, also, about the indispensable encouragement from instructors, the personal connections with students. In a focus group, one student described her memory of listening to her advisor explain how each barrier the then-tentative student named could be overcome; and how the student recognized that, finally, she was the only thing in her own way. I suppose I love that story because of what it says about recognizing the self as the principal player in learning. This student was already halfway there and didn't know it yet.

I suppose I would wish nothing more for all of us ... than we wish for our students: that starting from wherever we need to start, that we listen to each other with open hearts and minds, that we ask for and offer help when we need it, that we stay alert to the possibilities of change, and that we think of ourselves as good citizens in all the states in which we live.

Some of the logos that have represented CCV over the years.

"When you think about the future of higher education, it's not sitting and waiting for people to come to you. It's reaching out and providing pathways."

— Joyce Judy

Part Three

Inventing the Future

2001 to Today

Chapter 12

On a Big Playing Field Now

Tim Donovan, 2001-2009

People who in the 1960s and before had no voice, no path, now have a path to find out who they are ... and powerfully interact with their communities. You continually refresh the social, civic, economic and cultural blood of this state.

— Peter Smith, founding president,
from a September 2000 talk honoring
the college's thirtieth anniversary

The new century brought the college a new presidency and a decade of powerful growth and change. Some of that was grounding and stabilizing, some was expansive and diversifying, and a bit was painfully controversial.

Tim Donovan, who had served in various college posts since the late '70s, became the sixth president in mid-2001. He would lead the college until 2009, energizing and overseeing a period when student numbers almost doubled, enrollment in online courses surged to nearly 40 percent of the total, the college welcomed many younger students while forging new working relationships with secondary schools, and it finally began to build its own regional facilities.

"It was just a time of change," said Susan Henry, who became the first director of enrollment and advancement soon after Donovan's presidency started.

This was also a time when — very suddenly — the country changed.

When the month of September 2001 began, "I asked for two weeks off before I began my new position," Henry recalled. "We went to Maine, and 9/11 happened. When I got back, the mood had changed so much. I think there was a lot of innocence and maybe idealism of the '90s that didn't necessarily carry over."

The college, as it turned out, was entering a new, somewhat sobering phase of its own evolution. "In the '70s we were early childhood," Henry reflected. "In the '80s we were toddlers, then we became teenagers in the '90s. We got into the 2000s, and we were in our twenties — and we had to get serious about things."

"That's a great metaphor," said Dee Steffan, who directed the college's Western Region from the late '90s until her retirement in 2016. "What separated the 2000s for me was the really significant shift to younger students and the impact of having more new Americans, especially in Chittenden County."

Tim Donovan

By fall 2003, students aged eighteen to twenty-two, the traditional college years, made up 30 percent of the student body, and the number of high schoolers taking CCV courses had grown by a third from the year before. Minority enrollment had risen by 11 percent, compared to the previous year, largely in the center that served Chittenden County: In fall '03 almost one in ten students at the Burlington site came from a minority population, compared to about one in twenty in CCV overall.

INVENTING THE FUTURE

The college was especially challenged, during the century's first years, to accommodate a huge increase in online enrollment. Having begun with a single political science class in spring 1996, the number of online courses reached 37 in fall 2000, then 168 in fall '05. With the numbers of students signing up for online courses growing even faster, coping with all that felt like "drinking from a firehose," the late John Christensen said when he was guiding online academics in those years.

As CCV's overall numbers surged, "it felt like a very energized and expansion-focused environment," recalled Katie Mobley, who in 2008 became assistant director of the college's growing involvement with high schools and technical centers. "There was a lot of freedom, I think because we were expanding at such a fast rate. There was this element of 'run till you're tackled' — and because we had strong enrollment, we had some wiggle room to do that. The enrollment picture in the beginning of the 2000s also allowed us to hire a lot of staff, some of whom are still here."

"A lot of who were are now really came from that first decade," agreed Debby Stewart, who became associate academic dean in 2001 and is the present-day academic dean. "As Tim navigated the college through those times, we didn't know what the future would hold. We started to make transitions that have paved the way for who we are now."

For Donovan, three themes characterized the first decade of the 2000s. First, he said, "we had learned that technology could minimize the impact of geography." Second, "online teaching was ramping up — and hitting some roadblocks." And third, with everything that was happening, the college had the chance to do more than just cope: It was challenged "to create a culture of continuous change."

"People would say, 'We've had so much change the last couple of years, when are we going to stop?' The answer was 'Never,'" Donovan said. "Joyce has a much more articulate way of talking about this. She says, 'If we're not inventing the future, we're dead.'"

Joyce Judy, the college's current president, would take over from Donovan in 2009. Overall, "Tim and Joyce were very much ahead of their time," said David Wolk, who led Castleton University in the Vermont State Colleges System from 2002 to 2018. "They were doing distance learning and individualized education, personalized learning, well before the more traditional places who are now catching up.

"They certainly had the right approach," he observed. "Very student-centered, future-focused, affordable, accessible — frankly, the way it should always be for students, regardless of their age or their place in life or what zip code they were born in. I think they really perfected that model. And into the future, that will be the model going forward.

"Tim and Joyce," Wolk concluded, "really gave the place its wings."

The day after the 9/11 attacks, Barbara Martin went for an interview with Tim Donovan. For about fifteen years she had been working as UVM's financial affairs manager, a good job from which she expected to retire. Then she heard the community college was seeking a new dean of administration. She was intrigued, although she wasn't sure why she would want to leave the university.

"I mentioned it to my boss, a vice president at UVM," Martin said. "He looked me straight in the eye and said, 'You don't know this yet, but you belong at CCV. This job is your calling.'

"Tim was a big factor. You met this guy and talked to him and thought, 'I'd like to work for this man.'"

Barbara Martin

Barbara served as dean of administration, managing the college's "back office" of operations, from 2001 until her retirement in 2018.

I'm a fifth-generation Vermonter, and when I was in high school the only way you could go to college was to leave home. My father never got beyond sixth grade; my mother went to beauty school. [Barbara earned a bachelor's degree at Trinity College in Burlington, then two master's degrees at UVM.] I was one of those kids who was never supposed to go to college — and the more I heard about CCV, the more I wanted to be part of that.

You know how CCV was created, and what kind of an institution it was in the '70s. Thirty years later, we had a lot more to lose. We had a lot of students who really counted on us, and the world had changed. There were a lot more regulations out there that were kind of saying, "Hey, pay attention, because if you don't I'm going to come back and bite you."

The thing about Tim was, he always gave me the latitude to take the lead and to do what I thought needed to be done — yet I knew he was right there with his support and his wisdom. He challenged me. That was his style of leadership. He always supported his folks, and challenged them in a way that just made them feel such ownership and such pride in the work that they did.

"Tim has a remarkable combination of talents that are not usually combined in one person," observed David Buchdahl. "First, technology skills. He really is at heart a geek. He was teaching micro apps when we were introducing people around the state to what a computer was, and he loved it. He was an early subscriber to *Wired* magazine. He just liked the technology — so that's one area.

"Second was finance: Tim likes accounting and numbers and financial planning. The third area is interpersonal skills. Everybody *likes* Tim — he's a warm, outgoing guy, a big hugger."

"Tim is a very congenial guy," Dee Steffan agreed. "He's Irish, he's a storyteller, he brings people in. He relates through personal connection."

Donovan had worked with all the CCV presidents who preceded him. He was hired by Peter Smith in 1976, and under Myrna Miller (1979–1982), he directed the state college system's Office of External Programs, housed at CCV, through whose pioneering Assessment of Prior Learning program students could receive academic credits for what they had learned through work and life. Ken Kalb (1983–1991) brought Donovan onto the college staff, where he served as a regional director and led the introduction of desktop computers into student labs and administrative offices.

"I had this opportunity, with Ken, of having to take on things that I didn't know if I could do and discovering that I could," Donovan said. "My confidence built, and people's confidence in me built."

He became the director of the college's Western Region (1985–1987), then of its Eastern Region (1987–1991). He led the implementation of CCV's first college-wide network of staff computers after Mike Holland

(1991–1994) named him the dean of college services. He held that post through most of Barbara Murphy's leadership (1994–2001), until he was named dean of administration in 1999.

"My joke was always that my career path was taking on all the jobs people wanted done but nobody wanted to do," Donovan said. "Did anybody want to do computers? No. Did anybody want to do facilities? No. Over time I took on more of those things that were all new to me. I just felt like that's what had to happen."

In that process, he developed an approach to leadership. It centered on giving others the same chance he'd had, to learn what they could do and what they might become.

"You had to be creating the next generation of leadership constantly," he said, "and it's not a matter of keeping people in their comfort zones. It's stretching them. Not breaking, but stretching.

"I heard Peter Smith say to me at some point, 'Run till you're tackled,' and that was it. Every once in a while you'd tackle somebody, and they'd say, 'You told me to run till I was tackled!' and I'd say, 'And now you've been tackled. Learn from why you got tackled, and get up and run some more.'"

Deeper into the digital age

For much of Murphy's presidency, Donovan co-chaired a strategic technology planning group for the state college system, along with its Student and Administrative Services Initiative. From those positions he played a key role in moving the Vermont State Colleges into a new era of computer-enabled efficiency.

CCV had begun to discover that potential in the early '90s with its Virtual Campus project, then with its venture into online learning. "The next step, and there is always a fast-approaching next step for Internet-related technology," wrote Eric Sakai, then Eastern Region director, in 1996, "will be to provide students with the ability to apply for financial aid, register for courses, order textbooks, and consult their academic and financial records from the home computers."

But in the late '90s, the state college system's administrative technology was seriously outmoded.

INVENTING THE FUTURE

Tim Donovan

The VSC's central computing system sucked. It was twenty years old. The other colleges thought it was fine, but it couldn't scale to CCV's number of students. We pushed really hard, with great resistance, that the VSC needed to make a multimillion-dollar investment in new computing and software systems. That decision got made in about '99 and was going to be implemented over the course of about three years. So as I was coming in as president, the challenge was to make this work, in the ways you needed it to and in ways you hadn't thought of yet.

We had learned a decade earlier that you don't do these things halfway; you've just got to do it. I had good leadership credibility in the VSC on technology, so we were in a position politically to drive it. The VSC had all these teams: accounts receivable, accounts payable, payroll, student records, financial aid, billing. I put our smartest, best people on every team, and we created an internal group with those same people, working together across functions in CCV. We'd gone out on a limb on this; we were going to make sure we leveraged the hell out of it.

That became a huge part of my first couple of years. We were stuck in a system that was going to have to serve five colleges, and we were the oddball college. We knew if the system could be flexible enough to do what we needed it to do, it would be flexible enough for everybody else.

So that was one part. The second part was that we were ramping up what we were doing with online [education], and we were hitting some roadblocks. Part of that was that there were things we just didn't believe we could teach online. Meanwhile, this thing was really taking off. David Buchdahl had made a prediction that online would be a third of our enrollment — and now it was, even though our enrollment had doubled since he made that prediction. Online was a huge growth factor.

Through the course of my presidency, the question I kept asking was, okay, we've done a pretty good job of replicating a 1980s blackboard classroom online, "talk and chalk" — but what could we be doing online that we simply couldn't do in a classroom? Let's be looking for those opportunities. What are the programs we could offer that we can't aggregate enough market for in any one location?

An optometry program was the first one we did. It had two students in Newport, three in Burlington, one in Bennington, and one in Brattleboro — which was enough. We could never have run that program on the ground. So let's begin to exploit this.

All of that kind of begs the question, "How do you create a culture of continuous change?" My belief is that inertia is the most powerful force, not just in nature but in an organization. My analogy used to be, you can sit in the parking lot and turn the wheel all you want, and the car doesn't change direction. It has to be rolling. We can never stop changing, because if we stop changing, we're going to miss the next thing.

We had to stay skating on the edge, constantly — and technology was a place where we were ahead of everybody else. But that really requires people to be constantly saying, "It's okay that I'm letting go of stuff and starting to do new stuff." Once they get comfortable with that, it's a powerful force.

I didn't look to other educational institutions. I did not look to the *Chronicle of Higher Education* for ideas; I read *Fast Company*. What are innovative businesses doing? What are entrepreneurs doing? What can we steal shamelessly from them? We were trying to create a culture in which that amount of change was the norm. When you're the oddball, you've got to be running faster than everybody else.

Another hallmark of the first decade of the 2000s was that the college began to build new learning centers, to its own specifications, on property that the state college system had purchased at Donovan's urging. By the end of his presidency in 2009, the college had moved its leased St. Albans center into ownership; had built a new Upper Valley center in Wilder; had moved its main offices into the soon to be expanded former home of Woodbury College in Montpelier; and was constructing what would become its flagship learning center, for Chittenden County in Winooski.

"I think I was a builder," Donovan summed up. "But with a lower-case 'b'."

Teaching and learning in a changing college

Once every decade the college has faced its all-important engagement with the New England Association of Schools and Colleges, on which hinged the renewal of its accreditation. As the date drew near for the NEASC team's April 2002 visit, a group of CCV administrators and instructors labored to finish more than a year's work on a 100-page college self-study that the accreditors would scrutinize.

The self-study clarified the big challenges the still-young college was facing. As it worked to accommodate a major surge in enrollment, especially in online courses, CCV was pressed to deliver all that students and others expected of a "grown-up" college, while also keeping to the core values around individually determined education that this institution had always — at least, so far — held close.

"CCV is a college that is growing, changing and meeting new challenges," wrote Academic Dean Buchdahl in the spring '02 *CCV Instructor Newsletter*. "... As we make ready for the NEASC visit, you should know that this spring semester CCV achieved its biggest enrollment ever measured in course placements — over 9,900 — and the most students enrolled in over 10 years — over 4,800 statewide." (Students often took more than one class, of course; course placements count every signup for every course.)

Online course enrollment had doubled since the previous spring. "This year, we have also enrolled the largest number of traditional age students," the dean reported, "and this semester the percentage of men enrolled at CCV reached 30% for the first time.

"... Every NEASC institutional self-study is an opportunity to take a fresh, hard look at oneself," Buchdahl noted. "Sometimes this means reaffirming long-held views and values. Sometimes it means seeing how much an institution has changed in ten years, and sometimes it means discovering some areas where work needs to be done."

He summarized key findings of the 2002 self-study:

- "CCV is good at planning. We have used plans to advance important new initiatives such as online learning.... We are less adept at using data to evaluate outcomes, but we are committed to becoming better at this."
- "CCV is in the midst of a sea change in its own organization. On the one hand, it is becoming more fully integrated into a Vermont State Colleges system that is moving ... to a single, centrally managed system. On the other hand, it is creating stronger ties among 12 individual sites, and promoting regional delivery of programs and services."
- "Through all of this change, CCV's organization continues to depend on, and cannot be understood apart from, the role of the coordinator of academic services, a role whose ubiquity is, we believe, unique to CCV and absolutely vital to all CCV teaching and learning activities."
- "Through this self-study, CCV has reaffirmed its commitment to a 100% part-time faculty. It has more completely understood that the combination of full-time coordinators and part-time instructors is a novel alternative to a mix of full-time and part-time faculty typical of most community colleges."
- "CCV's facilities budget has gone from $.3 million in 1992 to $1.24 million in 2002. This represents major upgrades and expansion of rented facilities in all 12 CCV locations. Facilities in most locations — Burlington, Montpelier, Newport, St. Albans, Springfield, Rutland — would have been inconceivable a decade ago."
- "Each semester CCV hires approximately 500 faculty to teach credit-bearing courses and non-credit workshops and to serve in a variety of other roles such as committee members, mentors and tutors. Most faculty are returning instructors.... In the spring 2001 semester, 75% of course sections were taught by faculty with a master's degree or higher."
- "Recent substantial increases in instructor pay have improved CCV's ability to attract and retain highly qualified faculty. For the 2001–2002 year, the per-credit pay is $634. This is a 50% increase over the per-credit pay for year 1997 ($421), and an 81% increase over the per-credit pay for the year 1992 ($350), when NEASC last evaluated CCV. These increases are part of a purposeful four-year

plan to bring CCV faculty pay into parity with that of the other Vermont State Colleges' faculty by the fall of 2003."

- According to the findings of a spring 2001 faculty survey, "increased pay has led to increased faculty satisfaction, and better success in recruitment and retention of faculty. Faculty also appreciate that CCV devotes significant institutional resources to the support and training of faculty members. They report that small class size, motivated students and coordinator support are also major factors in their satisfaction."

- "Ten years ago, faculty did not serve on any committees. Today faculty serve on the Academic Council and nearly every academic committee.... Faculty are involved in the development of programs and courses. They are presenters at CCV conferences and in-service training. Instructors were members of the various committees involved in developing this self-study report for NEASC."

NEASC would renew the college's accreditation, but the struggle to meet the challenges of the new decade continued. As the fall 2002 semester began, CCV announced that its academics would now be guided by a new set of policies governing all five schools in the state-college system — and for the first time, instructors could assign the letter grades D and F.

For many at the college, that was a turning point. And a hard one to accept.

"CCV was a product of the '60s, you know — and for years, in the '70s and '80s, it was all about learning for learning's sake," said Joyce Judy. "But in the '90s, we started to see students wanting to transfer, and we were a pass/no pass institution. Yes they could transfer, but they had to go through a lot of hoops: You had to demonstrate all their learning, whether C or better, blah blah blah. And students were like, 'No, we want grades,' and they drove us to flip. So the default became grades, and you could request a pass/no pass.

"For some people, that was like we were selling our soul to the devil. 'This is not okay!' But you know, our students were changing, and we were not going to stand in the way of their success."

After an emotional debate in the mid-'90s, the college had shifted to an A, B, C grading system — but it kept the letter N, "which CCV has long used to indicate Non-satisfactory work and No credit," Buchdahl wrote in the *Instructor Newsletter* that fall. Now, in the early 2000s, the dean instructed his faculty that the grades they could assign were to include D and F. The N was gone.

"Please make sure you have a discussion with your students about the new policy," Buchdahl advised, "and make sure they understand that a D grade will not be able to satisfy degree requirements."

"It seems laughable now, but I remember speechifying about that," Dee Steffan said. "We felt like we did things for a reason, and that lack of a D grade was at the heart of our self-perception, an important difference for us.

"This was very much about, are we going to become more like regular colleges? Eric Sakai was like, 'Oh come on — we're on a big playing field now, and this is a silly thing to get hung up on.' But I was one of those who had tears in my eyes," Steffan remembered.

Clarifying the pathways to degrees

In 2003, CCV launched several new programs "to give students marketable skills for careers in fields with increasing opportunities." The additions offered associate degrees in computer network administration and performing arts, job-skills certification as a K-12 classroom paraprofessional, and preparation for the certificate in licensed practical nursing that students could then earn at Vermont Technical College.

Liberal studies was the college's most popular associate degree program. Students on that track could "take a broad array of courses in the liberal arts," said the 2003 course catalog, noting that most of those students "intend to transfer to four-year bachelor degree programs in other colleges." Other CCV degree programs that year were in accounting, business, communication, criminal justice, human services, office management, technical studies and visual arts.

The college and Johnson State were also providing statewide access to the External Degree Program, which VSC's Office of External Programs had created under Myrna Miller and JSC now administered. "This partnership allows you to stay in your community, work with a local academic advisor, and complete a bachelor's degree," CCV advised. "Courses are designed for students to earn degrees in business, elementary education, general studies, liberal arts, and psychology. Other degree options are also available."

With enrollment growing, program choices expanding, and VSC's new computer system speeding up administrative, registration and informational tasks, "I started thinking about how we could apply some management techniques that would help us get our arms around what was happening — particularly around planning classes, delivering programs," said Susan Henry, the associate dean of enrollment and advancement. "I teamed up with David Buchdahl to much more intentionally map that out."

David Buchdahl

Up until then, we hadn't really had much focus on program management. Take an example: We had a program in human services. Well, from a student perspective, if they wanted to earn degree in human services, how did they do that? How are those courses presented to them, over a two-, three-, four-year period? If you think about a regular college, you go to the catalog and find your program, and it says, "Take these courses your first semester, and these courses your second year, and there's a map to how you complete the program." We didn't really have that. There was a list of courses, but there was no responsibility on a particular site to make sure those courses were available.

Program management also coincided with our online development, so we could feel more confident saying, "Well, here's a way you can complete this program: If the courses aren't always available in your site location, we can make sure these are available online for you." So the coordination between online offerings and site offerings became more important, and we had to have people who were focused on the program level to make sure all that was happening.

That's basically what program management was about. I remember it required new staffing, which was a bit of a hurdle. Getting associate dean positions approved took a bit of persuasion. Debby Stewart and Rebecca Werner were the two first [associate academic deans, appointed in 2001].

We just became a lot more like other colleges. Some people thought that was good, and some people were regretful about that — but there's a reason colleges are organized in departments, with deans overlooking certain things. In a way, program management became CCV's version of academic departments.

As Buchdahl noted, some staff members had reservations.

Dee Steffan

Before, we felt like, "This is a journey of self-discovery: Here are the woods, now you find the trail." Then program management was, "Here's a road map, and these are the routes you can take to get where you want to go." We invested so much time into trying to figure it out — and to me it wasn't that interesting. I just remember so many meetings with faculty and staff: "Okay, we're going to develop this program tonight. We're going to serve you dinner, and then we're going to spend three hours." We did that again and again and again.

I do like the idea that CCV asked students to do a lot of that thinking in their work, so that when they got there, they knew how and why they got there. I felt that was an important part of their development. Because so many of our students started with feeling "less than," by the time they got to that goal, they no longer felt less than. They felt very accomplished.

It's like, "You write your owner's manual. Don't just read ours; you write yours." When I used to interview people to teach, that was important for them to understand, that this journey of discovery *has* to be individualized to some extent. And you have to help students understand the importance of critical thinking and putting some of this stuff together themselves. Understand why it's important.

Embedding the librarians

In the late 2000s, with David Sturges as its library director, the college unveiled a new Embedded Librarian program, available to any class that included a research assignment and used Blackboard, the online learning platform CCV had adopted.

"What does it mean to have a librarian 'embedded' in your course? Essentially, a librarian becomes a teaching assistant.... and creates a discussion forum in which students can ask questions about their research projects, including choosing and narrowing topics, finding and evaluating sources, and using citation styles," wrote Ann Schroeder, CCV's public services librarian, to the faculty in fall 2008. "The librarian also posts helpful tips specifically for your class: for example, how to use an art database, find a peer-reviewed journal article on nutrition, or research Vermont statutes about education.

"Faculty and students alike have been very enthusiastic about the service," Sturges added. "As a result, the program has grown to the point where in the spring 2008 semester, librarians were embedded in 50, mostly online, classes. Having a librarian available right where a student learns can really improve the chances of his or her success."

Community-based teaching: Rewards and challenges

As the 2002 self-study noted, CCV's approach to learning centered on its unique "combination of full-time coordinators and part-time instructors." By now there were some five hundred part-time instructors, "most of whom live and work locally," Buchdahl wrote.

"At CCV it is common to find an accountant teaching Accounting I, a writer teaching English Composition, a therapist teaching Introduction to Psychology," the academic dean wrote. This reliance on community-based teaching "is a direct response to the challenges of delivering higher education throughout a small rural state."

All instructors were hired from semester to semester; they had no guarantees of being offered a course or courses to teach in the next term. "Most CCV instructors tell us that they prefer to teach just one or two courses and are not conflicted by CCV's reliance on part-time faculty," Buchdahl maintained.

"I really liked it that all the faculty were adjunct faculty," said Rick Arend, who taught business and economics courses after a thirty-five-year career in the business world. "You didn't have to worry about tenure, you didn't have to worry about all this stuff, because you were hired for a semester at a time. I thought, well, this is a great model, because if the individual works out and they do well, you give them another course. If not, then you can not hire them again, right?

"If the student population grew, you could get more people," Arend noted. "If it shrank, you wouldn't have the issue that the traditional colleges have of, What do you do with your faculty? So I thought that was a very good model."

However, by now a growing number of instructors were relying on income from teaching multiple CCV courses. Many also worked as adjunct faculty at other local colleges, and often they struggled to piece together a sustaining livelihood. For those, the dean acknowledged, the unpredictability of course assignments "can be an issue."

"A small contingent would seek full-time faculty positions at CCV if they could," he wrote. "This is an issue that we revisit on occasion, since there are merits on both sides of the argument."

Instructor pay had seen a significant increase, and teaching at CCV offered other attractions as well. The average class size was just 12.5 students. The college was providing more and more training and support to its part-time teachers — and as the dean noted, CCV students were "traditionally motivated and mature."

"I think the thing about CCV that's so appealing is that when people come, they're interested in learning. They're interested in getting skilled, in not changing sheets any more — so they just approach it very honestly," said Jack Anderson, who had taught a CCV course in the early 1970s, then returned to teach the first-year Dimensions of Learning seminar, mostly at the Morrisville center, from 2006 through 2017.

"They'd make mistakes," he said. "And I'd say, 'This is great — you made mistakes. This is where you start. You can't be good at something until you fall down once or twice and you get back up. That's the key.'"

Abby Gelfer, a practicing psychotherapist, began teaching composition at the Burlington center in the late '90s. She had never taught before, but from those very first classes, she felt this was where she needed to be.

"It was really diverse, and people were really open," she said. "We were talking about commas in basic writing: Where do the commas go? But it was lovely and warm and people interacted well. They learned and were interested and motivated, so I kept doing it." She went on to teach English Comp, psychology classes, and the capstone Seminar in Educational Inquiry for some thirty years.

"One of the sweet secrets of higher ed is that there is nothing more pleasurable than having adult students in your classroom," said Mary Hulette, who began teaching business and computer classes at the Burlington site in 2001 and continued for many years. "When I first started at CCV, it was largely adult students. But as younger students and their families discovered the value from getting two years at the community college rate [of cost], classes started to become much younger.

"The younger students are fun, and they keep you on your game. They keep you sharp," she said. "You need to turn on a show for them, whereas the older students, you know: 'Just tell me what I need to know and I'll be happy.' So I did change over time, but I think in a good way."

"It was 2006 when I was hired, and I had just turned twenty-six," said Ian Boyd, who became a student resource advisor and also took on a course. "I taught an American history class, 1865 to the present. There were a lot of traditional-age students, but I remember being so nervous because there were five or six students who were probably around my parents' age — late forties, early fifties. They were lovely, they were great, and they shared their experience; they complemented the curriculum. But I would be lying if I didn't say that I wasn't expecting people who were *at* civil rights protests in the '60s when I was talking about them!"

Sharon Hopper

Sharon was a coordinator and an instructor at the Burlington center. The following is excerpted from a piece she wrote for the 2001 edition of Teaching for Development, *CCV's instructor handbook.*

CCV, formerly the college scene of the older, non-traditional student, is seeing an increasing number of students in the 18- to 24-year range. While some of these are so-called "traditional" college students who have come over from UVM or other colleges to take a few courses, what I have in fact seen more often in my classes is an emerging population of younger non-traditional students: single parents; working class kids who never thought they were "college bound"; creative types who shun the dorm- and-campus scene, etc.

However it is, I have seen among the younger students the same differences as occur among the older ones: differences in academic readiness, in intrinsic motivation, in socio-economic status, in intellectual curiosity, in vulnerability to distractions from life outside of school. So, whenever I am asked to comment on the needs or issues related to "the younger student," I am at a loss because, in my opinion, very few of the challenges we face regarding our students are age-based.

... As an instructor, I have always had to find ways for students to fill in frame-of-reference gaps. These gaps exist among students of different social classes, cultures, genders, and educational backgrounds as well as among students of different ages.... The bottom line for instructors is to take students from where they are to where they need to be in a given discipline. The bottom line for students is to entrust themselves to the process. And, since you asked me, I think the bottom line for any of us being here at all is not to focus so much on the differences as to learn from each other and become, each in our own peculiar way and time, more fully alive and human.

Hopper's bottom line could also be described as learning with the goal of discovering one's potential, of changing one's life. From its beginning, that had been central to CCV's approach.

"We believe that it's important to help students become self-reliant people who know how to learn individually and through cooperation with others," declared *Teaching for Development*. "When students leave CCV, we want them to be more effective as learners and citizens who have built a strong foundation of academic, critical thinking, and collaborative skills that they can use to learn a new subject, adapt to changing circumstances, and fulfill their career and personal aspirations.

"In that light, education at CCV should be a significant factor in the transformative processes of the student."

'It's a calling to do this work': One instructor's story

In the years since she started at the Morrisville center in 1989, Katherine Penberthy (formerly Veilleux) has taught as many as eight CCV classes a year: three in the fall, three in spring, and two in the summer.

It's so fulfilling to me. That's a good thing, because it doesn't pay very well! But it's really a calling to do this work. I think a lot of teachers feel this way.

Katherine Penberthy

The first class I taught was Dimensions of Learning, now Dimensions of Self and Society. The classroom was so tiny that the long folding table that you can sit about ten people around filled the entire room.

I walked in. There were ten students, they were from seventeen to seventy, and I just fell in love with teaching at CCV at that moment — because all of the students in the classroom were eager to learn, and they were there because they wanted to be. Lifelong learning has been our focus through all of these years, and it was so fulfilling to work with students who wanted to be lifelong learners. The older students were role models for the younger students.

The focus I've always had is to engage personally with each of my students, to get to know them on a personal level and have them share their stories. That creates a lot of trust in the classroom.

▶

KIND OF A MIRACLE

Penberthy developed a CCV course for single mothers called Transitions, teaching life skills and problem solving. Since 2004, she has taught Interpersonal and Small Group Communication at the Chittenden County center, now in Winooski.

> There are a lot of students in class who are refugees, who come from different countries, so I do a lot of work in that class on trust building. The staff and the rest of the faculty would put up with me having my students doing blindfolded "trust walks" up and down the hallways!
>
> When my students come into the classroom, I say, "Well, your advisor probably didn't tell you this, but you're now my adopted children. So you are required to email me and tell me what college you get into, and what job you have. And when you get married, about your children." And they do! I have students that are still in touch with me after like twenty years. I'm also a minister on the side; I've performed wedding ceremonies with them.
>
> CCV has always been very innovative. We're always analyzing what we're doing and how we're doing it, and how we can improve it. I'm on Academic Council, and we look at every single thing and think about, How can we make this more accessible to students? The strength of CCV is continuing to adapt and modify so we can reach out to the students.
>
> A couple of Christmases ago, I was at the Maplefields gas station in St. Albans, and the cashier there had been in my Transitions class as a single mom. She gave me a big hug and told me how she had gone on for further education and training — that she looks back on that class as being a turning point in her life, because it helped her to believe in herself and see that she could do things she never was told she could do before.
>
> When you're teaching, you don't necessarily see the result. It's like you plant the seed, and you're hoping that twenty years from now it will blossom.

•••

INVENTING THE FUTURE

'Each of them needing something different'

"The 2000s was also the decade of developing more support for faculty," said Debby Stewart. "That for us is a core part of being a teaching and learning organization — that teaching and learning is not just for the students."

In his message to the faculty in the *Instructor Newsletter* as the fall 2003 semester began, Buchdahl wrote: "We expect that about 700 of you will be teaching students in approximately 1,000 different class sections throughout Vermont.... almost 6,000 students, with approximately 1,600 of them taking CCV classes for the first time."

Many instructors were also teaching for the first time. So along with the Stewart-authored *Teaching for Development*, which in 2004 was published nationwide by the American Association of Community Colleges, CCV also developed a brief training for new instructors. It was a three-hour orientation workshop called Great Beginnings.

When he led the workshop, Buchdahl wrote in the college's autumn 2003 *Instructor Newsletter*, "I like to quote a statement from Dick Eisele, a wise old veteran CCV instructor.... 'Remember,' he said, 'we teach students, not subjects.'

> *A fairly simple and obvious idea, you might say, but how hard to practice faithfully. There we find ourselves in a classroom with ten or twenty students, each of them needing something different from us — attention, encouragement, understanding, compassion, challenge.*
>
> *... In Great Beginnings, we do a brainstorming exercise about diversity in the classroom. I ask the participants to name all the different kinds of diversity they might find in a CCV classroom, and I write them on the board. We usually end up with a list of 20 to 30 items, everything from age, gender, class, and race or ethnicity to learning styles, interest, skill levels, commitment, courage and charm. Then I ask: which of these kinds of diversity do you think will be most important in your classroom?*
>
> *Invariably ... we reach the conclusion that it all depends on who your students are.... You just never know. We teach this*

diverse crowd, and, if we are really skilled at our work, we find ways to reach each and every one of them, to push them or pull them along, draw them out, or rein them in on occasion so that everyone participates.... By the end of the semester, we want the class to respect each student's solo abilities and to also have learned to perform together, to create something new and even beautiful.

Is this idealistic? Of course it is, but it's also the very real spirit of teaching and learning at CCV.

The college decided in the early 2000s that all faculty members should have access to online resources to support their work and their development as teachers. CCV created a "top 40 anthology" of assignments to share with instructors. "We published that for our faculty," said Stewart, "so they could utilize resources and rubrics and assignments, and didn't have to make them all up."

Before he became president, Donovan served on half a dozen NEASC accreditation teams that visited other New England colleges. He chaired another four teams during his presidency and after, and then served on the accrediting commission itself.

"My observation suggests that CCV's commitment to faculty development and support is unprecedented, in terms of both focus and scale," he said.

Academic coordinators: A 'unique' range of roles

Some CCV instructors were professionally trained teachers. But because most were not, the academic coordinators were a vital resource for instructors to tap.

"The College's 51 full-time coordinators, from 17 at the largest site to just two at five of the smaller sites, work individually and in teams to design the local course schedule, advise students, recruit and assist faculty members, and manage the local program," said the 2007 President's Report to the VSC Board. "CCV's role of academic coordinator is unique in higher education in combining responsibilities for academic advising, instructional quality, program management, and community outreach. It requires both skills as an administrator and passion as an educator."

"Each site has at least one coordinator who works specifically with students who have special needs," Stewart's instructor handbook noted. "But all coordinators have responsibility for general academic advising pertaining to new student orientation, skills assessment, degree planning, transfer opportunities, and career development.

"The work of the coordinator does not stop with instructors and students," the handbook said. "It encompasses outreach in the community, service on college-wide committees, advertising and marketing of programs, and building strong relationships with other colleges and businesses, nonprofits, and social service agencies in the community."

Katie Mobley

I was twenty-six or twenty-seven when I started as a coordinator of academic services in Morrisville. In 2002, Morrisville was experiencing kind of a boom. There were four of us academic coordinators, because we were having enrollment growth that was unprecedented. Then a position opened in the Burlington location, so I moved to the largest academic center. I was an academic coordinator until 2008.

We used to joke that there were twelve academic centers and twelve ways of doing things — twelve ways of creating a class or twelve ways of storing syllabi. Over the 2000s, there was a continued movement to have consistency across the centers. We developed central objectives, so if you're taking Intro to Psych in Middlebury or taking it in Rutland, it's going to teach to those same objectives. I think as an institution we've been very strategic about wanting students to have a common high-quality experience while still being rooted in their local communities. That's sort of the balance that we seek to create.

This is a saying that gets said a lot at CCV: We are only as strong as our local relationships. As a community college, we are both a mirror of our local community — what the student population looks like in Winooski is different than in Newport, and different than in Brattleboro — and we also need our communities. We need those relationships in order to be successful as an organization. So there's always this balance, I think, between being rooted in our communities but also having a consistent student experience in the classroom.

We need strong connections as a college to what's happening in our local communities. We want to wrap that support around students, but we also want to be that access point for higher education. We want every community in Vermont to think, "We have a college that we can get students started at, and help them achieve the goals that they have set for themselves."

Opening doors for new Americans

"Since 1989, nearly 8,000 refugees from all over the world have resettled in Vermont, arriving from Africa, Europe and Asia," Andrea Suozzo reported in 2019 in *Seven Days*, the Burlington newsweekly. "… Given its relatively small population, Vermont has historically welcomed an outsized proportion of all refugees accepted into the U.S. each year…. Nearly all of those people landed in Chittenden County, the majority in Burlington and Winooski."

In the early '90s, the largest number of people entering Vermont from outside the country came from Vietnam, *Seven Days* reported, citing data from the U.S. Committee for Refugees and Immigrants. Most who arrived in the mid-to-late '90s were from Bosnia and Kosovo; in the early 2000s, most came from Somalia, the Democratic Republic of the Congo, and Sudan; and from 2010 to 1019, the majority came from Bhutan, Congo and Somalia.

As the number of resettled refugees grew in the early 2000s, CCV began to work with the Vermont Refugee Resettlement Program, providing free classroom space for the program's classes in English for language learners (ELL). And for a growing number of resettled refugees, enrolling in community college classes became a key step toward building new and successful lives here.

"When I started my job here in Winooski, we had like 5 percent new American students. Today it's more than 15 percent," said Tuipate Mubiay, a native of the Democratic Republic of Congo who came to the United States in 1994 and became a CCV academic advisor in Winooski in 2010.

"The impact of having new Americans in the Chittenden County center was big," Dee Steffan said. "How do we better serve these students? Their needs aren't the same as native speakers'. So we did a ton more ELL support, we made tutors available, and we did a program called Conversation Partners," in which CCV students who are learning English meet with native speakers for frequent conversations.

Inside the CCV classrooms at the Chittenden center, the impacts of new Americans could be profound.

"The seventeen-year-olds would just be in awe of some of the international students in class," said instructor Katherine Penberthy. "We had a student who talked about escaping from Rwanda and being shot at with blowguns as he was running through the forest. I've had students from Somalia, the Republic of Congo, Nepal, Bosnia, China, Japan. The students who had never left Vermont would just have their eyes opened to the world, and how privileged we are living here."

Tuipate Mubiay: 'This is not the office of the impossible, this is the office of the possible'

Tuipate Mubiay grew up as the son of farmers in the Democratic Republic of the Congo. He earned an associate degree in business in his home nation — but in 1994 he emigrated, fleeing the deep tensions that would soon erupt in the devastating Second Congo War, in which more than five million people died.

Mubiay had made it to New York City when he got a call from a friend from Niger who was living in Vermont, inviting him up. On a bus in Burlington full of people whose friendliness reminded him of home, he got off at Cherry Street.

"I asked the driver, 'How long does it take to get to downtown?' He said, 'Oh my friend, this is your first time? This *is* downtown!'"

▶

KIND OF A MIRACLE

He liked Vermont, and stayed. He worked a twelve-hour shift at the IBM plant in Essex Junction, part-time at Sears over the weekend, and one night each week at the Ames department store. In 2001, he became one of the first African immigrants to enroll at CCV.

"I had really wonderful teachers, and an advisor, Susan Henry, who made sure I had everything to succeed," he said. "She asked me so many questions because she wanted to know how to help me." He finished his CCV degree in 2003, then earned a bachelor's at Johnson State in 2005, and a master's in social work at UVM in 2008. All those years he continued to work, usually full-time.

Noticing that new Vermonters from Vietnam and Bosnia had each formed an association, Mubiay started the nonprofit Association of Africans Living in Vermont, which continues to serve new Americans from his home continent. He has since won several honors for his community service — including the Rising Star Achiever award from the Vermont Educational Opportunity Programs, a coalition of programs that serve low-income and first-generation college students.

Tuipate Mubiay

For fourteen years, Mubiay worked as the diversity coordinator for the Howard Center, Chittenden County's community mental health nonprofit; then he joined CCV as a coordinator of academic advising in the Winooski learning center. He started the college's Conversation Partners program for new Americans, along with the Winooski center's Racial Equity and Linguistic (REaL) Team.

"He is kind. Very patient. Passionate. Very focused," said Marianne DiMascio, regional director for the Winooski and St. Albans centers. "When students come here, he is available, and he's loving and firm. He wants to spend a lot of time with students early on, to let them know what college is all about: 'Here's how you have to show up; this is what you need to do, this is how you have to bring your A game.'

"I think students really appreciate that," she said. "And because of his lived experience, and all the qualities he brings, he is in a position to just rock it with a lot of students."

"I just tell them, 'Nothing is impossible,'" Mubiay said. "This is not the office of the impossible, this is the office of the possible. I tell them the CCV culture encourages every student: We're going to challenge you, and we want you to bring out your potential and succeed.

"When they see these awards and degrees on my wall, I say, 'You can do more than this.'"

•••

Ashraf Alamatouri

A native of Syria who taught at two universities in the Middle East before he came to the United States in 2011, Ashraf worked for the Vermont Refugee Resettlement Program as education coordinator from 2013 to 2018. He then became a coordinator of teaching and learning at the Winooski center.

I work with a team here called REaL, which stands for Racial Equity and Linguistic diversity at CCV. We started having workshops for staff and sometimes faculty, to make sure that we go over different perspectives and how students feel when they are new to the educational system.

You might have students who are lacking English to express themselves, but they already have the content; they are very keen with the content. So if it's math, physics, chemistry — they do need some help to express themselves, but that doesn't mean that we have to wait until they master English so they can express their knowledge of this area of study. So that that was something that I was very glad to work on with CCV.

The first thing we have changed is the foreign language program; we changed the name to World Language Program.

We changed English Language Learners to Multilingual Learners. We have also added a few classes, especially multilingual classes like English for academic purposes, where students can work on reading and writing in specific topics. We have added a few languages — we recently added Arabic, for example. When people are coming here and seeing that other students are learning their native language, it's a big push for them to learn English, and to feel that okay, I'm not alone in this.

We'd like to change the idea that our students from immigrant or refugee backgrounds are only receiving the service. We'd like people to see them also as a unique opportunity they can provide to their classroom, to their colleagues, to their instructors, and to the educational system in general. This is usually what I hear from my clients — they say "We'd like to volunteer." They say, "We are very proud citizens and want to give back to our country that helped us, that understands us and gave us our rights."

Ashraf Alamatouri

I think that having students from immigrant and refugee backgrounds just makes it clearer for other students to learn how valuable it is to attend college. How it's a privilege to come to a college. How it's a privilege to find a job. Some people take it for granted in the United States and in Vermont. Sometimes my kids take it for granted, and I have to remind them: No no, this is a privilege.

This is a privilege that you go to work, safe, and you know that you are coming back home. That you can drive a car, you can afford driving a car. That it's a great privilege to go to an educational institution.

'How well did we do it?'
Building a culture of evidence

As it worked to absorb steep enrollment surges during the century's first decade, CCV was swept up in a nationwide trend — one that spurred the college to take a fresh focus on measuring and improving student outcomes.

"Community college enrollments mostly grew during the first decade of the 21st century, accelerating rapidly at the end of that decade as the Great Recession hit," said a 2017 report on enrollment trends by the American Association of Community Colleges. "... Between 2006 and 2010, enrollments spiked to a record high of more than 8 million students, increasing by 20.3% over this period, or 4.8% annually."

During that time, said David Buchdahl, "people started looking at the student success outcomes and saying, 'You know, community colleges might be growing, but they're not doing that good a job overall.' The completion rate for community colleges was about 25 percent. Now, it wasn't quite as bad as 25 percent sounds, because a lot of those people transferred and got a degree from a four-year school."

Still, he said, "this became a major focus, a national issue. CCV was just like all the rest of the community colleges who were growing and growing and growing. How do we keep up with all this?"

"People who work here believe very strongly in the opportunity that it provides people," Debby Stewart said. "Then, a little before 2010, we began to think, 'Well, access alone is not enough; it needs to be access and success.' Part of that is also affordability, so it became access, affordability and success. And that three-legged stool is CCV's mission."

In 2007, Tim Donovan asked Buchdahl to move from being academic dean into a new position, the college's chief of planning and assessment, later renamed director of institutional research and planning. Staying in that role until his retirement in 2012, Buchdahl guided the college's push to better measure and improve student outcomes.

CCV was joining a national effort. In 2004, the American Association of Community Colleges came together with the Lumina Foundation and six other organizations working in higher education to create a new consortium, Achieving the Dream. Its aim was to lead a coordinated and supported campaign — "evidence-based, student-centered, and built on the values of equity and excellence," says Achieving the Dream's website — that focused on "closing achievement gaps and accelerating student success nationwide," among community colleges in particular.

"Achieving the Dream was an opportunity for us to move from a culture in which storytelling was at its core," Stewart said. "We all saw in so many ways firsthand the impact that CCV had on its students; we always had lots of anecdotal evidence, and those stories had so much power for us. Yet one of the things we had to shift, and this is part of what Tim saw, was that we had to help the college balance those perspectives."

That meant placing data-based evidence alongside the stories of student outcomes.

"David really instituted three questions to think about whenever we were evaluating our progress on anything," she said. "What did we do, how well did we do it, and how well do we know? What is the evidence? And what difference did it make?"

Susan Henry

"Building a culture of evidence was the main theme of Achieving the Dream," Susan Henry noted. CCV became a member of the national consortium in 2010, and was named an ATD Leader College from 2011 to 2014.

Those years, she said, "positioned CCV to carry forward ATD's key tenets: the value in building and sustaining a culture of evidence, and the practice of using the student-success measures of core course completion, persistence and first-term success, retention, degree or certificate completion, transfer, graduation, and closing equity gaps to evaluate our educational effectiveness."

"Back in the 1990s, we were flying by the North Star for directions," said Tapp Barnhill, who has directed the Brattleboro center since the late '90s. "Today we've got data-driven technology: slick spreadsheets, pivot tables, some really amazing tools now to help guide us. But in the end, what does it come down to? I think the thing that makes

CCV work so well is the autonomy and creativity that this organization has allowed me in my career and, hopefully, that I have shared with those I work with.

"It's about a belief in what our mission is, and about really holding true to that," she said. "As we've moved forward and grown over all those years, I think that's what has taken us to where we've come today."

A new basic framework

To give its students their best chance to succeed, especially when so many of them struggled or were not well-served in previous educational settings, CCV had sought since its earliest years to adapt and improve its general education curriculum, its basic framework for a liberal arts education. In 2007, the college declared that — following on all the advances in technology, the addition of VSC graduation standards, and its own new focus on success along with access — "the time has come for a fresh look at our curriculum and general education requirements," the *Instructor Newsletter* said that spring.

A task force chaired by Yasmine Ziesler sought college-wide input on how best to update those requirements. Their purpose, the group wrote, was "to develop engaged, self-directed and collaborative learners who demonstrate core competencies, recognize and apply strategies of inquiry, and embrace the challenge, complexity and wonder of our interconnected world."

CCV adopted its new general education program in fall 2008, aiming "to better prepare students for the work and educational demands of the 21st century," said its 2012 accreditation self-study.

The program now embraced three realms of learning:

1. *Core competencies.* Pegged to the VSC graduation standards, these eighteen credits aimed to develop skills in writing and communication, information and technological literacy, and quantitative reasoning. They included Dimensions, CCV's first-semester seminar that is now required of all students and gives them college-level experience in approaching, absorbing and discussing challenging materials. Long called Dimensions of Learning, the seminar would at this point be offered in two

options, Dimensions of Work or Dimensions of Freedom. Today it's called Dimensions of Self and Society.

2. *Areas of inquiry.* These nine credits "are broadly defined as the study of the natural world through the scientific method, the study of human expression through the arts and humanities, and the study of human behavior through history and the social sciences," said the self-study.

3. *Integrative approaches.* These six credits "explore the complexity of the natural and social world over time and with respect to others through the study of global perspectives and sustainability." Included is the Seminar in Educational Inquiry, CCV's interdisciplinary capstone course that, with Dimensions, bookends the learning experience for degree students. "SEI provides a forum for critical thinking about ethical and substantive issues, problems, and themes that affect the world, our society, our communities, and ourselves," the self-study said. "It is also the course in which students complete a culminating project of their choice, which is used to demonstrate their ability to meet the graduation standards in writing and information literacy."

Inviting high schoolers to 'Rise to the Challenge'

During the first years of the 2000s, the college continued to offer Vermont high school juniors and seniors free enrollment in the twelve-week Introduction to College Studies course it had created in the late 1990s. The course helped high schoolers build skills in note- and test-taking, communications and studying, managing time and stress, setting goals, and planning for college.

"Many schools offer high school credit for successful completion of this class," said an early brochure for the course. By 2003, five learning centers were providing it, in Bennington, Burlington, Morrisville, Rutland and Springfield.

CCV also began offering "Rise to the Challenge" scholarships that enabled high school juniors and seniors to take regular CCV classes at any of its centers. The stipends were for high schoolers who had limited

financial resources, "may be the first in your family to attend college, or may be unsure of your ability to succeed in college, or may need certain classes to meet basic college-entry requirements," said the '03 catalog. The program was supported by grant funding from the federal GEAR UP (Gaining Early Awareness and Readiness for Undergraduate Programs) initiative through the Vermont Student Assistance Corporation, the state-created nonprofit that connects Vermont students with financial aid resources for higher education.

To connect more high school juniors and seniors with Rise to the Challenge's dual enrollment opportunities, by 2008 the college was working with high schools and technical education centers all over Vermont.

"I think that has been one of our most strategic and best decisions, to really invest in each community throughout the state in that way," said Katie Mobley, who became assistant director of secondary education in 2008.

"When we think about who our target population is, sometimes we use the term *middle majority*," said Mobley, who went on to serve as director of secondary education and now oversees admissions, marketing and financial aid. "We serve anyone, and we want to serve all students, but we absolutely want all *potential* students to know they can be successful in college."

"The Rise to the Challenge program is targeted at high school juniors and seniors who have not considered college or do not realize that college is an option for them," said a CCV publication. "They move through high school in the middle of the pack — not in college prep, not in trouble."

"That work with high school students to change their aspirational trajectories is a really important piece" of the college's history, Debby Stewart agreed. Before Rise to the Challenge, she said, "we had really seen ourselves as a college that supported adults. We didn't realize that the same approach would also support traditional-aged students — especially those who didn't see themselves going to college."

Not every high schooler is ready for college classes. So in 2008 CCV redesigned Access to Success, its curriculum for students who needed to build basic skills in math, reading and writing before enrolling in a college-level course. The redesign was funded by a grant from the Nellie Mae Foundation, New England's largest education-focused philanthropy.

'A fundamental disconnect'

In 2009, an influential report titled *Postsecondary Education* from the Vermont Community Foundation pointed up a startling gap. "While Vermont's high school graduation rate exceeds the national average," it said, "just 45% of Vermont students attend college immediately after graduation, compared to 57% nationally."

"It was a real crisis," said Emerson Lynn, longtime owner and publisher of the *St. Albans Messenger*. "In Vermont, pre-K through 12 is a very successful system, and we have a really high graduation rate — then we go all the way down, from top tier in the number of kids that graduate from high school, to forty-seventh in terms of the kids that go on to college. It's stunning. It's such a fundamental disconnect."

"In Vermont, as in the rest of the country," said *Postsecondary Education*, "middle school students are optimistic about higher education but lose momentum as they progress through high school." The report also noted that nationally, 40 percent of college students "require some remediation in English or math."

"College graduates are more likely to have healthy families, have children that perform well in school, vote, volunteer, serve on civic boards, and patronize the arts," wrote author Holly Tippett in her report. "Research suggests that college graduates are also more likely to engage in entrepreneurial endeavors," and that "college graduates earn nearly double that of high school graduates over the course of a lifetime."

Postsecondary Education was funded by the J. Warren and Lois McClure Foundation, a supporting organization of the Vermont Community Foundation (meaning that VCF provides it with administrative and other supporting services). Vermont philanthropists Warren and Lois McClure had created their foundation in 1995. Joining them on the board in 2001 was their daughter, Barbara Benedict, an educator who had worked as a middle-school librarian in Arizona.

"We were approving all sorts of projects," Benedict recalled, "and every year the common theme was, 'We can't get enough nurses, we can't get enough engineers, we can't get enough trained people for the needs of Vermont institutions.' So that's when we funded the report."

Benedict and her husband had raised their children in the Southwest, where "I had years of being familiar with county-based community colleges," she said. "The perception in Vermont, as I thought of it, was: There are tons of colleges here for people. Wonderful colleges. Well, then I became aware of my husband's family, who were still based here. All my nieces and nephews needed an education, but they couldn't afford any of these institutions."

Even amid its "dismal data" about Vermont high school graduates going on to college, *Postsecondary Education* showed Benedict a bright spot — CCV's Introduction to College Studies (ICS) course. So in spring 2008, the McClure Foundation awarded a grant that enabled the college to make ICS available to every high school student in Vermont.

That began a dynamic and ongoing relationship between the community college and the foundation, whose funding continues to make it possible for high schoolers to attend CCV, and also helps the college support students who are military veterans.

Within a year, enrollment in ICS rose by 90 percent. All over the state, some 1,400 high schoolers were getting a taste of the college experience at CCV. And since 2008, those who complete ICS have received a voucher for a free course for college credit at CCV.

"We had been trying to find ways to get college courses in the high schools," said Tim Donovan. At first, "we had the most luck with small schools, like Danville — they were happy to have one more thing they could offer.

"Our first iteration of it, I always referred to as the 'car wash coupon book.' We sold coupon books for ten CCV courses to high schools at a discount, for them to hand out as they saw fit. If a guidance counselor was sitting with a student and was struggling to find something that would interest them, they could say 'You know, you could take a course at CCV,' and give them a coupon."

"It was kind of a novelty," said Ian Boyd, who became an academic coordinator in 2010. "You got a voucher to take a college class, which was a big deal." As a free noncredit course, Intro to College Studies "is low-stakes," he noted — "but it's introductory, for students to have that experience of being at CCV. They have a student ID number; they have an email address. They're very much connected to CCV."

'Leave that baggage out in the parking lot!'

"I took this class because I wanted to get a better understanding of how college works, and so I could help others figure it all out," said Nick Cain, who was a student at Brattleboro High School when he completed Introduction to College Studies at CCV Brattleboro.

"Most kids only think they know how college works because they've been accepted, but that doesn't mean they understand the many aspects of college," Cain said, according to a college publication. He went on to take an international business course at CCV, then enrolled at The Cooper Union in New York City on a four-year scholarship.

For students taking ICS, "the biggest benefit is that they start to become self-directed learners," said Nina Lany, who taught the course at the St. Johnsbury and Newport centers. "They realize they have choices about what, when and where to study. In this class, students get to explore their assumptions about what is and isn't possible for them to accomplish, and in that process the reality of how many choices they have becomes apparent.

"It's not tied to hard academic skills," Lany said in CCV's *Rise to the Challenge* newsletter. "It's about success strategies, defining your own goals, and thinking critically about what's next in life."

In 2010 the *Rise* newsletter profiled Kathy Whitney, who was teaching ICS at the St. Albans center. Said the profile: "A passerby might be puzzled at the sight of Kathy and her students walking across the CCV St. Albans parking lot as she called to them, 'As teenagers, you may have some baggage that you are bringing with you. Leave that baggage out here in the parking lot. Shake it all off!'

"The information students learn in ICS can be really helpful, especially for juniors or fall semester seniors," Whitney said. "... When the semester begins, some students arrive for class a few minutes late. A couple of weeks later they arrive on time, and by the end of the semester, they are early. It is those moments when students 'get it' that make teaching ICS such a pleasure."

"Since 1995, approximately 45% of all ICS students have used a dual enrollment voucher to take a college course," the program's newsletter reported in spring 2010. "In 2009, the most popular CCV course for dual enrollment was English Composition, followed by Foundations of Reading & Writing and Basic Math."

A vision of learning:
The rise of online education

When the college delivered its first online course, Bill MacLeay's Introduction to Political Science, to twenty-five students in 1996 (see page 223), the moment was ripe.

"Only a year ago, Internet access was a very expensive proposition for many Vermonters, who had to make the connection through a long-distance telephone call," wrote Eric Sakai, then Eastern Region director, that summer in the *Valley Business Journal*. "Now, virtually everyone in the state with a computer and a modem can get on the Net with a local call.

"None of MacLeay's students were computer nerds with special expertise or equipment," Sakai noted. "Ranging in age from their late teens to early 70s, they were among the growing number of Vermonters who have gone online using their home computers and a commercial Internet provider."

Conversations in that first class could be a little awkward. When U.S. Sen. Patrick Leahy did a pioneering virtual visit with MacLeay's students, they submitted their questions through an online forum. MacLeay would type up and post Leahy's responses — so by the time an answer appeared on a student's screen, the session had moved several questions further on. Still, one student's evaluation said the course was "a great way to learn; very convenient."

"I continue to be proud," another wrote, "that I was part of an institution on the cutting edge of post-secondary course delivery."

That summer, the Emerging Technologies Committee decided to add two online courses, on the Constitution and on Science Fiction Literature. The latter was taught by John Christensen, who would go on to be the "guiding light," as Sakai put it, of the years when online learning at CCV blossomed.

"We bought some web servers, and we bought this software called Web Crossing. It was a business tool, basically a discussion board," said Megan Tucker, who was cobbling together the tech side of CCV's online course delivery.

"The fall of '97 is when it really started to get rolling," she said. "We had eight classes that were taught online; I built all those by hand. Then it just blew up. In spring 2000, I was building thirty classes by hand."

At a Chicago gathering of the League of Innovation, a tech association for community colleges, Tucker met the two co-founders of an online learning management system called CourseInfo, which the two had created as a student project in grad school.

"I came back and said to Tim, 'This is what we need, so that our faculty can build their own,'" Tucker said. "In the interim, CourseInfo became Blackboard. Somewhere I still have the starter kit. It came in a cardboard box, with a mug."

The state college system adopted Blackboard at Donovan's urging — but "CCV was the only one to really engage with it," Tucker said. "We've always been, and still are, pushing the envelope on that sort of thing. We were just much more flexible in terms of trying things, to see if they would work or not."

When Donovan became CCV president in 2001, he pushed for each state college to name a representative to the newly formed VSC Distance Learning Advisory Group. Sakai, who had just become CCV's director of learning technologies, was the founding chair.

"Our goal," Donovan wrote in an October '01 email to the group, "is to develop a sustainable distance learning infrastructure that can support ever-changing technologies in teaching and learning. We also hope to use distance learning strategies to improve teaching and learning, increase enrollments, and boost revenues from a variety of sources."

INVENTING THE FUTURE

"We used to call Tim VL, visionary leader," said Tucker. "From the very moment I met him in 1988, he was always pushing technology. He was the person that got us all computers on our desktops."

When online teaching started, she said, "that was the big push. Let's take this and run with it, and see if we can figure it out."

'Instruction of a very high order'

"If you look at the spreadsheet, the growth curve of online learning is quite astonishing," Sakai said. "In those first years we were growing anywhere from 50 percent to 100 percent a semester. And that was exciting — for one thing, it wasn't happening throughout higher education. We always like to talk about making it up as we go along, which is what we largely did."

Along with the academic side of online, in the early 2000s "we also explored the idea of students not having to come into an academic center to register," said Sarah Corrow, a former CCV work-study student who had become assistant director of academic technology. "Megan Tucker created that; we called it Meganware. She's a genius at figuring out how to make stuff work. Students could go to a web page and fill out a form, which would generate an email to me, and I would then get the student registered, process the payment, all that stuff."

KIND OF A MIRACLE

In spring '02, the college exceeded one thousand online-course placements. "That was just amazing," Corrow said. "We emailed Tim Donovan and Susan Henry and said, 'We broke a thousand, we broke a thousand!' The next day, Tim showed up here in Newport with a bottle of champagne and a bottle of sparkling cider. I still have the cork."

For John Christensen, shaping the academic side of CCV's online education meant challenging "the ideas about teaching and learning that I have always taken for granted," he wrote in an essay, "Authenticity and Liberation at the Online Education Frontier," from which the following is excerpted.

John Christensen

From its inception, online learning emphasized and highlighted the role of the student as an active learner.... Teachers play a vital role in the process ... but an essential part of the driving force in the virtual classroom is expected to come from the students.

Current online education programs extend and broadcast a vision of learning that invites students to be active and engaged: following leads, distinguishing the substantial from the trivial, synthesizing insights drawn from different sources, and formulating new questions. If I think I can bring my old teacherly habits and attitudes into this new world, I'm going to waste my own time and that of my students.

The innovative educator understands that the future depends on creative and unexpected applications of new technologies. The success of online education programs will be located in intuitive leaps.... Creativity in education will flourish so long as minds remain open to chance, intuition and mystery.

... As the technology of online education becomes less expensive and more common, traditionally disadvantaged groups will find startling new ways to exploit the medium.... For the isolated student, the online classroom may not be quite the same as a traditional classroom, but it may literally be a lifeline. More than once I've encountered such students and observed that for them the computer monitor is a doorway out of a dungeon, an escape from a community that can't begin to meet their needs....

In the virtual classrooms of my experience as a community educator in rural Vermont, I meet all kinds of weird and wonderful people who have finally found their way out of some nightmarish oubliette where they could not communicate with anyone, let alone with kindred spirits. Countless more people are still in those oubliettes, desperate for some kind of contact with the rest of humanity. Online educators will often be the first to bring them out of captivity.

To this end it is most helpful ... that we insist on some form of dialogue between teachers and students, between students, and between students and the means of instruction. A lecture to 1,200 students in an auditorium is on campus and face-to-face, but it is nonetheless a sad kind of distance learning. On the other hand the teacher who has 20 students online, liberated from moorings in space and time, and reading and discussing, say, Plato's *Meno*, is providing instruction of a very high order.

... Students and teachers enter the online learning environment as pioneers and explorers, and they will break precedents, if necessary, to rebuild the culture of higher education. But because no one really knows much about online learning, we're all de facto learners. I consider myself fortunate if I'm a step or two ahead of my students. At the end of the day I think that's much healthier for me as an educator.

The saga of Harvey

In 2003, as online course numbers and enrollment were growing steeply, Megan Tucker and CCV network specialist Tony Harris attended a presentation at MIT on using metadata terms to organize and provide access to a variety of online resources. Back in Vermont, they asked consultant Dave Macleay to use the new approach in building for the

▶

KIND OF A MIRACLE

college a searchable content repository — an online directory of digital materials that could be searched by author, title, topic or keyword.

This was a new resource, which not everyone would be confident in trying. "How do we draw people into stuff they might be a little resistant to?" Tim Donovan asked.

As it happened, the resource needed a name. At a meeting, Tucker recalled, staff member Elmer Kimball "said, 'Oh, let's just call it something like Harvey.' It was a very off-the-cuff thing."

The idea recalled the well-remembered 1950 film Harvey, in which James Stewart's character has an imaginary best friend named Harvey, who's a rabbit — and for Donovan, that resonated. He began telling CCV's people that the new Harvey "is your rabbit," Tucker said. "It's always there with you, even though you can't see it."

Harvey

To introduce the new resource, Rebecca Werner, an assistant academic dean, showed up in full rabbit costume at CCV's fall 2003 convocation. Soon after, Tucker spotted a stuffed rabbit on a staircase in the children's section of the local bookstore in Norwich, Vermont.

"He had the same expression that [the claymation dog] Gromit has in the Wallace and Gromit films — sort of bewildered and beleaguered," she said. "So I bought the rabbit, put it on top of something in my office, and took a picture of it. Somebody had sent me a new digital camera; that was a big deal then." Tucker posted the photo on the landing page of the content repository, and people liked that. It drew them in. Before long, she was posting new photos of Harvey on the landing page.

"At first it was just my husband, my son and me making little scenes with him," she said. "At Thanksgiving he was in the turkey roaster. He went to the beach. He was skiing, all this stuff. He got friends!"

Each Monday, the landing page began featuring a fresh Harvey image in a new setting — "and it just snowballed," Tucker said. "I had to buy

INVENTING THE FUTURE

more Harveys. They went on study abroad trips to Belize, to Ireland, to Italy. People made their own vignettes with him. I was willing to let anybody do anything with it, because it was such a draw for people."

Donovan and Tucker were learning Photoshop — "he was really geeking out over this stuff," she said — and they began inserting Harvey into images they'd found. A "Register Now" ad showed Harvey writing "I will not forget to register at CCV" multiple times on a blackboard. Another image had Harvey in a Red Sox cap, photoshopped onto the Fenway Park scoreboard as it flashed a message (this part was real) that welcomed CCV and Castleton staffers on their annual trip to a Sox game.

Tucker and Donovan produced a Harvey calendar with a different image for each month, and gave one to everyone at Convocation.

"People sent me things for Harvey — clothes, a little lounge chair," Tucker said. "Everyone really glommed onto it for a couple of years."

In 2007, the whole state college system adopted Blackboard, which by then included a content repository. An image was posted of Harvey packing up for retirement. "He was ready to retire," Tucker said.

But then in 2016 CCV built its own new content repository, and Harvey was reintroduced.

"Most of the current employees have no idea why," Tucker noted.

•••

'Online learning was CCV's future'

As the technology for online learning continued to evolve, CCV went with it. By 2004, Blackboard was in use in over 400 courses across the state college system, and was the primary instructional medium for some 150 online courses. That spring, CCV led the launch of the VSC Portal, which integrated web-based services and learning resources "into a single online environment that will also provide new tools for communication and collaboration for CCV's students, instructors and staff," said the *Instructor Newsletter*.

"A Blackboard course site is automatically created for every credit course offered each semester," the newsletter said. "Course sites provide instructors and students with a variety of useful tools, including discussion forums, chat rooms, a grade book, individual and small-group Web pages, online exams, and content areas for sharing documents and Web links. Additionally, CCV staff use Blackboard to support committees, work groups, and other organizations that need to communicate and share information."

In 2011, the college shifted to Moodle, a newer software package. Later that decade it migrated to Canvas, which it currently uses.

The years of surging growth in online enrollment and course numbers — what Christensen called "drinking from a fire hose" — continued through the aughts. By fall 2011, almost 25 percent of the college's course enrollment was in online classes.

"In the last decade, the College has seen enormous growth in its online course offerings, where enrollment has more than quadrupled since 2001, with 261 courses offered per semester accounting for 3,655 course placements," said the college's 2012 accreditation self-study.

The college's pioneering of online learning was also winning wider attention. "We quite regularly presented at EDUCAUSE, which is a national educational technology organization," Sakai said. "Their national conferences were attended by seven thousand, eight thousand people, faculty and IT folks from all over the country. We presented at other, similar conferences — the League for Innovation, places like that. We're still pretty small fish in the national scope, but we had some interesting things to present."

"When Joyce Judy became president, she also realized that online learning was CCV's future," he observed. "Tim had long been recognized as Mister Technology throughout the Vermont State Colleges System — but when Joyce, who's not a techie, started saying, 'We need to stay with online learning and make sure that's an integral part of CCV's educational model,' I think that was very important."

Under Sakai, the college created a five-week Introduction to Online Teaching course for faculty who were new to the approach. "Faculty have to buy into what is necessary for the students to have a good experience online," said Jennifer Alberico, who revised the course after she became online learning director in 2019. "What that takes, honestly, is humanizing the experience, not making it feel like I'm sitting alone on my computer typing and there's no human interaction. How to make that come alive is really the key.

"There are a lot of different types of live interaction where you are actually really engaged in conversation, through discussion forums and that sort of thing, in a very active way across time during a week of the class," she said. "It's a wide-open world of resources in best practices, from all kinds of places that have done online teaching and great training around that — so there are constantly ways to renew and improve how we do it."

"When I was first asked to teach online, my mouth just dropped open. I am *so* not a techie person," said longtime instructor Katherine Penberthy. "One of the associate deans that knew me really well asked me to do it. She said, 'Katherine, you're a good teacher — just transition what you do in the classroom to the computer.' So since 2006 or 2007, I've been teaching Intro to Psychology online, and it's amazing. I'm really surprised I can say this, but it's possible to build a wonderful class climate on the computer.

"Every student posts a two- to four-paragraph response to a question that I ask, and then I respond in detail to that. Then they respond to me, and then I have them question-and-answer each other every week. You can develop a wonderful class atmosphere with that.

"I had to transition my Interpersonal Communication class to the computer. I'm very animated in that classroom — so I figured out how to do that. I do videos, I do photos, I have them do a lot of activities on their own, like trust walks. I love classroom teaching, but it's so much more flexible to teach online. You can teach from anywhere in the world."

Eric Sakai

Excerpted from Eric's 2016 essay "Reflections on 20 Years of Online Learning at CCV."

New technologies have expanded the curricular breadth of distance education. Who would have thought 20 years ago that CCV would offer courses like Anatomy and Physiology, Drawing I, and Effective Workplace Communication online? The majority of CCV's 15 degree programs and seven certificates can now be completed entirely online, although most students mix on-ground courses with online courses that allow them to fit college studies into busy work and family schedules. Advances in the delivery of videoconference-based courses at CCV and the VSC promise another option to help students progress toward their degrees.

As we celebrate two decades of online learning at CCV, we are also extremely proud of what has not changed. Our online courses are still small, averaging 14 students rather than the more typical 25 elsewhere, which allows them to be as richly interactive as our classroom courses. They still conform to the same College-prescribed learning objectives required of on-ground courses, and students benefit from online advising, tutoring, and other support services also available at CCV academic centers. Almost 80% of CCV online students complete their courses successfully — the same high rate as that of on-ground students and including nearly 200 high school students who learn online through Vermont's Dual Enrollment program.

John Christensen, heart and soul of CCV online

A gifted and soulful educator, John Christensen was devoted to the community college. He had been teaching history and literature courses since the mid-1980s, and was working as a coordinator of instruction and advisement out of the St. Johnsbury office in 1990, when he was diagnosed with throat cancer.

A laryngectomy took his voice. With the whisper he had left, Christensen continued to teach, do his administrative work, and serve on college boards and committees.

Then, in the late '90s, came the advent of online education.

"He helped to motivate it and push it," said Sarah Corrow, assistant director of academic technology. After the first course succeeded,

Christensen began teaching science fiction online, and in spring '97 he took on the management of online learning for the college. All that, for him, was a way to go on doing the work he loved.

"Dr. Christensen's pioneering work in online instruction resulted in part from a deep personal motivation," Tim Donovan wrote in 2002. "Largely deprived of one of a teacher's most valuable tools, his voice ... he found a new voice in the electronic dialogues of his online courses.

"... Dr. Christensen almost single-handedly built online learning at CCV," Donovan wrote, "from a pilot offering for 15 students in spring 1996 to a program with over 1,500 students in more than 150 courses each semester."

At the same time, Christensen earned a Ph.D. in higher education curriculum and instruction at the University of Sarasota. "His dissertation, 'Students' Learning Experiences in Community College Humanities Courses Delivered Online,' makes a substantial contribution to the scholarship on distance education," Donovan wrote, "and a convincing case for the effectiveness of online teaching and learning."

John Christensen

"He combined high standards of instruction with sympathy and sensitivity," wrote faculty member David Seager. "John hired me for online teaching in 2004, and nurtured my development as an online instructor.... Whenever there was an issue or conflict, John supported and guided me.... When I have some questions about what to do in a certain situation, I'll reflexively think to ask John his opinion. I will forever miss him."

Christensen died in 2015. "The cancer came back two or three times," said Corrow, who was also his neighbor and a close friend. "He did treatment, but even on the days that he was not able to come into the office, he would let me know what needed to be done and we would make it happen.

"He was so intelligent," she added. "He wrote the most beautiful emails and poetry. He was an amazing guy."

•••

KIND OF A MIRACLE

A union drive raises tough issues

In the early 1990s, the adjunct faculties voted to unionize at Vermont's four residential state colleges — but two previous efforts to organize CCV staff by the American Federation of Teachers had failed. The first, in 1979, was withdrawn for lack of support, while a campaign in 1985 led to a 34–3 vote against joining the union.

From the late '90s through the mid-2000s, seven years of annual increases boosted CCV instructor pay by 86.9 percent in total, to $910 per credit (compared to a 45.5 percent per-credit rise in CCV tuition those same years). That made it possible for more instructors to try piecing together a livelihood by teaching multiple courses. A growing number of the roughly five hundred instructors were involved more deeply than ever before in the college: Along with teaching up to three courses per semester, many were serving on committees and other panels.

And in early 2004, a number of faculty members began to organize a union drive.

"Although CCV courses are taught at 12 different sites around the state as well as online, technically speaking there is no 'workplace' to organize," wrote *Seven Days* reporter Cathy Resmer in "Class Conscious: CCV's adjunct faculty are thinking union," a September 2004 article in the newsweekly. "Instructors come in just once or twice a week, teach one to three classes, and then leave. And therein lies a prime motivator for forming the union."

"The nature of part-time teaching is very isolating," said Catherine O'Callaghan, a teacher of comparative religions who was a lead campaign organizer, in Resmer's article. "You tend not to know anybody else because all you do is go in and teach your class.... A culture of collegiality or community of scholars is not promoted."

The community college had grown "into one of the largest institutions of higher learning in Vermont," *Seven Days* noted, "each year serving more than 5,000 traditional and non-traditional students." And while "everybody who's involved in this [union] loves CCV and loves our student population," O'Callaghan told Resmer, "we've found that the basics of how to treat instructors aren't really in place at the college."

"O'Callaghan started CCV's union drive late winter by calling other instructors to gauge their interest," Resmer reported. "The grievances she heard most often involved what she describes as 'issues of professional respect.'"

CCV instructors were not paid for keeping office hours, "even though many do," the article noted. They received no benefits and had no tenure, seniority or job security, even though "community college earnings are the sole income for a growing number of instructors.... Hired on a semester-by-semester basis, CCV instructors can teach the same class for a decade and then not be asked back, with no explanation."

The issues were real and difficult, and over the next months the union drive gathered steam. CCV asked the Vermont Labor Relations Board to take the unusual step of holding the coming ballot by mail, to enable the largest possible number of instructors to vote.

"Our point was, this will change things," Donovan explained. "For some people it might be better, for some it might be worse — but don't let it be decided by a few people. And the Labor Board agreed."

The mail-in vote was set for October 4, 2006.

Under CCV's letterhead, Donovan sent three single-page letters to each instructor at their home, laying out the college's case for voting no.

"We take this position because of the likely effect unionization will have on the College," Donovan wrote. "How will our mission to provide students a better education, while keeping it accessible and affordable for all Vermonters, be sustained or changed by the vote you will cast? Should the unique nature of CCV be preserved, or will this effort bring fundamental changes that will make CCV a more mainstream and traditional post-secondary institution?"

After a two-and-a-half-year campaign by the prounion organizers, the October 4 vote was 260–144 against. "Nearly 90 percent of CCV's all-adjunct faculty who were eligible to cast ballots did so," reported Jill Fahy of the *Burlington Free Press*. "In moving forward, Donovan said the college intends to listen to input from all faculty who have questions or issues."

In the vote's aftermath, Donovan recalled, "we found new ways to involve faculty in programmatic decisions. It also gave us a way to talk about some things. Why are there only part-time faculty? People would say, 'You're trying to save money.' Fair enough observation, but if you have just a few full-time faculty [in each center], how will a student get a broad educational perspective? It provided an opportunity to talk about that."

The question whether to unionize would come up again, a decade later (see pages 345-349). This time, the result would be different.

A nomad no longer: Building for the long term

> *CCV is unique in the sense that it didn't start with a main campus and then expand. More than any other community college system, certainly in New England, CCV is in the communities.*
>
> —Barbara Brittingham, President Emerita,
>   New England Commission of Higher Education
>   (formerly NEASC)

"There had been an unwritten prohibition on CCV owning anything," Tim Donovan said. "I could never find where it was written, but it was pretty well understood: You're the traveling circus; you're a moveable feast."

But as its enrollment grew late in the twentieth century, the college struggled to find affordable downtown spaces, with nearby parking, that could accommodate daytime classes. Then passage of the federal Americans with Disabilities Act in 1990, requiring that all public accommodations be accessible to all students, put an end to the early years of making do with whatever spaces could be found and refitted for classrooms and offices.

Under presidents Mike Holland (1991–1994) and Barbara Murphy (1994–2001), the college began to lease larger facilities, some designed and built by landlords for CCV's use. The first of those was opened in 1992, on Main Street in St. Albans.

Tim Donovan

During Barbara's tenure we continued to improve our leased facilities, and shortly after I took office, I began laying the groundwork to prepare the [VSC] board for the notion that there's nothing worse in the world than a ten-year lease —

because you've been there long enough to almost pay for something, and you have nothing to show for it.

It's just like, do you own a house or do you rent? I was bringing that over and over to the board, because we'd seen the benefit, with the building in St. Albans and then on Pearl Street in Burlington, of having a distinctive location that said "CCV."

The first opportunity came. We had a horrible place in Wilder, and enrollment there had grown to the point that we had an annex, an equally horrible building across the parking lot. A developer down there came to us and said, "I think I can put together a piece of land out of two small ones by King Arthur Flour, right off the highway."

The board had people who had business savvy. I said, "I've got this opportunity; here's the financial plan that makes this worth doing. We're going to build a building, and we're going to include Vermont Interactive Television, because they need a space down there, and we're going to have room for Vermont Technical College to have a nursing lab. So we're partnering."

I was able to put the financing together. VSC was issuing a bond for some dorm space at the same time, so I was able to hop on that. We were able to commit quickly, or we would have lost the land.

My goal was that by the time I was done, a majority of our square footage would be owned.

The first academic center built and owned by CCV opened in Wilder in 2005.

KIND OF A MIRACLE

"Community College of Vermont: A Borrower and a Nomad No Longer," said a four-column *Valley News* headline on June 7, 2005, the day after CCV opened its newly built, 15,000-square-foot Upper Valley center in Wilder. The college had bought its St. Albans facility earlier that year, but that building was already in service; so when he spoke at the Wilder event, Donovan was able to say, "This is the first building dedication in the history of the college."

It would not be the last.

In 2009, the college purchased a place on Elm Street in Montpelier that had once been the barn-like home of the city's Poor Farm. The capital city sheltered its most impoverished residents there for about a century, until the facility closed in 1956 — and for decades after, the words *Poor Farm* remained visible in large letters built into its roof.

The old barn was purchased in 1989 by Woodbury College, an innovative small college that rebuilt and expanded the structure. After Woodbury was absorbed into Champlain College in 2008, CCV bought the building in 2009. A 2011 expansion added 12,000 square feet to what now houses both the college's central offices and its Montpelier academic center.

In 2012, the college and Gov. Peter Shumlin cut the ribbon on a newly built academic center on West Street in Rutland, a 32,000-square-foot leased facility that doubled the size of the previous Rutland center.

The biggest challenge, and opportunity, for a new learning center came in Chittenden County. As enrollment grew by more than 40 percent from 2002 to 2010, close to eight hundred students were being shoehorned into classrooms at the site on Pearl Street where CCV leased space in the state's Health Department building. CCV then leased more space in a building next door — but "by 2008, the two Burlington buildings had maxed out all the available space at 42,000 square feet," said the college's 2012 self-study.

"The city of Winooski wanted us badly," Donovan recalled. Eyeing prospects for a new center in that small city across the river from Burlington, the college began to work with Ray Pecor, Jr., a prominent local businessman who owned the Lake Champlain Transportation Company, operating ferries across the lake. Pecor had also brought minor-league baseball to Burlington in 1994 as owner of the Vermont Expos, later the Lake Monsters.

Donovan, Pecor and the City of Winooski worked out a deal whereby Pecor would buy property that held several rundown buildings on a city corner. One structure was an apartment building that housed a number of former refugees; the college worked with the city to make it possible for those residents to relocate to new housing along the river that had been built with federal funds. Pecor, meanwhile, would buy the corner property and rent it to the college for a period of years so that the city would continue to receive property taxes on the land. Then he would sell it to CCV.

"Ray would refer to himself in the third person," Donovan recalled. "I said to him, 'Ray, I need you to buy this property and lease it back to us, and then sell it to us later and not make any money.' We were doing this over tuna salad sandwiches in the basement of the Champlain Mill. He said, 'Ray can do that.' Afterward, I said, 'Ray, I only ask for one thing: I'd like to throw out the first pitch at a Lake Monsters game.' He said, 'Ray can make that happen.'"

'We're going to put the money aside'

"Tim said, 'If we're going to have a building in Winooski [on leased land],'" David Buchdahl recalled, "'how do we save for it over a period of five or six years, so we can afford to do it without increasing prices?'

"That was a huge, huge issue for him — we're not going to build a building and then suddenly charge fees and raise tuition to pay for it. We're going to put the money aside for five years. He did that, and that enabled us to build the Winooski building without adding any additional cost to students. And that is kind of amazing."

By 2014, CCV had saved the money it needed to purchase the land from Ray Pecor.

"CCV Plans to Build Campus," the *Burlington Free Press* announced in a December 2007 headline. "Tentative plans call for construction of a building near Winooski's downtown redevelopment area," wrote reporter Tim Johnson.

Emerging from the consideration of architects' proposals for the new center was Tom O'Brien, who had been working with CCV since the early '90s to design and set up its rented and leased spaces. Donovan said that when he called O'Brien to say that his Northern Architects had been chosen to design the new flagship building, "he cried. He said, 'I've always wanted to do this. This is a dream.'"

One challenge was central. The Winooski center had to be built affordably, yet it had to meet the needs of the college and its students — and it had to have flexibility for changing enrollment.

"The charge I gave Tom was: It needs to look like a real college to our students," Donovan said — "but their first reaction can't be, 'My tuition is paying for this?' How do you balance that?

"So there were a lot of choices we had to make. The building was designed so that if our enrollment shrank, it could be partitioned; we could rent some of it out. If we needed more space, we had the infrastructure built into one end of the building so that we could expand."

For Donovan, what best sums up how CCV met the challenge is the story of the leftover stone.

In 2004, Middlebury College, the prestigious private institution an hour's drive south of Winooski, had opened its new Davis Family Library, with facing of handsome quartzite sandstone. The college had found a quarry in upstate New York that could supply the stone, and the quarry had spent a winter preparing the facing to the college's specifications.

"They ended up with a bunch left over," Donovan said.

"The poetic part of this story is that we faced the base of that building in Winooski for less than we would have paid for concrete block, because of the leftovers at Middlebury," he said. "Middlebury had returned the 'extra' to the wholesaler, and it was just enough for our use. So we bought it for about twenty cents on the dollar. Beautiful. The downside was, I had to be able to tell that story to anybody who said, 'What are you doing, paying money like that for that kind of material?'"

Construction began on the Winooski center in 2008. Then came the Great Recession of 2009.

"Our general contractor, E.F. Wall & Associates out of Barre, was able to get the best subcontractors in the state, because they didn't have work and were trying to keep their crews together," Donovan said. "The price of copper plummeted; we saved enough on copper for the electrical

INVENTING THE FUTURE

The main entrance to the Winooski center is rounded, so that students can see the bus coming from either direction.

system to pay for anything else that went over. So we ended up with a building that had been built with far more care and attention to detail than we could have expected normally for commercial construction.

"The other thing was, the guy who was the foreman for E.F. Wall said to me, a number of times: 'You know, the guys working on this building really care about this, and not because it's lousy times everywhere else. They know this is where their kids can go to college.'"

CCV's new Chittenden County facility opened on June 30, 2010, on the corner of East Allen Street and Abenaki Way in Winooski. Five years later, it was christened the Timothy J. Donovan Academic Center.

"Funded as a capital investment approved by the VSC board in 2007, this $17 million project is part of a $72 million construction effort by the VSC that included construction projects at all five state colleges," said a college fact sheet. "CCV will pay for this facility without charging additional fees to students."

The 65,000-square-foot facility has thirty-five classrooms, four science labs, three art studios, study space, office space for administration and student services, and the Evelyn Donovan Learning Center, funded by Donovan's siblings and named for their mother. The plaque at the Learning Center reads: "Each of us has a special gift awaiting our discovery."

"When you go into that building, there's a cylinder on the corner," Donovan said. The rounded three-story element features the center's main entrance. "Tom [O'Brien] said, 'I want somebody to be able to stand here and see the bus coming in either direction,'" Donovan said. "To me, that's kind of a culmination of all the little things we put together."

By the time the Winooski center opened, Tim Donovan had become chancellor of the Vermont State Colleges System. When he left the CCV presidency in mid-2009, the college had met his goal: Over half of its total square footage — the centers in St. Albans, Wilder, Montpelier and Winooski, with the main offices in Montpelier — was owned by CCV.

The lasting legacy of Elmer Kimball

Through two decades of CCV's June graduation ceremonies, Elmer Kimball was the catcher on the side.

"He stood at the side of the stage and helped steady the graduates as they walked down the stairs," Joyce Judy said. "The graduates could be very nervous and distracted, and they could wear some pretty strange footwear, too — so it was great to have strong, calm Elmer there to save them from an embarrassing fall."

That was just one small role among the many Kimball played in more than twenty years with CCV. A self-effacing native Vermonter, he joined the staff at the Chittenden center in 1993, just before its move to downtown Burlington; and aside from a break in 1994–1995 to work for the VSC-IBM Education Consortium, he stayed with the center, becoming its office manager and then co-regional director, until his untimely passing in 2014.

"His initiation was to manage every detail" of the move to 119 Pearl Street, Burlington, Judy recalled. Kimball capped his career by doing the same, and more, as the college developed its Winooski center at 1 Abenaki Way.

"Elmer was just a gem," said Dee Steffan, who came to share the Western Region directorship with Kimball, handling academics as he managed operations. "He was brilliant, but you would never have known that because he was also through-and-through Vermont.

"Whatever needed to be done, he learned how to do it. He never said no. If someone approached him and said, 'Would you do this?', it didn't matter how outside his experience it was, he would just tackle it.

Elmer Kimball, with Kathi Rousselle

"When we were moving into new centers," Steffan said, "he took on the role of managing the move — which included pulling us all together to design the building, pick out paint colors, decide how many classrooms, how the classrooms were going to be set up, everything about the physical layout and the organizational aspects of the move. Of course, he didn't know how to do that, so he just started learning programs to teach himself how to design classrooms, to furnish them, to look at electrical systems. He had a mind that was spongy — a very, very wry sense of humor, and game for anything."

"He got things done well and done on time," Donovan said. "Elmer believed they were done well because he benefitted from hearing everyone's ideas, everyone's desires, and, indeed, their needs.

"Nothing exemplifies the range of Elmer's contribution to CCV so much as 1 Abenaki Way," Donovan said. "That started with a vision for a building that would strike the balance of looking like college for students and community without being extravagant. Bringing that to fruition meant tens of thousands of decisions that we all entrusted to Elmer."

▶

> One of those decisions involved a tree.
>
> "At the eleventh hour, when the building was nearly ready for classes to begin and the landscapers were digging into their work, the landscape architect came to Elmer with a problem," Joyce Judy recalled in the eulogy she gave at Kimball's memorial. "The design called for a sycamore tree at the center of the lawn, and the designated Vermont sapling, at the nursery, had a defect in its trunk. The landscaper said not to worry, he had located a sapling in New Jersey and could send someone down to pick it up.
>
> "Elmer said, 'Not so fast,' and went to see the sapling. It had, as he called it, 'a hitch in its giddyup' at the base of its trunk. Knowing that CCV was a place of second chances, Elmer insisted that this tree would take its place on the lawn."
>
> By the time Kimball died in 2014, the Winooski center had been open for almost four years — and "each spring as the tree buds and leaves, it is a happy sight," Judy said. "It is becoming a magnificent tree."
>
> "The last time I conversed with Elmer was two weeks before he passed," Donovan said at his memorial. "There were several of us in his hospital room, laughing at stories that shouldn't repeated in public. When Elmer wanted to contribute, he kept circling back to a theme that was clearly on his mind: being sure people had a chance to be heard.
>
> "We should all be so lucky as to have an Elmer Kimball saunter into our lives."
>
> •••

'To reach beyond its walls': Summing up a vibrant time

Tim Donovan

> This was something I didn't talk about in any public way: I had watched over the years how every five to seven years, somebody — the governor, the speaker of the House, somebody — was going to say, "You know, the problem with the state colleges is, they have too many colleges. We need to close one or two of them down." I'd watched that conversation happen, and the only successful defense had been, "Okay, which one do you think we

ought to shut down? The one in your district or the one in that district?" The easiest one to settle on was CCV. Its economic impact was distributed, it didn't have one political base, it didn't bring in out-of-state students. It was serving the poor end of the spectrum.

What Barbara Murphy succeeded at more than anything else, in my mind, was that she raised the quality of the college's educational programming. The UVM recognition was the demonstration of that. So my driving goal, for as long as I was president, was to move CCV from the least likely to save to the most important one to save. Barbara raised the academic performance of the institution; my job was to raise the public's perception of the institution. How do you do that?

The first thing, and this is something Susan Henry really made happen: We undertook a very thorough branding exercise. Susan convinced me that branding was something more than our logo. It's the promise we make, and it's the promise our customer expects from us. More important, we've got to be sure we can deliver what people expect — and only part of that was marketing.

The other part was partnering. The phrase I used to use was, "I want to be on everybody's dance card." When somebody's putting a group together to work on something — say, workforce development in the Northeast Kingdom — we're going to have somebody at that table. Not just anybody; we're going to send somebody who's in a position to internally influence the college's direction, somebody with leverage.

So we were actively involved in workforce development stuff in other corners of the state. We were actively engaged with the superintendents' association when we were working on dual enrollment. We wanted to be the partner of choice, the ones who say, "Yes, we will be there" — and mean it.

If I point to only one thing that happened during my tenure, because of the work of a lot of people, it was that we raised our public perception, up to the level that Barbara had raised our programs.

KIND OF A MIRACLE

At the naming ceremony for Winooski's Timothy J. Donovan Academic Center: from left, Susan Henry, Mica DeAngelis, Pam Chisholm, Tim Donovan, and Mary Tharp, Tim's spouse.

On March 16, 2009, Gary Moore, chair of the Vermont State Colleges Board of Trustees, announced that Tim Donovan would become the seventh chancellor of the VSC System.

"Donovan brings outstanding strategic thinking, fiscal management and an energetic, collaborative leadership style that will help us fulfill our mission," Moore said.

The new chancellor's achievements as CCV's president, the announcement noted, had included "expansion of CCV's collaborative partnerships with high schools, development of extensive distance learning programs, improvement and ownership of several CCV facilities, including the 65,000 square foot flagship facility currently under construction in Winooski.... Enrollment at CCV has grown more than 40% during Donovan's tenure as president."

To many, the unspoken message of choosing, as chancellor of all the state colleges, someone who had devoted his career to CCV was clear: At long last, the community college had arrived. It was now a full partner in the system, whose leader Donovan would be from mid-2009 until his retirement in 2014.

One month after the VSC's announcement, six of Donovan's colleagues at CCV cosigned a letter nominating him for the Vermont Leadership Institute's annual Excellence in Leadership Award.

INVENTING THE FUTURE

The institute is a program of the Snelling Center for Government in Burlington; all those signing the letter had attended it, most of them during Donovan's presidency, when he made the Leadership Institute a professional-development priority.

The letter aptly sums up what Donovan's residency, capping his twenty-six-year career at the college, meant to CCV. It was signed by Susan Henry, John Christensen, Debby Stewart, Natalie Searle, Katie Mobley and academic coordinators Yasmine Ziesler and Bill Morison:

> *Part visionary and entrepreneur, part storyteller and historian, part baseball manager and pinch hitter, Tim encompasses such a breadth of leadership skills it is difficult to imagine a better or more deserving candidate for recognition.... Becoming president of the Community College of Vermont in 2001, he challenged CCV to reach beyond its walls, creating a new era of collaboration with high schools, agencies and businesses in local communities across Vermont. More than 1,300 Vermont students are now dual-enrolled at CCV each year. Partnering with Vermont businesses and the Department of Labor, CCV now delivers a Career Readiness Certificate for unemployed and under-employed Vermonters.*
>
> *A leader in the adoption of technology for both academic and administrative uses, Tim envisioned an online learning program that would provide access to an unprecedented array of courses and programs to the rural reaches of Vermont. CCV now enrolls nearly 1,800 Vermonters per year in its online learning offerings. During Tim's tenure as president, the number of Vermonters pursuing a higher education at CCV has increased by more than 40%. Tim has helped make CCV's value apparent to public opinion and to public policy leaders.*
>
> *Most college presidents have a master facilities plan for a campus — CCV's master facilities plan involves the landscape of our entire state. CCV now owns its facilities in Wilder and St. Albans, a new flagship facility is under construction in Winooski, and CCV recently purchased the former Woodbury College campus in Montpelier. These developments have come about*

through Tim's masterful fiscal leadership, and they have not come at the expense of students. Tim has long ensured that CCV tuition is affordable, and at a level fully funded by federal Pell grants.

On a first-name basis with all who know him, Tim has created a culture of inclusion, shared problem-solving and genuine respect. So often Tim has stood before a group of CCV faculty and staff and said, "I need your help." He looks for ways to empower the voices of our youngest professionals, and he can't resist the chance to buy them a beer on a Friday after work to learn what they are thinking about.

… If you've ever sat next to Tim at a meeting, you know that he is not one to sit still for long. Tim thrives on interaction and momentum, and his energy is contagious. Whether you are enthralled by his telling of a good story, swept up in his deep laughter, or bobbing along with him on a bus to Fenway Park (an annual event he personally organized for the CCV community), you can't help but admire the passion with which Tim wraps his heart around his every task and challenge. "If it's not fun," he says, "it's too damn much work."

As an era at the community college came to a close, the Snelling Center presented its 2009 Excellence in Leadership Award to Tim Donovan.

Chapter 13

Changing Lives, One at a Time

Joyce Judy, 2009 to Today

CCV graduations are real celebrations, made all the more meaningful because of how much the graduates have overcome, in so many cases, to get there. The June 4, 2011, ceremony was no exception, as almost four thousand people came to see nearly five hundred students accept their diplomas.

To be their student speaker, the graduates had chosen a single mother from Brattleboro who had completed high school seventeen years before.

Angela Givens was receiving an associate degree in education, and she had been accepted at prestigious Smith College to study for a bachelor's degree. But, she told the gathering, "if you met me three years ago, you would not recognize me.

"I had hit bottom. I was 130 pounds overweight and in the last throes of a very unhappy marriage. I was also unemployed, and in June of '08 I was homeless and living in Fort Dummer State Park with my son. Ironically, this unfortunate set of circumstances was perhaps the best thing that ever happened to me."

Abandoned by her husband and caring for their bright four-year-old son, "I ended up in Morningside Shelter in Brattleboro for six months," Angela said. "After years of trying to do everything on my own and failing, I was forced to ask for help.

"The staff at Morningside saved me and my son. They not only helped me find housing, they helped me realize my dreams! They connected me with people who could help my son with his unique needs, and they connected me with the programs that allowed me to go back to school."

Angela would go on to graduate from Smith in 2015, with a bachelor's degree in mathematics and education. "Her eyes flash with humor and passion as she talks about math, breaking it into its most beautiful concepts, and builds it into the language of the universe," said "Making her way from homelessness to Smith College," a 2011 article about Angela in the *Brattleboro Reformer*.

"I am the mother of a seven-year-old with insatiable curiosity," Angela said in her CCV commencement speech. "He is constantly asking me and his teachers questions. My son's eyes shine whenever he learns something new; that is when I think he is happiest. He has a thirst for knowledge that is unquenchable.... I can only hope that all of us can follow his example and never stop learning.

Angela Givens and her son, at her CCV graduation.

"Human beings are social animals," she continued. "We need each other. There are no limits to what we can achieve when we work together. We are all connected and we need each other to achieve success.... I ask of each of you to honor your own achievements, ask for help when needed and to give of yourself when you can. I truly believe these are the keys to a happy life when combined with the desire to keep learning."

After college, Angela taught high school math in Vermont for several years; she is currently personnel manager for the Sociology Department at the University of Massachusetts, Amherst. CCV included much of her graduation speech in the 2012 *Dimensions Reader*, a publication the college compiled to support its integrative seminar for first-year students.

And that June day, CCV president Joyce Judy later wrote, "Angela Givens of Brattleboro captured the hearts of everyone who heard her story."

A new decade's different challenges

The college's seventh president began as an academic coordinator in 1983, then rose to become dean of students and CCV's first provost. In March 2010, after a nationwide search, the VSC board chose Joyce Judy for the college's top job, even though she had warned the search team in her interview that — though she had spent her career at this institution — she wasn't about to let the college remain the same.

Joyce Judy

"I said, 'If you want CCV to stay as it is, then I'm not the person for you,'" recalled Judy, who became the college's longest-serving president and still holds the post. "I am a believer that CCV has always been an agent of change — and we always are changing."

She had served as interim president since mid-2009, when Tim Donovan left to become chancellor of the state college system. In her years on the staff, Judy had built a wealth of positive, collaborating relationships. That was central to the way she worked, and it would be central to her presidency.

"Joyce would visit with people and get to know them on a personal level," said David Buchdahl, who like Judy had worked at the college since 1983. "She was completely trusted, and is."

CCV celebrated its fortieth anniversary at its June 2010 commencement, and all six former presidents came to mark the occasion. Two days earlier, the college had opened its flagship learning center in Winooski. In between those two ceremonies, the seven presidents joined longtime staff and others on an evening cruise aboard the *Spirit of Ethan Allen* on Lake Champlain.

Proposing a toast, Buchdahl paid tribute to each of Judy's predecessors. Then he turned to the new president.

"I said, 'I do believe that Joyce is going to be the strongest president yet,'" he recalled. "The reason I felt that is that Joyce has no ego investment in this job. She is completely dedicated to the mission of the college."

Judy's first decade as CCV's leader would bring different challenges from the one that preceded it. After years of steady enrollment, growth had peaked — and in the 2010s, CCV's student numbers began to decline, as did those at community colleges across the country. Between fall 2011 and fall 2019, enrollment at the college would sag from 7,116 students to 5,104.

CCV would respond in part by boosting its engagement with secondary schools, using new state funding to make it possible for students to do their final year in high school as a first year of college at CCV, tuition-free. For even younger students, an innovative new outreach offered middle schoolers around Vermont the chance to sample a day's college experience at CCV. And with Judy's encouragement, college staff reached out to build new collaborations with Vermont employers, meeting workforce training and education needs in newly flexible ways.

"I have always been a believer that we are only as strong as our relationships are deep," Judy said. "It's relationships that get people through our doors."

The years 2009 to 2019 were a time for the college of creative adaptation — and that was before Covid-19 struck in 2020 and CCV scrambled, along with most everyone else, to adapt even more.

For a community college that began by creating itself, with no role models to follow — then has creatively adapted to each new decade, while keeping its student-centered core — Joyce Judy's first decade as president stayed true to the promise she made to the search committee. CCV did continue to both change and be an agent of change, one engaged actively with Vermont communities.

"I would have my evaluation meeting with her," said Dee Steffan, "and she would often ask, 'So what are you doing in the community? Who's working with this group, or who's working with that group?' She was absolutely attentive to that."

"I am just a huge believer that we can only be strong in Vermont if we're out there," Judy said. "I feel like that's been a major part of my presidency. I feel like I'm out there all the time."

All seven CCV presidents, together at the 2010 commencement ceremony. In front, from left: Barbara Murphy, Joyce Judy and Myrna Miller. In back: Peter Smith, Mike Holland, Tim Donovan and Ken Kalb.

"Joyce leads in many ways by example, but she's also incredibly strategic," said Katie Mobley. "She sort of embodies the values and mission of CCV. She's funny, and she can be a little irreverent. I would say that's true of most of our leaders at CCV: We don't take ourselves too seriously, but we take the work really seriously.

"Joyce is a fascinating college president," she added. "I think her upbringing gives so much insight into her work style. You know, she goes to the farm every weekend to muck stalls."

'Just do what you've got to do'

Bill and Hazel McNamara, Judy's parents, wanted to start a farm. He loved horses, and Hazel had grown up on a dairy farm in Vermont. But six weeks after their wedding in 1947, "a horse carrying Bill stepped into a woodchuck hole, and the resulting fall left Bill severely injured and in need of a lengthy hospital stay," wrote Greg Fennell in the *Valley News*.

Bill came out of the hospital paralyzed from the neck down. He would regain very limited use of his limbs, just enough to operate a pickup truck.

"We could get him into his pickup, and one hand could grab the steering wheel — and he had enough mobility in one wrist to go back and forth," Judy said. "He had enough mobility in two feet that he drove. So he conducted his work from his pickup."

In 1950, Bill and Hazel bought a rundown farm with no electricity or running water on the banks of the Connecticut River in Plainfield, New Hampshire, across from Vermont. They had five children. Hazel worked as a visiting nurse and kept everyone on the farm fed, while Bill supervised the workers they hired — and when they were old enough, his children too — from his truck.

"My mother never complained, and she never looked back," Judy told the *Valley News* after her mother passed away in 2020. "That was not in her DNA, nor in my dad's. They could have had their lives flipped upside-down after they were married … yet they moved on and lived life."

"My dad just figured out how to do things," she said of her father, who died in 2004. "He was not able to do anything by himself, but both my parents were very determined, and together they figured out how to get things done. That's why I think 'just do what you've got to do to get it done' has always been my approach."

The family farm thrives today as McNamara Dairy, producing milk in old-school glass bottles along with maple products, eggs, meat and butter. Her brothers run the operation, and Judy returns often to pitch in, as she always has.

"We were always expected to work," she said, "but we also played a lot of sports. We had no money, but I never grew up thinking we were poor. We always had what we needed.

"I tell people that the reason I can manage a community college budget is because of all those things. I'm very frugal; my mother was really clear that you don't buy things unless you see a way to pay for them. I take pride in the fact that every year, our budget has always been on the positive side. It has forced us to make the really hard decisions up front. We are pretty creative — and I believe that the training in my background has helped me figure it out."

"One of Joyce's special focuses has always been accessibility from a physical perspective — being able to help students with disabilities, make sure they are able to attend," said David Buchdahl. "That was important for Tim, too, when we were designing these new buildings."

"The thing about CCV that I always admired, and it was always sort of a function of the top leadership, is how entrepreneurial they were," said instructor Mary Hulette, who has taught CCV courses since 2001. "They would put up a program, give it a try, and if it didn't work, it didn't work. And we try something else.

"If there's a way," she said, "Joyce will find a way."

A snapshot in numbers

From the college's 2012 accreditation self-study:

As an open-admissions college, CCV provides the entry point to higher education for a broad spectrum of students, particularly for educationally, economically and socially disadvantaged Vermonters. Sixty percent of CCV's students are first-generation college students. The vast majority (about 83%) attend college part-time, and more than three-quarters hold full or part-time jobs. Almost one-third are new to college each semester; nearly half of them are academically unprepared when they enter CCV and thus require developmental skills preparation in writing, reading, and/or math.

Reflecting Vermont's population as a whole, only 7% of students report minority ethnic backgrounds. Of the 70% of degree students who received financial aid in 2010-11, 28% had incomes under $10,000, and 48% had incomes under $20,000 (looking at both student and parents' adjusted gross incomes). More than a third of CCV students support children.

Notwithstanding these data, CCV students are wired: 98% report having a personal email address, and 80% say they go online daily or several times a week. Students cite low cost, proximity of classes, and availability of financial aid as the most important factors in their decision to enroll at CCV.

By national standards, CCV's tuition ranks among the highest for community colleges, though the cost of attending remains by far the lowest of any college in Vermont. The annual appropriation from the State of Vermont represents just 12% of CCV's cost revenue; student tuition and fees make up 56%. Low state support results in high tuition costs, yet carefully considered operational efficiencies have kept the cost of delivering CCV's programs below the national average.

▶

> ... CCV offers a wide variety of courses, 11 career-oriented certificates, and 17 associate degree programs in liberal, professional, and technical fields. As is typical for community colleges, CCV's programs and courses attract students who want to upgrade job skills, prepare for transfer to a four-year college, or earn a degree.
>
> ... For much of CCV's history, because of the lack of a critical mass of students to enroll in upper-level program requirements, students in Vermont's most rural areas had limited options for completing their preferred degrees. This made the advent of online learning particularly attractive to the college. CCV dove into distance learning with two primary priorities: the convenience of asynchronous learning and a commitment to providing the same individualized, interactive classroom experience that has become a hallmark of CCV. To support this commitment, CCV's online classes average 14 students and rarely enroll more than 18.... With over 20% of CCV's overall enrollment in online classes today, distance learning has become a very significant aspect of CCV operations and an essential strategy for expanding access for students.
>
> •••

From school into college: Opening new paths

One day in spring 2011, a conversation between education leaders and Vermont's governor gave rise to a breakthrough in early-college opportunities for young Vermonters — one that took off from and built on a CCV initiative.

At the time there was shared concern that although the state's high school graduation rate was high, its rate of students continuing on to college was among the nation's lowest. (It still is.) In particular, noted Judy, "the discrepancy is huge among students who are low-income and from first-generation families," compared to students from families with college experience and middle or higher income levels.

CCV had been taking steps to help close that gap:

- It was working with high schools and technical centers around the state to offer all students its free Introduction to College Studies course, with funding from the McClure Foundation.

- In 2008, the college began offering a discount on tuition for CCV courses to high school juniors and seniors around the state. Through this dual enrollment option, students continued full-time at their high school while also taking one to two courses at a CCV academic center.
- The college was providing free dual enrollment to some high schoolers with limited financial resources through its Rise to the Challenge scholarships, funded by VSAC's GEAR UP grant.
- CCV was also using federal Perkins Act funding to offer free dual enrollment to students in career and technical education (CTE) secondary schools.

By 2010, Tim Donovan, now the Vermont State Colleges chancellor, felt that CCV had proven dual enrollment could work. "There was enough of a track record on this, enough [high] schools doing it," he said — and even though the community college was the only one in Vermont offering dual enrollment on a significant scale, the chancellor believed it should become statewide policy, backed by state funding.

At the 2014 commencement ceremony: graduates with Governor Peter Shumlin.

After Gov. Jim Douglas said he would not stand for reelection and several candidates began to campaign for the fall 2010 primaries, "I went to candidates in both parties," Donovan recalled. "I said, 'I'm willing to help you develop your education platform, if you're interested.'"

Only Peter Shumlin, a Democratic state senator from Windham County, accepted his offer. When Donovan talked with the candidate and brought up dual enrollment, he found Shumlin to be "kind of receptive to this notion."

Shumlin won the primary, then the election. In early 2011, the new governor convened a meeting with CCV President Judy, VSC Chancellor Donovan, state Commissioner of Education Armando Vilaseca, and the governor's policy director.

The group also included John Fischer, who was then both state director of career and technical education and director of the High School and Adult Division at the Vermont Department of Education. Fischer had been talking for some time with Donovan and David Ruff, executive director of the New England Secondary School Consortium, about the potential of dual enrollment to help close the gap in high-school-to-college continuation.

Shumlin asked the education leaders how the state could encourage more young Vermonters to enroll and succeed in college. Recalled Fischer: "He was saying, 'What can I do about that?' So we said, 'Well, you've got a little bit of a dual enrollment program at CCV, but it's not state-supported.' It was not codified, and it was limited to CCV."

What followed over the next two years was an expanding series of conversations among leaders of the education department, the VSC, the Vermont Superintendents Association, the Vermont Principals' Association, the governor's policy office, state legislators and others. The Department (now the Agency) of Education did a policy-research study on dual enrollment and other "flexible pathways" to successful learning in high school.

"Vermont was part of the New England Secondary School Consortium. The six New England states are in this," Fischer said. (The consortium is a project of the nonprofit Great Schools Partnership.) "The goal," he explained, "was to improve the high school experience for students and not rely on seat time or the Carnegie unit," a time-based measure of educational progress, "to be the determination of [high school] completion.

"So a lot of things started coming together at that time. Policy change doesn't happen quickly, and many of these conversations occurred at various levels."

Out of those policy discussions and the education department's research, leaders of the Vermont Legislature's education committees developed a bill that they introduced in the 2012 session.

It did not pass.

"I'm not surprised, because it challenged the status quo," Donovan said. "The School Boards Association and the Superintendents Association unfortunately saw it as, 'You're going to take the best students out of our schools' — which was nobody's intent."

When Gov. Shumlin gave his second inaugural address at the start of the Legislature's 2013 session, he focused entirely on education and its importance to the state's future. "Sixty-two percent of job openings in the next decade will require post-secondary education," he said. "Yet only 45% of Vermont students who begin ninth grade continue their education past high school, and that percentage drops as family incomes decline."

State funding for dual enrollment was among the measures the governor promoted, along with expanded opportunities for students to simultaneously complete both their senior year of high school and a full first year in college. He also proposed that all students develop personalized learning plans that would follow them through public school, helping them to expand their options.

That spring the Legislature adopted Senate Bill 77, known as the Flexible Pathways Initiative. It became Act 77, a landmark new law with several important and connected impacts.

At the heart of Act 77 was the concept of flexible pathways to high school graduation. Traditional classroom time could now be blended with virtual learning, work-based learning and/or dual enrollment — "any combination of high-quality and experiential components," said an Agency of Education summary of the law.

Act 77 "set the groundwork for proficiency-based graduation," said Fischer, who went on to become deputy state commissioner of education. "No longer does a student qualify [to graduate] based on seat time; students must demonstrate proficiency." The State Board of Education left it up to local school districts to determine the needed proficiencies.

Act 77 required that all students in grades seven through nine develop a personalized learning plan. If that plan included early college and the student was academically ready, starting in 2015 the state would pay the college tuition for dual enrollment programs.

"This was taking the early CCV model for dual enrollment and scaling it to all higher education in Vermont, if they agree to certain conditions set out in Act 77," Fischer said. In developing dual enrollment, he noted that CCV had aimed especially to raise aspirations among Vermont students of limited means. "When you see the aspiration rise, you see enrollment follow."

Act 77 also built on an innovation by Vermont Technical College, which was inviting high schoolers to spend their senior year as a first college year on VTC's Randolph Center campus, through its Vermont Academy of Science and Technology (VAST). The new law called for the state to fund a full year of early college for high school seniors who had put that into their learning plan.

Act 77's support for dual enrollment included students at career and tech ed centers. Said Fischer: "We wanted that to be a catalyst — to say, 'You know, dual enrollment is not just for elite students in the top 10 percent of their class. It's for all students, including career and tech ed.'"

Students at Vermont's CTE centers can still earn CCV credits through the college's Fast Forward program. "CCV led the way, and still does lead the way," Fischer said, "in not drawing conclusions that just because you're a CTE student doesn't mean you're not college-bound."

'It just keeps escalating'

"Act 77 funded dual enrollment and early college and all these other pieces; it sort of put everything we'd been doing up tenfold. It just keeps escalating," said Natalie Searle, who in 2000 became the college's director of secondary school initiatives.

Since 2014, Early College at CCV has given high school seniors the chance to enroll full-time at any of CCV's twelve academic centers, to earn one year of college credit, tuition-free.

In Vermont Tech's VAST program, "kids literally left high school and became students at VTC," Tim Donovan said. "Act 77 allowed for something that was a little less disruptive." In CCV's model, Early College students stayed enrolled at their high school while studying at a CCV center, so the high school kept its state funding for each student in the program. Negotiations also won an agreement that those students could still participate in their high school's athletic and other extracurricular activities.

Enrollment in Early College grew steadily. CCV accepted 119 seniors into the program for the 2016–2017 year, almost twice as many as the year before. As chancellor, Donovan persuaded the other state colleges to accept Early College students, even though each student came with funding set at CCV's tuition level, "which was less than half of theirs," he said.

"They did not like that, but they tended to do it with the local [high] schools," Donovan said of the other state colleges. "CCV was saying, 'We'll do it with anybody — every student in Vermont.'"

Overall at the community college, between Introduction to College Studies, the Rise to the Challenge scholarships and Early College, from 2006 to 2017 a total of 19,139 Vermont high schoolers took at least one CCV course. In the 2017–2018 academic year, about 400 took what had been renamed Introduction to College and Careers, and high school students used about 1,500 dual enrollment vouchers to take free classes through the college.

The McClure Foundation has been a key player in helping make all this happen. Having begun its work with CCV by helping fund the Intro to College Studies course in 2008, the foundation expanded its commitment after Act 77 opened up more early-college opportunities.

"We support the whole suite of CCV's secondary education initiatives," said Carolyn Weir, the foundation's executive director — "everything from the middle school Access Days that they offer throughout the year to dual enrollment and early college, and the outreach to all the public high schools in Vermont that are serving students who could benefit from these programs."

At present the college offers over one hundred dual enrollment courses, now taught at both its centers and in high schools during their school day. "From fall 2016 through summer 2019, nearly 4,000 students participated in dual enrollment at CCV," said the college's 2022 self-study. Among dual enrollment students at career and technical education centers, 56 percent were first-generation college students. Within sixteen months of graduating secondary school, 73 percent of all dual enrollment students were enrolled in a post-secondary degree program.

Compared to the average cost of attending a full year of college, the self-study reported that dual enrollment in the 2020–2021 academic year "saved Vermont students and their families over $900,000 in total."

Access Days: 'It just sticks in their memory'

Inside CCV's Rutland center one April morning in 2022, Dana Oliver and Nathan Astin waited for a bus crammed full of eighth graders.

Oliver coordinates Access Days, the college initiative that brings middle school students into a CCV center for a half day's experience of what it's like to be there and learn at the college level.

"It just sticks in their memory that they can be here. And belong," she said.

This morning's group, from Fair Haven, would become eligible for CCV dual enrollment in tenth grade, noted Astin, a student advising coordinator at the Rutland center.

Between the first Access Days in 2015–2016 and a pause in early 2020 for the Covid-19 pandemic, CCV centers hosted 103 of these visits for 4,718 students. The great majority were middle schoolers, plus a growing number from high schools and career-technical centers. The program is supported by federal funding through a GEAR UP grant from the Vermont Student Assistance Corporation.

Instructor Mario Hankerson at a 2019 Access Day, at CCV Montpelier.

"People are really recognizing the value of introducing students, especially first-generation and low-income students, to the idea of college early on," explained Natalie Searle, CCV's director of secondary education initiatives. "Not in their senior year of high school: 'Have you thought about college?' It's really important that they start thinking about it in middle school."

When the forty Fair Haven middle schoolers filed uncertainly that morning into a meeting room at CCV Rutland, three college instructors were waiting in their classrooms, each ready to lead a fifty-minute sample of a course they teach. But first, Oliver welcomed the students and took them through a slide-show introduction to the college, with some key numbers: a thousand courses per semester at twelve sites and online; an average class size of thirteen; 77 percent of students attending part-time.

"How many know," she asked, "that college can be very expensive?" Young people all over the room murmured that they did. Oliver told them about CCV's free Introduction to College and Careers course, then about dual enrollment.

"You can earn credit for both high school and college at the same time," she said. "All you have to do is talk to your guidance counselor — say, 'I want to use my dual enrollment voucher.' You can spend one free year of college as a high school senior." CCV's Early College Plus, she said, offered a $1,000 stipend for enrolling in one of five certificate programs to build skills for in-demand careers.

And CCV's newest initiative, just announced and funded by the McClure Foundation, would enable anyone who completed the Early College year to do their second year at the college for free, thereby earning an associate degree. "This applies to everyone [now] in the eighth grade and up," Oliver said.

One aim of her talk and slide show was to introduce middle schoolers to college terms: credits, transfer, financial aid, associate degree. As CCV staffers passed out college-branded notebooks and pens, she urged the students to take a few notes. The day would end, she promised, with "College Lingo Bingo." There would be prizes.

'How do we raise aspirations?'

Access Days began, as many innovations at CCV have, with an idea and the encouragement to go ahead and try.

"It was very local and homegrown," said Kate Hughes, an academic coordinator at the Upper Valley center who first organized the program. "Just a small group of caring people, trying to think creatively about how you connect kids with opportunities."

Hughes wasn't only talking with instructors and students. "There's always been an outreach component, where we try to make partnerships

▶

with schools and other community partners," she said of the coordinator's job. "Not overlooking those natural relationships."

As Hughes talked with people in the Windsor school district, "we were thinking about, how do we raise aspirations? There's research that supports the idea of middle-level focus — so the idea was, Can we create a hands-on experience? Because people can talk to you about all the things that would be good for you, but seeing is believing. It exists. You've been there."

After a couple of early experiments, where small groups of volunteering high schoolers came to events at the Upper Valley center, Hughes and her partners decided to invite middle schools in the area to bring in larger groups by bus for a two-hour or half-day experience tailored to them. Those first Access Days in 2015–2016 brought in 690 students, from nineteen schools. The program quickly caught on; in 2018–2019, 1,450 students from twenty-eight schools all around Vermont had an Access Day experience.

The pandemic forced CCV to pause in-person Access Days and do its best with short videoconferencing options, offered over the course of a week. It wasn't the same. But in spring 2022 the in-person events started again. After this one in Rutland in April, fifteen more were scheduled around the state in May.

"We're getting a ton of requests," said Oliver. "I'm back on the road again."

'To develop your brain'

To teach its Access Day sample classes, the college tends to ask instructors who are known to be engaging. That April morning, veteran professor Philip Crossman led a discussion on the philosophy of ethics; astronomer Catherine Garland introduced the science of galaxies and black holes; and Melissa Holmes, an emergency responder and former police officer, led a hands-on sampling of the work of crime scene investigators.

Said Crossman to his listeners: "The number-one reason to take a college philosophy class, or any college class, is to develop your brain."

"In the early 1900s, we only knew of one galaxy," said Garland in her astronomy class. "Today we know there are billions and billions out there

— and each star has at least one planet." What if, she mused, "there's an Access Day going on right now, in another galaxy?"

In all three classrooms, even those eighth graders who had started the session slumped or looking out a window were soon visibly engaged. Holmes had students taking their own fingerprints, then learning how to gather clues by analyzing a skull. "I like this class," one student said as her group left that session, headed for a lunch downstairs.

As the eighth graders consumed their pizza, several at one table were asked: Had today's experience changed their thinking about college?

"In many ways," a student named Cody affirmed. "College is cool ... ish."

"Now that I've gotten to kind of see what it's like," said Noah, "I get the gist of it."

"I've been thinking about college since sixth grade," said a boy named Dante. "I want to look at medical technology."

At a 2016 Access Day, instructor Martha Rainville gave a glimpse of the course she teaches on anatomy and physiology.

Two boys said they still weren't thinking about college. One planned to make movies, the other to play pro basketball. But a girl named Gracianna said of CCV, "I think it's an awesome opportunity for kids who don't necessarily have the money or the resources."

"College helps people," said Ayden. "Especially community college. If it costs less, more people would be able to get good job opportunities."

'Well sure, try it'

"We originally designed these for middle schools, then we started to get a lot of requests from high schools and tech centers," said Searle. "They would say things like, 'We have this group of students and they don't know what they want to do. We want to explore some careers, or just show them what college is like.' So we changed the name, from Middle School Access Days to just Access Days."

▶

KIND OF A MIRACLE

> "CCV has a culture of encouraging people to run with things," said Kate Hughes, the original organizer. "I think that's one of the many things that makes this such a great place to work — innovation and creative thinking, and sort of empowering people to try things. I think that's why we've been successful: 'Well sure, try it.'
>
> "We've brought kids here to experience a college setting and a college opportunity; and they go home and talk about it," she observed. "We don't know all of the ways in which those tentacles spread. Sometimes we'll hear stories of how it would result in a sibling coming, or a parent coming.
>
> "To me, that's the magic of working and teaching here. All kinds of people find their way to CCV."
>
> •••

Intro to College Studies: 'You can do this'

Introduced in the late 1990s, CCV's free course for high school students — first called Introduction to College Studies, renamed Introduction to College and Careers in 2017 — has had a demonstrated impact. Open to all Vermont high school juniors and seniors, the course "provides an important foundation for students to begin their college experience," said the college's 2012 accreditation self-study.

"Of the 75% of students who successfully completed ICS in spring 2009," the study reported, "65% subsequently enrolled in college, nearly three-quarters (71%) of them in Vermont."

Today, Introduction to College and Careers, or ICC, is offered to students in grades 8-12, "with a special focus on ninth and tenth graders," said the college's newest self-study in 2022.

With several different modules that can be added in various combinations to the course's core, "ICC introduces students to career exploration, college financing, and academic skill formation," the self-study said. "Although free to all students, ICC targets students with barriers to postsecondary education that include being low-income or first-generation or having a documented disability."

The course is offered at high schools in addition to CCV centers — and "between fall 2016 and summer 2019, 1,338 students enrolled in ICC across all 14 Vermont counties," the self-study said. "Of these, 739 (55%) were first-generation students. The overall course success rate for ICC in 2019 was 79 percent, up from 69 percent the previous year.

"Among the 515 ICC completers who graduated from high school in 2018 and 2019, 370 (72%) matriculated in college within 16 months of graduation, which is higher than the continuation rate of Vermont high school students who go on to any postsecondary education (52%)."

Linda Lawrence is one of today's ICC instructors. The course, she said, is "exactly what I wish I had had."

After graduating high school in 1987, Lawrence worked for Domino's Pizza for twenty-two years, managing stores in Vermont for much of that time. She became pregnant, left the franchise, and got involved with Reach Up, Vermont's support program for parents of limited means who have minor children.

"My Reach Up worker said to me, 'You know, you could go to school for free,'" Lawrence said. "I was like, 'Whaaat?' I had never even thought about going to college."

She took a word-processing class at CCV's Burlington center, did work-study in the financial aid office, then took a full-time job at the center while completing her associate degree. She went on to earn a bachelor's degree at Trinity College in Burlington and a master's at St. Michael's College in Winooski. Along with teaching an ICC course, Lawrence is now CCV's assistant director of operations.

Her ICC class typically has between ten and seventeen high school students. "There are different modules that you can choose to teach," she said. "I do a module on career and work interests. They do a career research chart, after looking at their personality and learning styles or preferences — kind of figuring out, 'OK, what careers fit that?'

"We do a college module, which is thinking about the career that they've looked at and what degrees they would need for that. It's not always what they think. Then they do a college comparison chart; they look at three different colleges.

"We do a project at the end of the class that we call the Game of Life. They write down the college that they're going to go to, the career they want to have when they get out of college. I have them look at where they might want to live, and do they want to rent or do they want to own a home? They have to look up either a home or an apartment, and write down how much the cost of that is.

"They have to look at the utility bills for that: how much for gas, electric and cable internet. Are they going to take the bus, use public transportation, or buy or lease a car? How much might their health insurance cost, what is the average debt for the college that they would go to? At the end, they write a paper based on what they've learned and make an oral presentation.

"There are so many Vermonters that don't have a college education," Lawrence reflected. For her, much of the aim of teaching Intro to College and Careers is "reaching out to them, getting them to the point where they understand, 'You *can* do this.'"

Not traditional students: Welcoming and working with vets

After the September 11, 2001 attacks gave rise to the U.S. military presence in Afghanistan, and American forces then invaded Iraq in 2003 to topple Saddam Hussein, some 1,700 Vermont Army and Air National Guard troops were deployed to those theaters of war. When they and others who had been on active duty began returning to Vermont, a fast-growing number of veterans enrolled at CCV. The college began to work on building its capacity to help veterans — both in transitioning from the military to college and in navigating the complexities of securing G.I. Bill educational benefits.

Crucial to that effort was the active support, financial and advisory, of the McClure Foundation.

"That was when I really met Joyce for the first time," said Barbara Benedict, the foundation's president. Benedict's son had served in the infantry, in both Iraq and Afghanistan. "He had seen that in garrison, every soldier has their laptop in front of them," she said, "and there's a chance to take courses online if they can — and they were being marketed to by for-profit colleges in a huge, huge way. Money was being siphoned off to other institutions, and students were being siphoned off when they came home."

Eager to learn how the Vermont National Guard was informing vets about educational opportunities in the state, Benedict helped organize a meeting that included herself, Judy and the Vermont Guard's education officer.

"Between the beginning of the meeting and when Joyce was going to talk," she said, "the National Guard put up this map of the institutions of higher learning in Vermont — and there was no CCV on it. At all. We were in shock."

"The perception of so many people is that a four-year degree education is what the goal is for everybody," Benedict said. "Well, we have all learned that's not always effective for the workforce training that's needed, or for individuals. So we realized we had work to do to promote what CCV had to offer."

"That opened the door," said Carolyn Weir, the foundation's executive director, "to what has now been a ten-year grant relationship of supporting and expanding CCV's capacity, not only to support veteran and military-connected students, but also to invest in the training and professional development that staff and faculty at CCV need to serve those students well.

"Soldiers need one point of contact," she said. "They're used to a clear vision of who they talk to next, go up the chain of command. We decided we would help fund an advisor who would be this one point of contact."

For several years, Kyle Aines served as that advisor. A combat medic who had done two tours in Iraq and five total years in active duty, he left the military in 2009 and earned a degree in criminal justice. In 2014, he spotted a CCV job posting for a student resource advisor for veterans; he would fill that position until 2022. His narrative below is excerpted from a 2022 interview.

Kyle Aines

They wanted somebody who could speak to how to access the benefits and navigate them, and who could direct people to the different tools and resources that the college has. This particular position was kind of new; the rest of it would be defined as we went along.

When any veteran comes in and engages with the college, they're going to get an automatic email from me. If they're using benefits, in particular, they're going to want to speak with me. If they have questions about how to access the benefits, or what it means to use them during the semester, I give them all the details. Sometimes they're eligible for multiple benefits; we try to work out their specific situation, what's going to work best for them.

These are not traditional students. They come back and they've got families, they've got jobs and homes, a plethora of other responsibilities outside of CCV and school. Education is important, but it's not top of the list sometimes, right? So just being patient is important. When they're ready to do something, access something, you've got to go with it quickly. When they're ready, they'll let you know. When they're in crisis, they'll email or call — and getting back to them quickly with the right answers, with a solution, really means a lot to them.

We focus a lot on faculty and staff training. PTSD has always been around, but with our understanding of it now, as a society, it's recognized on a different level. We provide some training around that. TBIs [traumatic brain injuries], what that looks like in a classroom setting, what you can expect. Trying to see signs; suicide prevention, when it comes to that. Recognizing some of these things in the classroom, trying to jump on them quickly.

[Veterans] sometimes have issues in the classroom, particularly in being with students who are younger than they are, or at least inexperienced. I mean, they've done a lot, they've seen a lot. Their worldviews have changed quite a bit. The majority of the time, our veteran students are leaders in the classroom — right now, 52 percent of our veterans are eligible for our Salute Honor Society. It does happen occasionally, though, where we've got to talk about, "Well, this isn't the military anymore. You can have a difference of opinion. You don't have to agree with them; you can say that's not how it is. There's just got to be some tact involved."

The biggest part is the advising piece. The Montgomery G.I. Bill is Vietnam era, and I have to be familiar with how that works. There are students using it today. Once people deploy overseas and produce active duty time, then they start being eligible for the post 9/11 G.I. Bill, the newer one that's been changed to increase some of the benefits and some of the services. That's just two; there's a bunch more. Reserves and Guards each have one that is very specific on how to use it and when to use it.

Federal tuition assistance, the National Guard tuition benefit program — there's a lot that students can access. It's really rewarding when I get to work with a student, or with their spouse or dependent, who wasn't aware that they were eligible for something. I reach out, I talk: Let's have that conversation. And that happens every semester.

I think it's a civic responsibility for everybody to understand what we expect of our military — because when push comes to shove, if we ever need them we will call on them and expect tremendous things from them. So I think it's really important that we sit and listen and help shoulder that burden of what it means to fight.

We have a wellness scholarship. It was made for the intent of using it with the Warrior Connection, a retreat for veterans that are suffering from PTSD, anxiety, depression, any of those sort of symptoms from their military experience or from military sexual assault. It's weeklong. Spouses can go for this too. We started with, "We'll pay the commitment fee; we'll pay for a tutor for two weeks before the retreat and two weeks after. Give you time to get ahead, then give you time to catch up at the end."

Now the scholarship doesn't have to be just for the Warrior Connection. Anything a student would like to use it for, in terms of improving their own wellness, we'd like to follow up with that. Because if we make this available, they can really help themselves. I've helped students get food, housing. If they don't have to think about that stuff, they're going to be much more likely to succeed in this world.

Jack Anderson

A former CCV assistant academic dean, Jack taught courses at the Morrisville academic center from 2006 to 2017. He submitted this recollection to the online "CCV Stories," where it was published on August 7, 2013.

I could cite many success stories that would document students' change and growth. But the one story that I like the best is about Nate, an Iraq veteran who came to my Dimensions class with some PTSD and certainly a no-nonsense, outspoken and fairly entrenched approach to everything. Nate laid it all out, and in language that was more fitting for an angry pirate. It even encouraged some of the other male students to think they could get away with it too, despite my constant reminder that such language was not appropriate anywhere and especially in college classrooms. Nate got better, but still needed reminding about his choice of adjectives.

Nate showed up in my class the next semester, and I was glad of it. We spoke at the beginning of the class about using appropriate language in class, and he said he'd give it his best try. He made it through the entire class without one swear word. On the last day, we had a potluck lunch and enjoyed the last opportunity to socialize as a class, and Nate hung back to help clean up. He said after we cleaned up, "Did you notice that I didn't fucking swear once during your class?" I responded, "Yes, I did and that is just one example of your growth here."

The last I heard about Nate was he enrolled in the nursing program at Norwich University. It is my observation about students, if you can visibly see some growth in them, you know they are open-minded enough to [keep] learning new and even complicated things.

> **From the college's 2022 accreditation self-study:**
>
> Once largely ignored by the larger higher education, governmental, and business communities, CCV now enjoys an extensive network of partners and relationships. CCV is regularly invited to "sit at the table" to explore, collaborate, engage in shared problem solving, pursue funding opportunities, and partner to get new programs up and running....
>
> Similarly, partnerships have allowed CCV to make progress in its mission of providing the most affordable tuition possible for students. This has been a continual challenge for CCV. Historically, Vermont has funded K-12 education at one of the highest levels in the nation, while ranking last or near-last in support for public higher education. These policies made CCV ... highly tuition dependent. CCV grew to become one of the most expensive community colleges in the nation, while at the same time remaining the most affordable college in the state.
>
> For decades, CCV has chipped away at the problem of affordability by being frugal, creative, and conservative in budgeting. As a top priority, CCV has held tuition within range of the Pell federal grant.... A key funding partner established the Endowment for Life Gap Grants, providing just-in-time grants to help students pay for textbooks or meet basic needs for food, transportation, and child care. These grants are an unprecedented, highly flexible resource for CCV students that can make the difference between staying in school and dropping out.

Making the difference: The impacts of giving

When Laura Dailey came back to college in her late thirties, aiming to finish her associate degree, she took on several part-time work-study jobs to make the finances work. "One night after work her vehicle broke down, leaving Laura unsure how she could continue both work and school without transportation," said the college's 2020 *Donor Gratitude*

Report. "Thanks to a Life Gap grant, her vehicle was fixed, and she was able to continue toward her goals."

After Laura took her degree in accounting in 2020, CCV hired her full-time to join its Northern Lights program, which provides training, career advising, technical assistance and support for Vermont early childhood professionals.

"College has opened doors for me to a better life," Laura said. "My journey has and will continue to inspire others around me."

A gift from private donors enabled CCV to create its Life Gap Fund in 2017. "Whether it's the internet bill, new tires to pass inspection, or simply an expensive textbook, Life Gap grants help students overcome financial hurdles that get in the way of school," said the gratitude report. "Since its inception, Life Gap has helped 1,525 students stay in school."

Donor support has also enabled the college to gradually build up a modest endowment. And for a community college, that's not an easy achievement.

"Graduates tend to donate to the schools that handed them a degree, which is often the four-year college where they continued their education," wrote Sarah Earle in a 2019 *Valley News* article, "Community College of Vermont Focuses on Building an Endowment." "As a result, community colleges lack the endowments, which provide investment income to support their programs, that many four-year colleges and universities have amassed.

"In recent years, however, Community College of Vermont has gotten in the game. The school ... has built up its endowment to about $2.2 million over the past two years. Compared with Dartmouth College, which boasts an endowment of $5.7 billion, that's pocket change.... But CCV administrators say the endowments, which go primarily toward student scholarships, have a big impact.

"'Small amounts of money can make a huge difference to students,' CCV President Joyce Judy said in a telephone interview," the paper reported. "...CCV's Endowment for Student Success, its first and by far its largest endowment fund, was established 20 years ago by a $25,000 gift from former Vermont State Colleges trustee Jan Gillette.... The fund now contains about $1.1 million and will provide $50,000 in scholarships in 2020."

Support from individual and organized philanthropies has done more than fund scholarships: It has also helped the college continue to innovate, finding new and expanding ways to connect Vermonters with college and help them succeed.

"I have to give full credit to philanthropists in the state," said Judy. "The McClure Foundation has been a huge partner with us; they've just been right there with us. They will let us try some things and fund them. Sometimes those things don't work, but our goal is always, help us try. If it's of enough value, the college has to figure out how to fund it. I often think of them as the R&D of what we have.

"Dan Smith at the Vermont Community Foundation has been incredibly helpful, in terms of matching philanthropists who are interested in access with CCV," said the president. "Patricia Fontaine came to us through the Community Foundation: She has provided support to be able to expand our Learning Centers, for example, and our peer mentoring program. There are a number of philanthropists who have come to us through the Community Foundation."

Dan Smith

Dan is president and CEO of the Vermont Community Foundation.
We organized at the Community Foundation in 2017 or so around the idea of closing the opportunity gap that exists in Vermont. The opportunity gap is really the systems and structures and conditions that hold people in Vermont back by virtue of where they're born, what their racial or ethnic background is, or what the family background is.

CCV and the community colleges nationally are a silver bullet when it comes to economic mobility. They're essentially low-cost or low-tuition points of access and support for people who have historically been unlikely to continue their education after high school. Thirty years ago, forty years ago, you had a shot at being economically self-sufficient without a college degree; in the twenty-first century, that's simply not an option. So when you think about economic security and economic mobility, the key challenge is figuring out how to get people, from families who are not economically mobile, access to the skills and knowledge and tools to be economically self-sufficient. Community college is the best mechanism in Vermont.

When it comes to funders, I can articulate almost anything into a recommendation to fund CCV. Is it poverty, is it economic resilience of single parents, is it rural economic development? The CCV academic centers are distributed in places where the underlying economy can use a jump start. Is the [funder's] interest in helping people coming out of corrections? CCV ran a philanthropically funded, excellent partnership with [Vermont] Corrections, getting people college credits so they can come out with some focus and a sense of potential. Is it disaffection of youth, is it youth development? Dual enrollment and Early College are incredible programs to support young people who are struggling in their own high schools, in those social and cultural environments.

So there are very few problems for which community college, and in particular CCV, is not a component of the solutions on which the state would be well-advised to rely more heavily.

Workforce education: Innovating for opportunity

Ian Boyd

Ian is a coordinator of student advising in Winooski.

In the crash of '08 and '09, I was seeing dozens and dozens of students who were recently laid off, who needed to retool and retrain. That was a wave of students responding to the situation we all found ourselves in. In the past five or six years, I've been talking with students more and more about technology and health care careers. I think largely that is based on the way the economy is driven and the needs of all employers. You need some basic level of tech skills, and every year that's becoming more the case. CCV has retooled our programs and courses to meet that need.

INVENTING THE FUTURE

> There's a sense of urgency from students — which I guess was always there, but I feel like it's more pronounced now. They really want coursework to be available at times that they need it to be available. They want to complete their degree very fast, and they're more results driven: What will I get out of this?
>
> We've designed some Flex courses, which allow students to complete them at their own pace, whether slower or faster. We have stackable programs. I really ask students to take it one step at a time — break up their ultimate goal into smaller steps, encouraging them to utilize the resources that CCV has.

"In a world of accelerating change, about 100,000 Vermonters between the ages of 25 and 64 have a high school degree/equivalency, but no college degree," noted CCV's 2018 Strategic Plan. "For many of them, postsecondary credentials that deliver on the promise of relevancy, expediency, access, and value will be the key to employability.

"... A growing share of non-traditional students will look to us for easy entrance/exit points and workforce credentials acquired through microcertification courses," the plan predicted. "Meeting this market demand will require us to rethink the traditional college classroom experience."

The very first courses CCV offered in 1971 included typing, cosmetology and something called the "Career Opportunity Program." By the mid-'70s, more than a third of students listed "the desire to acquire job-related skills as their primary reason for attending," said *Wampum*, CCV's '70s-era first guide for instructors. The college responded by expanding its array of skill-building courses, from accounting to welding. Many of those were not part of degree programs; instead, completion earned a certificate that could be shown to a current or prospective employer.

In the early '90s under Mike Holland's three-year presidency, the college greatly expanded its programs and employer partnerships in workforce development and job-related training. "From a few clients in 1986, TOP [the college's Training Opportunities Program] has expanded its customer base to over a hundred businesses today," Holland reported to the Vermont State Colleges Board in 1992.

"CCV over the years has had different waves of looking at how to help businesses," said Tiffany Walker, who began coordinating these efforts in 2008. "There was a time frame when every staff member had a group of businesses. They visited them, and that's how it worked for a while. There were different programs in helping businesses connect to CCV, so their people could take classes. If somebody had interest in the community and expertise [to teach the subject], then we did that."

From the mid-1990s to the mid-2000s, as the college focused on building its academic strength and reputation — and developed articulation agreements with dozens of bachelor's degree-granting institutions that would now accept student transfers and CCV credits — "there was a little bit of a lean away from workforce education," noted Walker, who joined the Rutland center in 2006 as an academic coordinator.

Tiffany Walker with her daughter Hannah Lattuca at Hannah's CCV graduation in 2019. "I had the absolute joy of handing the diploma to her," Walker said.

"After about fifteen months, I told Tim I wanted to do something for the whole college. He invited me for pancakes one Sunday morning and said, 'I have an idea. I'd really like for you to head up a new venture in workforce education.'

"I thought, I would love to give that a try."

'Pieces of innovative learning'

Walker was paired for the new effort with another coordinator, Bill Morison in Newport, who had experience working in business. "Bill and I just went for it," she said. "Tim let us be creative in figuring things out. We visited businesses and tried to understand the landscape of the state, what were the needs, asking economic people to tell us what they were seeing in what was coming for Vermont.

"There was a level of basic skills that people didn't seem to have, that they needed," said Walker, who is now senior director of workforce education. "Businesses would tell us over and over: 'This is what we're struggling with. These are the skills people need: basic computer skills, an understanding of computers, things like that.' Math was a big part of it, and the soft skills: timeliness, email etiquette, interviewing skills."

Late in the first decade of the 2000s, CCV developed a Governor's Career Readiness Certificate, which could be paired with the ACT's National Career Readiness Certificate. The latter focused on harder job skills, such as math and reading for information. To complement it, the free ten-week certificate course that CCV built with the state Department of Labor "took on the computer skills and the soft skills people seemed to be needing," Walker said.

"We started with companies like Energizer and Green Mountain Coffee Roasters," she said. Both firms accepted the career readiness certificates. CCV worked with them to design ways of enabling people to fill gaps in the skills the company needed.

"Those early years, for us, were a lot of very individualized work with specific businesses like Energizer and GMCR [later Keurig], to figure out what would work best for the pipeline of new workers," she said.

In spring 2011, CCV and Vermont Tech launched Vermont Corporate College, a joint venture "for people struggling with the next step," Morison told the news site *VTDigger.com*. The venture's services "include needs assessment, training design and execution, and customized degree programs," the site reported.

A turning point came in fall 2011. The college was awarded a three-year, $2.5 million grant from the U.S. Department of Labor to support "trade adjustment" programs for workers who had lost jobs and needed new skills. With that grant and a second in 2014 from the same Department of Labor initiative, cumbersomely called TACCCT (Trade Adjustment Assistance Community College Career Training), CCV aimed its efforts at *preventing* trade adjustment — building the skills people needed to keep their jobs and rise in their careers.

Said Walker, "That let us start changing from a focus on 'What does an individual Vermont business need,' to 'Can we bring one program to the state that can help all manufacturers?'" CCV soon unveiled its Certified Production Technician (CPT) program, which builds manufacturing production skills for four certifications — in safety, processes and production, measurement, and maintenance.

"Since 2015, nearly 400 Vermonters have participated in the CPT trainings," Joyce Judy wrote in 2019. "Between 2015 and 2018, those who completed the CPT program have seen an average wage increase of $5,798 after one year."

"This is now the state's number-one requested entry-level manufacturing certification," Walker added.

The program shifted to all-online delivery during the Covid pandemic in 2020–2022. That allowed the instructor, an engineer in Morrisville, to work with a combined cohort of students from two different firms: the sock maker Darn Tough in Northfield and the outdoor outfitter Orvis in Manchester.

CPT training in 2023 "has multiple pieces of innovative learning in it," Walker said. "It's credentialed, and it's embedded in apprenticeship, which is a huge piece of what we do now. *Earn and learn* is our new way of working with businesses."

A new federal grant in 2018 enabled the college to expand its apprenticeship offerings beyond the building-trade fields — plumbing, electrical, and so on — in which this means of skill building had long been used. "We wanted to show Vermont employers that you can apprentice in other areas," Walker said.

'It's a huge stepping stone'

As Vermont hospitals struggled with a deepening shortage of nurses and other allied health professionals, CCV began working in 2016 with Brattleboro Memorial Hospital (BMH) on a new approach to making it more affordable and practical to train for those careers.

The college called this the College to Career Pathway, and the initial focus here has been on medical assisting.

"At a place like BMH, medical assistants are widely used," Walker explained. "It's a huge stepping stone; a lot of people go on to be nurses, or they pick other career paths within the medical field. We sat down with the head of the hospital, Joyce [Judy] and the rest of us, and said, 'What do people need in order to do this job?'

"We took five courses and put them into one semester, which meant that people were going to school full-time. We weren't sure if people would be able to do that, but we had a full class immediately. The students got a scholarship, and after fifteen weeks of instruction, they would have employment at BMH. Basically, it was the hospital taking your employee tuition benefit that you would have earned five years from now, and giving it to you up front — which was a really innovative way of hiring."

In that first class, "a lot of the students were women who'd been working at convenience stores and places like that," Walker said, "and in fifteen weeks they had white coats on and were working in the hospital. We went to the cake ceremony to congratulate them, and HR was there handing them their assignments. It was just so powerful to watch that happen."

"Since 2018," said the college's 2022 accreditation self-study, "CCV has established three new registered apprenticeships and one new pre-apprenticeship: medical assisting, manufacturing production technician, and pharmacy technician, plus an LNA-LPN [license nursing assistant to licensed practical nurse] pre-apprenticeship to apprenticeship program."

Among those programs, the college has been partnering since 2019 in St. Albans with Vermont Technical College and Northwestern Medical Center. Students can earn CCV's Allied Health Certificate, then shift into Vermont Tech's LPN or RN degree programs. In Berlin, a similar collaboration with Vermont Tech and Central Vermont Medical Center allows hospital employees who are licensed nursing assistants to stay at their jobs while taking courses to become licensed practical nurses.

The allied health "pre-apprenticeship program," preparing students for LPN courses and apprenticeship at Vermont Tech (now part of Vermont State University), has become CCV's largest certificate program. In fall 2020, it accounted for 47 percent of all students enrolled to earn certificates, attesting to new, career-focused skills and knowledge.

'I have been moving mountains'

India Martin was in a serious auto accident in 2005. Her best friend died, and she spent four months in a wheelchair. "I remember the medical staff — the compassion, empathy and knowledge that came with the treatment and care they gave me," she wrote years later. "After that, I knew I wanted to help people the way they helped me. I want to be that support, that comfort, that someone needs during a difficult time."

India Martin

She became a licensed nursing assistant. Then she had four children, "so that kind of pushed everything out the window." Martin was a working mom with a couple of jobs in Brattleboro when, one hot summer day, she decided, "I want to go back to school."

She enrolled in CCV's Clinical Medical Assisting certificate program, and got a scholarship through Brattleboro Memorial Hospital, the college's program partner. Interviewed as she completed an introductory course in medical assisting that prepared her for a summer internship at the hospital, Martin said she had decided to continue beyond the certificate — to work toward a Health Science associate degree, and to become a nurse.

"I want to be an advocate for women, especially women of color," she wrote in a "statement of purpose" for her medical assisting course. "Growing up in a small town in Vermont, I didn't see many people who look like me, especially doctors and other medical staff. Later, learning that black women's maternal mortality rate is two or three times higher than our counterparts shocked me." Knowing, too, that "our demographic would experience more bias in the healthcare system also inspires me to want to make a difference."

In the medical assisting class, Martin and fourteen fellow students learned basic health care skills: taking vital signs, drawing blood, performing an EKG, and more. Other courses in the certificate program cover human biology, anatomy and physiology, medical terminology, pharmacology, and a general introduction to health care.

The college brings in financial aid from several sources for students in the certificate program. "The hospital pays for some cohorts and some classes within some cohorts," said Tiffany Walker, workforce program director. "We also have an apprenticeship grant and are able to pay for registered apprentices." All this is typical of CCV's workforce education, she said: "We do a braided funding model, so we put together funding sources when they are needed."

On the last day of their class with instructor Ryn Gluckman, R.N., several of Martin's classmates also shared their stories. Claire Betit, a grandmother, had worked for thirty years in an industrial cotton bleachery — "we didn't make anything, we just washed cotton" — and had volunteered with her local rescue service in Jacksonville, Vermont. "I'd often thought about doing medical assisting as a retirement career," she said. "So that's what I'm doing."

Makayla Narushof of Burlington had been taking courses for two years at CCV Winooski and online. She needed Clinical Medical Assisting to graduate, so for two and a half weeks (this was a "super-accelerated" version of the typical seven-week class), she drove to the class from Burlington to Brattleboro, three-plus hours each way.

"I definitely missed a couple of classes," she said. "But I'm proud of myself for holding myself accountable, and being here."

Hayley Slayton had been driving to the Brattleboro classes from her home in Springfield, where she was working full-time as a receptionist in a doctor's office. "My work started to offer a professional development program through the state of Vermont and CCV and our hospital system," she said. "I applied and got in; the state provided grants so tuition would be covered and some textbook expenses as well."

Slayton's great-grandfather was a physician who helped found what is now Central Vermont Medical Center in Berlin. She wants to become a doctor, too.

"I've been taking one class at a time, trying to pace it so I don't get overwhelmed," she said. "I'm getting trained on the clinical side by

▶

the nurses I work with, and I have a great support system. My goal is to get my associate's here, then maybe transfer to Castleton for their health science program. Then I want to go to either UVM Medical School or Dartmouth Medical School. Either of those would be wonderful."

The next week, India Martin and several of her classmates would begin their BMH internship with a two-week rotation. After that, she said, they would be placed "where they need you, what you like — just where you fit."

"I have been moving mountains," Martin wrote in her statement of purpose, "and I haven't been this proud of myself in a long time. This semester I made the dean's list, and I was over the moon. This journey will not be quick or easy, and I'm OK with that. I trust this process and myself."

After completing CCV's certificate program, India went to work at Brattleboro Memorial Hospital's Four Seasons OB/GYN & Midwifery practice, as a certified medical assistant.

•••

Affirming knowledge and pointing up paths

"I like to say that CCV is one institution that never gives up," said Scott Giles, president of the Vermont Student Assistance Corp. He summed up the college's approach: "We'll try and reach you as a traditional-age student, and get you into this affordable pathway that will give you a credential that will lead to a good livable wage. But we are still available to you four years from now, ten years from now, or fifteen years from now.

"The other area that I think is going to be equally revolutionary is the [college's] expansion of what we call stackable credentials," he said. "Each of those paths recognizes the credential that preceded it. It's affirming what you know — not feeling, as an adult with some experience and some knowledge, that I'm being asked by my institution to start over."

Since 2018 — building on its longstanding Assessment of Prior Learning courses, in which students develop a portfolio that demonstrates for credit the college-level learning they've acquired through work and other experience — CCV has developed twelve "competency-based pathways," or CBPs. These allow students "to earn credit for courses based on their college-level learning achieved through life experience," said the 2022 self-study. "CBPs include Introduction to Business, Computerized Accounting, Principles of Management, Principles of Marketing, Spreadsheets, and Professional Field Experience, plus six options for early childhood courses."

"As we move toward stackable credentials," Giles reflected, "the model doesn't have to be all-or-nothing, 'I pursue a certificate or I pursue a degree.' A degree is expensive, and what if I don't really know what I want to do? What if I get a job and don't like it? A stackability model allows me to progress at my own pace, my own comfort level, and my own career goals."

Early in the 2010s the college produced *College and Career Guide*, a color publication aimed at high schoolers and built on a model from Arizona that Barbara Benedict, president of the McClure Foundation that funded the project, had admired.

With concise text, brief profiles of students and graduates, and key information graphically displayed, the publication showed how students could balance college costs with financial aid, how they could get credit for prior learning, and how they could earn workforce readiness credentials. A spreadsheet-style display, "Choose Your Path," showed each area of study at CCV, from Accounting to Web Site Design: the featured courses, what they prepared you for, and what you could expect to earn in that field in Vermont.

"It had a lot of good information," Benedict said. "We funded the first *College and Career Guide* in 2012. There were a couple of issues after that, and then the information all went online."

'We'll develop it and do it'

"We work with businesses, or on a large grant, to get cohorts of people together in a certain area," Walker said in 2022. "When a business says, 'I need this course to help my people,' we'll develop that and do it.

"We help employers figure it out by listening to them. What kind of skill set do you need? Here's a credential. Somebody will come to us and say, 'Do you do this, or do you have this?' If we don't, we'll connect them. We've helped people get grant funding; businesses will say, 'We don't know how to go about this,' and we'll help with that.

"We have community breakfasts where we bring people together, in a certain industry or across industries, and let those conversations happen. At one point here in Rutland, we had Adecco, the large temp agency, and GE downstairs doing one of our community events, and a student came walking in. She said, 'I just lost my job, and I'm probably going to have to leave school because I can't afford to stay.' We said, 'Do you want to come downstairs and talk to the people there?' She went downstairs, and by the time she left she had a job again.

"It's an exciting department to be in," Walker concluded. "We're juggling so many things at any given time; we constantly have an extremely large project plan, and we go through that every week to see where we are and what needs to be done. It's just really exciting."

Shining a light: College in a correctional center

"When somebody said there were college courses in jail, I didn't believe it," Scott Barber said.

It was 2017. He was incarcerated at the Northern State Correctional Facility in Newport and he signed up for classes that CCV, working with the Vermont Department of Corrections, had just begun to offer at the facility.

"What happened for me, stepping into a classroom, is that I was welcomed," Barber said. "I was no longer an inmate, I was a human being looking for an education."

CCV's Newport classes were a pilot project in offering college courses within a correctional center. At a roundtable discussion about the project with then U.S. Representative (now U.S. Senator) Peter Welch of Vermont in 2021, Barber and two fellow students shared their experience with what came to be called ReSet VT.

"Being able to go to CCV made me able to go back to the functioning person in society that I was," said Walter Clark. "That label gave me some self-pride back." By 2021, Clark was taking three online CCV classes and was working toward an apprenticeship with an electrician.

"The way the CCV staff treats you ... they actually treat you like a person, like a student," said Sean Bailey, another Newport student, in an article on the Welch roundtable by CCV communications chief Katie Keszey. "I have been out for about four months now. I'm working full-time. And I'm ready to pursue an education."

The work that led to college courses in Vermont prisons began in 2016, when Joyce Judy and two other CCV administrators sat down with leaders of the state Agency of Human Services, Department of Corrections and Office of Economic Opportunity.

"It was about exploring scope for collaboration," said Heather Weinstein, the college's dean of students and strategic priorities. "What are our mutual goals, where are there overlapping populations that we serve, and how might we partner to better serve Vermonters?"

Ongoing conversations found a focus on bringing college to incarcerated Vermonters. The state's Community High School of Vermont has a program of courses within correctional centers, but there were no similar college-level opportunities.

"We started unpacking what the challenges might be to offering classes in Vermont," Weinstein said. "We started to recognize a path."

The stumbling block was money. How to fund this?

By chance, the McClure Foundation, which had been supporting CCV's work with high schoolers and veterans, once again reached out to the college. "They said, 'We'd like to invite you to apply for an additional funding opportunity. Think about what the foundation might support,'" Weinstein said.

The college wrote a proposal, and the foundation funded a two-year pilot in Newport. The first courses, delivered in fall 2017, were Dimensions of Self and Society and English Composition. Added the next spring were Effective Workplace Communication, Statistics, and Introduction to Psychology.

It's not uncommon for Vermonters to want to go into correctional centers to do good work, noted Dana Lesperance, head of the Community High School. But what CCV did, he said, was to "take the time to understand the setting and the folks you're dealing with.... And that's what made the difference."

Heather Weinstein was herself among the instructors in the pilot.

"I saw such a desire to have an opportunity to contribute to their communities," she said. "I heard so often that they wanted to make their families proud. It was an opportunity for them to redefine themselves, to think about themselves differently. You'd assign a reading of chapters one and two, and you'd come back and they'd have read the whole book."

Before the Covid pandemic forced it to pause in 2020, ReSetVT delivered twelve in-person classes, plus academic coaching and career-preparation advising, to a total of one hundred students at the Newport facility.

The program found an ongoing source of support in 2020, when CCV became one of three New England institutions named a Second Chance Pell School by the U.S. Department of Education. Second Chance Pell allows college students who are incarcerated to qualify for federal Pell Grants. Then in 2022, U.S. Senator Bernie Sanders of Vermont secured a $4.5 million Department of Justice grant for CCV that "will bring postsecondary educational opportunities to all six Vermont correctional facilities," Weinstein said.

"The project will provide staffing, funding for contracted courses and tuition, education supplies and technological infrastructure to each facility," she said. "Most importantly, it will help CCV and Vermont Department of Corrections develop a deliberate process of relationship-building at each correctional facility, identifying the best programmatic options to address the barrier particular to each prison." The project will also, she said, enable CCV and Corrections to work together on supporting inmates in continuing their education after release, and will enable CCV to build the capacity of prison staffs to support higher education.

"Now we have a funding source to support this program," Joyce Judy noted. "But we would never have been able to apply if the McClure Foundation hadn't worked with us to be able to prove the concept."

"I just want to use the word *gratitude*," former inmate Scott Barber summed up in the conversation with Rep. Welch. "I can't be grateful enough for the experience I had, that shined a light in a very dark place."

INVENTING THE FUTURE

Higher wages and job security: The faculty unionizes

When he was CCV's first director of special services from 1980 to 1987, Roger Cranse led the team that created the integrative Dimensions of Learning course for first-year students. He returned to teach at the college in 2004. After other instructors organized a vote in 2006 over whether to join a union, "I probably voted against it, if I voted at all," Cranse said. "I didn't think it would do much good."

That 2006 union ballot was the first for CCV instructors, and it failed by a wide margin. But by early 2016, faculty members were again working with the American Federation of Teachers (AFT) to organize for a new vote.

This time, Cranse joined the leadership team for the union campaign.

"I would say our campaign was more organized," he said. "I remember meeting with people and talking it up in the faculty lounge, having coffee with people to get them to vote. Others were doing it too."

He also wrote and sent out a "Dear CCV Colleagues" letter.

"After 46 years (the College was founded in 1970)," Cranse wrote, "CCV faculty still work, like the longshoremen in 'On the Waterfront,' in a 'shape-up' system. We're hired semester by semester at the discretion or whim of the coordinators.... Further, we're all paid the same, regardless of seniority. A brand new hire gets the same pay as a teacher who's been with the college for, say, ten or twenty years.

"I'm not much of a joiner ... but it's really clear to me that we need a good, solid union contract."

By 2016, pay for CCV's part-time instructors had fallen well below what adjunct faculty were earning at the other Vermont state colleges. "For me it was a part-time job," Cranse said. "I like teaching, and I was making some money. But a lot of people put their living together doing this."

One of those was Jennifer Elizabeth Brunton. A Columbia University Ph.D. who had been teaching for eight years at CCV Brattleboro, Brunton decided in autumn 2016 that she had had enough. She laid out her reasons in a long, intense open letter to the CCV administration that was posted in October on the news website *VTDigger.com*. Here are excerpts:

Jennifer Brunton

I am a passionate, engaging, committed, caring, knowledgeable, extremely hard-working teacher. I bring many years of teaching experience at Columbia and Barnard to my teaching at CCV, and I offer CCV students the exact same high-quality learning experience that I offered students at those expensive, exclusive schools. In fact, because teaching at a community college was always my dream job, and because I believe community college students deserve every advantage their more privileged peers receive, I have tried even harder at CCV than in my prior work.

... I really loved my first few years of teaching at CCV. First, I knew I was making a huge difference in students' lives. I relished introducing students to new ideas, and I always told them — from my own experience — that they were just as worthy as students at fancier colleges (several of my students indeed continued on to places like Smith and Marlboro colleges).... I was a single mother, but I had some savings, and the reality of my earnings for the job I labored so hard for took a while to sink in. For a few years, I puttered along, doing my best — and seeing my savings disappear. I began to worry about such matters as heating my house and clothing my children. But I continued to do my best at CCV.

... What does it mean to "do one's best" as a faculty member? In order to actually do a good job, worthy of the needs of our students, each three-hour class takes a bare minimum of 10 to 12 hours of prep time. That's not counting additional research to stay up-to-date in our fields, or the barrage of emails, texts, notes, and calls we faculty must answer — daily, and ideally, "within 24 hours" — from students every week. These 10–12 prep hours don't necessarily include office hours — or meetings, such as the many I've had with students when reporting plagiarism, or with coordinators to discuss academic and behavioral issues.... Also, they don't include the additional five to 10 hours — weekly! — of preparation needed the first time one teaches a class. To do a really great job of teaching, as students deserve, requires so much more than is recognized or recompensed at CCV.

If we work 15 hours a week (12 hours of preparation, three of teaching) for 15 weeks at the going pay rate, we make about $16/hour. Remember, this estimate is a minimum one for a class one has taught before — and the hourly wage is calculated BEFORE taxes and Social Security are taken out, with no other benefits included WHATSOEVER. If pre-semester course prep (crafting syllabi, handouts, and grading rubrics; building online platforms in Moodle and Blackboard) and the required midterm and final narrative grades are added into this equation (a minimum of 20–30 hours), which seems reasonable, the hourly wage descends still more.... We community college teachers thus take on challenges that faculty at other institutions either rarely encounter or navigate through extensive institutional support, yet we earn much, much less.

... There are many worthy reasons to teach at CCV for those who can afford to do so. We stay because we desperately want to use the professional credentials we've sacrificed so much to obtain, and to serve our students, because we believe in community education, and some, the lucky ones, stay because they have other sources of income. Most of us, however, feed ourselves and our families by the grace of the SNAP program (food stamps) and rely on Medicaid for health insurance.... How is it possible that those of us who are on the front line with students on a daily basis, actually teaching them — which I at least think is the purpose of CCV — are "rewarded" in this way?

... I am sure you are aware that CCV faculty are trying to unionize. I applaud my colleagues' intentions and actions, and have been involved in this effort, but cannot sacrifice my family to poverty any longer while hoping against hope for change.... I do not presume to speak for every faculty member, but you should know my experience is similar to that of many, many faculty at CCV who believe that being a good teacher should be more valued and better-recompensed by your administration.

Currently a freelance editor and writer, and speaker about neurodiversity, Dr. Brunton is the co-author of The #Actually Autistic Guide to Advocacy *(London: Jessica Kingsley Publishers, 2022).*

KIND OF A MIRACLE

'A very exciting moment for faculty'

On June 30, 2017, the CCV faculty filed a petition signed by a majority of its 539 members, asking the Vermont Labor Relations Board for a vote on joining the Vermont State Colleges Faculty Federation, AFT Local 3180. Casting their ballots by mail over a three-week period in the fall, this time 300 CCV instructors voted yes. Just 132 voted no.

"This is a very exciting moment for faculty," said instructor Emily Casey, quoted in a college news release on October 17, 2017. "We have been organizing our union for years."

As 2018 began, the new union got ready to open contract negotiations with the Vermont State Colleges administration. "We seek improved job security, benefits and an institutional culture that recognizes faculty expertise as essential to the core mission of the college," wrote Elisabeth Lehr, lead negotiator for the faculty.

By May 2018, the two sides had met nine times. The union declared an impasse, and the two sides engaged a mediator. About fifty people, many of them CCV teachers, picketed in a heavy rain outside the offices of the state college system.

"Part-time faculty members are asking for higher wages and job security," reported *VTDigger*'s Emily Neubauer. CCV's instructor pay, she wrote, was now roughly 45 percent below that received by adjunct faculty at the residential state colleges. And "since instructors are currently neither salaried nor permanent, union spokesperson Emily Casey said each year instructors do not know if they will be asked back and many have two or three jobs because of the inconsistent nature of the job."

In June, the college and the union finally reached agreement. "The three-year contract ... provides for a pay increase and ensures that faculty with seniority teach at least one course per semester," *VTDigger* reported. It quoted Casey: "We've created a first step, or a first level, of job security that is a really good spot to build off of."

"I think that I need to underscore how important faculty and staff are," Joyce Judy told the news site. "So I am thrilled to have this behind us."

Underneath, a much larger issue

Two years after the first union contract was signed, "it has redefined some of how we work with faculty," President Judy said in late 2021. "It defines who you have to offer courses to, and it pretty strongly leans towards seniority. There are other factors that are considered in hiring; but you know, we offer 850 classes, and now it's very defined.... Based on how many courses they've taught and how many years, [faculty] are in different tiers. The contract spells out, 'You have to do this for people in tier three, and tier two and tier one.'"

"Instead of the flat pay for everybody," Roger Cranse explained, "we have three pay grades, and those are based on seniority. Every year there is a guaranteed pay increase, and for people in pay grades two or three, you're guaranteed a course. There's a schedule for requesting courses and a schedule for offering. That's all formalized."

Instructors, he added, "are still hired semester by semester; there's no yearlong contract, but there are criteria for hiring: experience, student evaluations, diversity. Then there's sick leave, mileage reimbursement for going to college-sponsored events — a lot of good stuff like that."

Underlying the faculty's move to unionize is an issue much larger than CCV itself.

As a portion of the total operating revenues of Vermont public higher education, state funding for Vermont's higher ed institutions declined from 40 percent in 1988 to 12 percent in 2018, while the share borne by families rose from 60 percent to about 78 percent, according to a 2021 report from the National Center for Higher Education Management Systems.

"The state of Vermont has not fully lived up to its promise to increase funding for its higher education system," union negotiator Lehr wrote in a January 2018 *VTDigger* commentary. The low level of state funding, she added, "financially pinches our institutions, our students, and our faculty.

"CCV students currently pay the country's highest community college tuition rate," Lehr noted. "... We believe that a strong union is the best path to increased state funding, which will ensure fair tuition for our students and fair wages for community college faculty."

Teaching and learning, through the pandemic and beyond

When Covid-19 invaded the nation in spring 2020, colleges and universities were forced abruptly into conducting all, or nearly all, of their classes online. For many across the nation, that challenge was akin to lurching from a standstill to full speed — but for CCV, it was more like shifting to a higher gear.

After online course signups surged to nearly 40 percent of its total enrollment in this century's first decade, the college had begun offering instructors a five-week training course in online teaching and had asked all faculty to work with its online course-management service: first Blackboard, then Moodle, now Canvas.

"It became business as usual," said Megan Tucker, administrative technology director. "It was just, 'This is how we do it,' right up until the pandemic."

"Even among our faculty who had never taught an online class," said Academic Dean Debby Stewart, "there were expectations for them to be using Canvas — doing their grades online and having their syllabus and other materials in there, so that if a student were sick or unable to get to class, they could see them. Fast-forward to Covid: All those pieces really helped us make a transition to where we had to move the entire learning community and all classes online."

When the pandemic struck in March 2020, 50 percent of the college's classes were online. Stewart wrote to instructors that a team of faculty and staff was "here to support you and answer any questions you may have as you move your class online." To its online resources for instructors, she said, the college had added "a page dedicated to Alternative Course Delivery, containing links to discipline-specific and general online teaching guidance and resources."

By the start of the fall semester, all but twenty-five of the college's seven hundred courses were being conducted remotely, in one of several fast-evolving forms.

"It was a big lift," Tucker said. "But it wasn't unbelievable."

> **From the college's 2022 accreditation self-study:**
>
> Amid the many dramatic events of the year 2020, CCV held a shortened celebration of its 50th anniversary, convened the nine standard committees to undertake the drafting of this self-study, and did the unthinkable — temporarily closed all 12 academic centers, transitioned staff to work from home, and moved all classes to a fully online format.
>
> CCV took a hard look at issues of diversity, equity, and inclusion, not just out in the world, but within its own community and in its policies, assumptions, and behaviors. CCV formed its first college-wide DEI task force to advance diversity, equity, and inclusion. Several groups and committees across the College were asked to identify at least one goal or initiative to advance equity within CCV, and the DEI task force was charged with supporting and coordinating these goals. Academic Council and its committees reviewed the College's curriculum through the lens of diversity, equity, and inclusion and implemented curricular changes to strengthen those perspectives.

Equity and flexibility

The pandemic made digital equity more of a pressing challenge to address, noted Jen Alberico, director of online teaching and learning.

"One thing we did was communicate to all the students where the hotspots were, where the free WiFi was, and making hot spots available through internet providers. We don't hand out free laptops; we can't do that. But often, when the offices were open, we let students come in and use our technology. We have computer labs that are always available.

"We also made sure we developed a digital equity statement so that students knew they weren't going to be left out because of these issues. We built that component into the [teaching online] training so that people are aware of the equity issues — if a student doesn't have a laptop or doesn't have WiFi. Or, this came up a lot: 'I'm in a family of five, we're all doing online learning right now, and we have one computer.' If these are issues for you, talk to somebody at the college who will attempt to solve them."

Up until the pandemic, CCV's approach to online coursework had been asynchronous: Students could choose when to log on to do their work and join in discussions, as long as they did so several times in a typical week. As courses that had been taught in person shifted now to online, instructors often adopted a synchronous approach, combining regular group Zoom sessions with online tasks.

"When we went mid-semester to all online, some faculty continued to hold classes at the same time, but maybe for a shorter period," Tucker said. "If it was a three-hour class, they might shorten it to an hour. They didn't want to drop students from that face-to-face contact. Synchronous evolved from that, and now we do quite a lot of it."

In 2018, the college received a McClure Foundation grant to develop flexible, self-paced online courses that led to digital workplace credentials. These Flex courses — more than twenty-five of them in spring 2021 — replace weekly participation requirements with modules that students complete at their own pace during a semester. During the pandemic, Flex courses "offered the perfect solution for unemployed Vermonters wanting to pivot to a new career when the State provided Coronavirus Relief Funds for free training," said a 2020 college publication.

CCV also now offers accelerated courses, which range from weeklong in-person to seven-week online courses, for which students do significant work both before and after the course is delivered.

"The College has developed several resources to assist faculty and coordinators of teaching and learning (CTLs) in assuring the quality of academic programming and delivery across all formats," said the 2022 accreditation self-study. "Examples include Best Practices in Online Teaching, Course Design Rubric, and Faculty Guide for Flex Courses. A Canvas site was also created to support synchronous course faculty."

INVENTING THE FUTURE

Academics: The ongoing evolution

As they have throughout CCV's history, academics at the college continue to evolve in other significant ways:

Health science and technology have become the most popular degree programs. First offered in fall 2019, health science grew in a single year, fall 2019 to fall 2020, from 5 percent to 11 percent of all degree-seeking students. The most popular certificate, with 47 percent of certificate enrollment in fall 2020, is allied health preparation, whose students prepare for entry into Vermont Technical College's licensed practical nursing program. Other popular certificate programs include medical billing and coding, clinical medical assisting, childcare and bookkeeping.

"Over the last decade, CCV has shifted its traditional academic programs to a model that focuses on meta-majors designed around career clusters," said the 2022 self-study. "The new approach balances both structure and flexibility, allowing students within a cluster area to align their course work with their goals without losing momentum toward the completion of a credential or degree. The approach also addresses the demands of career paths within Vermont, which often require generalization rather than specialization due to the rural nature of the state."

The core intent, said Academic Dean Stewart, is "giving students the most value for their educational dollar. That's really the way we think about this: What is going to provide students with the greatest amount of value for their educational dollars. That's how we design a lot of these pieces now, around that."

"A re-imagined curriculum moves from programmatic silos to a model of meta-majors that offer students meaningful credentials within a variety of career clusters," the self-study said. "Meta-majors provide the flexibility students need for smooth transfer along CCV's many 2+2 pathways and ensure students can complete their four-year degrees within 120 credits. The trend ... has been accompanied by the creation of short-term stackable certificate programs to meet immediate workforce needs, such as after-school and youth work, clinical medical assisting, cybersecurity fundamentals, funeral director, graphic design, and pharmacy technician."

Each year, from 4 percent to 10 percent of CCV's graduates secure some degree credit through the state college system's prior learning assessment programs, which the community college pioneered in the 1970s. Most CCV students who earn prior-learning credits build portfolios to demonstrate what they've learned, either through a one-credit "focused portfolio" course or a three-credit assessment of prior learning course. "The focused portfolio course has a 12-credit average award with a successful credit request rate of 90 percent," said the self-study. "The average award for the full portfolio course is 30 credits, with a 75 percent success rate."

Students often begin the portfolio courses "feeling not confident, feeling kind of bad about themselves, about their lives," said instructor Mary Hulette. "They haven't been able to get as far as they wanted to professionally because they keep bumping up against this barrier, they don't have a degree — but they know a lot of stuff. In the course, students absolutely come alive, realizing there is a lot they've learned in their lives. So that course to me has been a career highlight."

Students can also win assessment of prior learning credits through an examination or a "course challenge," in which faculty evaluate the student's learning against essential objectives for CCV courses.

Each CCV associate degree requires thirty-three credits of general education among its sixty total credits of college-level learning. In 2020 and 2021, faculty from the state college system worked to develop a new framework of seven content clusters, each with specified outcomes, including those that show learning in diversity, equity and inclusion. The VSC's Academic Council adopted the new general-ed framework in spring 2021.

Every degree student now participates in CCV's integrative "book-ends" of general education. Dimensions of Self and Society, the first-semester seminar that's now also required of certificate students, builds college-level skills in critical inquiry and analysis along with an exploration of career options. The capstone Seminar in Educational

Inquiry concludes each degree student's CCV experience. In it, "students explore interdisciplinary strategies of investigation, reflect on the knowledge and critical thinking skills they have gained in their educational career, and apply those skills to the holistic examination of ethical and substantive issues, problems, and themes," said the self-study.

Offered at CCV since the late 1980s, Dimensions became a graduation requirement in 2008. Through the years a key piece for most classes has been reading and discussing "The Allegory of the Cave" from Plato's *Republic*.

Once his students had read the allegory, instructor Jack Anderson said he would ask them, "So what?"

"They'd always say, 'What do you mean so what?'"

"'Well, how is that relevant to you?'"

"You really hope that people are going to grab hold of this stuff and grow from it," he said. "I always felt not so much as a teacher but as a learning facilitator — that you provide information to people, let them think about it, talk about it, write about it."

Data from 2015 showed that 46 percent of students who had recently taken Dimensions in the fall semester were still enrolled at CCV the next fall, compared to 31 percent who had not taken the course. College data continues to support what has become known as the "Dimensions effect."

The Seminar in Educational Inquiry "is an opportunity for community college students to take a liberal arts seminar," said instructor Abby Gelfer. A critical piece is each student's final paper, "not just for outcome assessment but to show the student can write and do critical thinking, research and an oral presentation," she said. The final paper is now part of a portfolio each student puts together.

In the process she sets out for her students, "first they give me their thesis statement and their sources; then they do an updated bibliography," Gelfer said. "Then they do a first draft, a peer-reviewed draft, and a final draft. So it's a lot."

Long central to the way CCV operates, the role of coordinator of academic services had grown to encompass an ever-wider array of tasks, from recruiting and supporting instructors to student advising and community outreach. "I and many others in leadership grew up with that — that's where we started," said President Judy. But as the college grew larger, the work of its now forty coordinators "just got bigger and bigger and bigger," she said.

So as part of a major staffing reorganization, in 2019 CCV split the coordinator position in two. Coordinators of student advising, or CSAs, now work with students to help them identify their academic and career goals, select programs, register for classes, and develop the skills they need. Each of the college's twenty-four CSAs works with about 220 degree and nondegree students. That's a large load, but it's still "well below the median of 441 students per advisor in community colleges" across the nation, said the 2022 self-study.

The college has also invested significantly in training for these coordinators, President Judy said, with the aim of "moving from an advising model to a coaching model, having students be far more in charge of their approach and their learning. It's a culture shift."

Coordinators of teaching and learning, or CTLs — sixteen of them at present, across CCV's academic centers — hire and supervise faculty. CTLs are "deployed regionally and according to their areas of expertise," said the self-study. "This ... was designed to address a longtime desire among CCV faculty for their hiring coordinator to have more knowledge in their discipline area."

The college began to offer short-term study abroad programs in 2003, with a trip to Ireland that focused on Irish folklore. In developing new opportunities, "we would find a class at CCV, or propose one that we thought would be popular" and would satisfy one or more degree requirements, said Marianne DiMascio, regional director at the Winooski center. After a semester spent completing that course, students then travel to the country of focus for a week to ten days, accompanied by instructors, for a focused period of study.

"We've gone to Belize for forest ecology. We did folklore in England; we did a history class in Greece," she said. "When students challenge themselves — and for some, it was getting on a plane; for some it was leaving their kids or their home for ten days, going into a new culture or a new country — they start to challenge themselves when they come back home in new and wonderful ways."

In numbers: CCV in 2023

- Classes offered in 12 locations statewide and online
- Associate degrees: 12; career certificates: 22
- Associate and/or certificate programs available 100 percent online: 30
- Awarded in spring 2021: 410 associate degrees; 177 career-focused certificates; 96 industry-recognized credentials
- 455 part-time faculty
- Most affordable college for Vermonters. In-state cost per credit: $280 (out-of-state rate: $560/credit)
- Classes offered days, evenings, weekends and online; average class size: 16
- Over 200 online, hybrid, accelerated and flexible-start courses each semester
- Students each year (three semesters): 10,239
- Vermonters: 94 percent
- Average age: 28
- Students in dual enrollment (taking courses for credit while still in high school): 2,010
- Female students: 72 percent
- Self-identified member of minority racial or ethnic group category: 15 percent
- Students seeking degrees: 60 percent
- Degree students with full- or part-time jobs: 79 percent
- Degree students enrolled part-time: 85 percent
- First generation in their family to attend college: 56 percent
- Degree students receiving a Pell Grant: 57 percent
- Portion who graduate with zero debt: 65 percent
- Graduates since 1973: 14,133
- Graduates in the Class of 2019 who reported being employed, continuing their education, or serving in the military within 6 months: 91 percent

Source: ccv.edu, based on fall 2023 semester numbers.

A college for tomorrow

In 2015, the Georgia Institute of Technology organized a commission on the future of higher education. It asked the panel's forty-eight members to imagine what a public university might look like in 2040 — and among the "many compelling ideas" they produced, wrote Arizona State University professor Jeffrey Selingo in the *Washington Post*, "three point to the possibility of a very different future for colleges and universities."

Here are those three ideas, as Selingo described them in his July 6, 2018 *Post* article, "The Future of Higher Education: Students for Life, Computer Advisors and Campuses Everywhere":

> *1. College for life, rather than just four years.*
>
> *The primary recommendation of the Georgia Tech report is that the university turn itself into a venue for lifelong learning that allows students to "associate rather than enroll." Such a system would provide easy entry and exit points into the university and imagines a future in which students take courses either online or face-to-face, often in shorter spurts over the course of a lifetime....*
>
> *2. A network of advisers and coaches for a career.*
>
> *If education never ends, Georgia Tech predicts, neither should the critical advising function that colleges provide to students. The commission outlines a scenario in which artificial intelligence and virtual tutors help advise students about selecting courses, navigating difficult classes, and finding the best career options....*
>
> *3. A distributed presence around the world.*
>
> *Colleges and universities operate campuses and require students to come to them. In the past couple of decades, online education has grown substantially, but for the most part, higher education is still about face-to-face interactions. Georgia Tech imagines a future in which the two worlds are blended....*

INVENTING THE FUTURE

If you replace "around the world" with "around the state" in their third prediction, Georgia Tech's forecasters could have been describing the Community College of Vermont.

Nor would they have been alone.

In a 2017 post on his blog Rethinking Higher Education, CCV's founding president, Peter Smith — who has authored several books that urge higher ed to reimagine itself for a new era — wrote that "the college of the future will be organized around the learner/user experience just as surely as traditional colleges were organized around teaching and the campus experience."

And through all of its changes, innovations and real-world accommodations over the last fifty years, CCV has held fast to that core idea: that it would shape itself to meet the needs of learners, rather than the other way around.

"When you think about the future of higher ed, it's not sitting and waiting for people to come to you," said current President Judy. "It's reaching out and providing pathways."

Over the years, she said, "we've had to find the balance between honoring [educational] tradition — doing that in the right way for students — and not being traditional. The focus is on student learning." Even as its classrooms have grown more age-diverse, she said, what has stayed consistent are the college's decentralized structure; its part-time faculty, made up largely of practitioners in their fields; and a flexible, outreaching responsiveness to Vermont's communities, students and employers.

"We are continually adapting to the evolving needs of Vermonters and our state," Judy wrote in a 2019 blog post.

In recent years and especially in response to the Covid pandemic, "we have diversified our course delivery models, which now include flexible, synchronous and accelerated options," she wrote in a 2020 post. "We are developing more short-term credentials that easily build toward certificates and degrees in high-demand fields such as manufacturing, child care and IT. We continue to work closely with businesses throughout the state to ensure CCV programs are aligned with employer needs."

"Something we've held true to, throughout, is that we've tried to make sure students were at the core of our decision-making,"

Judy reflected in an interview. "Sometimes we were more successful at that than others, but it's always on our mind."

"I think the future of higher education looks more like CCV than it does like traditional institutions," declared Tim Donovan, CCV's president from 2001 to 2009. "Number one, we've never assumed that going to school is the defining element in a student's life. You have to make college fit into *their* defining elements. Those might be geographic, they might be financial, they might be family, they might be work.

The late Burlington couple Alfred and Marguerite Couture had nine children — and five of them, Paul, Janice, James, Bernard and Gerald, have taught or worked at CCV, as has Paul's daughter Kimberly. The Couture family sponsored Room 406 at the Winooski academic center, where Janice, shown here, has served as a coordinator of academic services.

"Number two, education is not sequential. It isn't high school, then college, then career. Our federal [education] policy is the way it is because it was written by congressional staff who went to Middlebury, then went to work for their congressperson. Or law school. So that's their view of how you need to support colleges and universities, and it's just not the reality for a majority of students.

"Going to college is not sequential — and it *shouldn't* be sequential. That requires you to think about a whole bunch of things differently. You took this course four years ago, so that doesn't count any more? That's ridiculous! We need to be much more forgiving about how and when and where someone learned what they've been learning. Assessed prior learning should be a huge part of this: Yes, you learned that someplace. Let's value it.

"It's constantly asking yourself what's important and what isn't," he summed up. "That I think is why CCV has been, and continues to be, a directional beacon of some sort."

'As they go, so goes the country'

American higher education is, in general, struggling to cope with or adapt to a world of concerns — over high tuition costs and the burdens of student debt; over how to meet the needs of learners beyond traditional ages and outside traditional structures; over tightened budgets, declining enrollments, and a pool of potential students that seems, more and more, to be questioning whether college is really essential after all.

From 2004 to 2015, student loan debt "more than tripled, at an average annualized growth rate of about 13% per year," said a 2019 blog post from the Federal Reserve Bank. "Since 2016, about 18% of the population has held student loans, up from only 10% in 2004."

"The financial void families must fill between the price of college and the aid they receive has steadily widened in recent years," wrote Arizona State's Selingo in the *New York Times* in 2020 ("So You Got Financial Aid for College. But How Do You Pay for the Rest of It?"). "The average gap amount is roughly $11,000 at public colleges, up 72 percent since 2008; and $16,000 at private colleges, an increase of 43 percent since 2008. The gap in financial aid is growing because family incomes remain largely stagnant even as college prices continue to rise."

Largely as a result of rising costs to attend, operational costs and declining numbers of high school graduates, many small private colleges — especially those without big endowments they can draw on to provide financial aid to students — are struggling just to survive. In 2019 alone, Vermont lost three: Southern Vermont College in Bennington, Green Mountain College in Poultney, and the College of St. Joseph in Rutland. Dimming the picture further, the Gallup organization reported in 2019 that "younger adults are now less likely than middle-aged adults and seniors to consider college as very important."

From 2013 to 2019, Gallup's polling found that the portion of Americans who viewed college as very important dropped from 70 percent to 51 percent. Among those from eighteen to twenty-nine years old, it fell from 74 percent to 41 percent.

The Covid pandemic made budget pressures even tighter. "Across the country, colleges are in crisis," CNBC reported in late 2021, citing an 8 percent drop in undergraduate enrollment across the country, "putting some colleges in severe financial distress."

"While the drop in college and university enrollments occurred across public and private institutions with two- and four-year programs," CNBC said, "community colleges have been hit the hardest, falling 6% this year after a staggering 9.4% decline last year."

"Community colleges, long the unsung foundation of higher education in America, have reached a perilous turning point," warned Nick Anderson and Danielle Douglas-Gabriel in the *Washington Post* in March 2021 ("Community Colleges at a Crossroads: Enrollment Is Plummeting, but Political Clout is Growing"). "No other sector of higher ed lost as much enrollment — a devastating development for these schools that serve large numbers of disadvantaged students and are open to all who apply.

"'As they go, so goes the country,' said Josh Wyner, executive director of the College Excellence Program at the Aspen Institute and author of a book on quality community colleges," Anderson and Douglas-Gabriel wrote. "'Without them,' Wyner said, 'we're really going to be hard-pressed to make good on the promise of equal opportunity for a good life and a good career.'"

'What remains a challenge is cost'

CCV has hardly been immune to the pressures. After its student numbers surged during this century's first decade, the college's enrollment declined from 7,116 in 2011 to 5,104 in 2019. But then the numbers held steady from fall 2019 to fall 2020, even as the pandemic's impacts deepened and community-college enrollment plunged across the nation.

The stabilizing of CCV's enrollment came despite "the decreasing population of young people in New England," wrote Madeline St. Amour in *Inside Higher Education*, and it contrasted with an 8 percent enrollment decline in Maine's community college system. By spring 2022, CCV's enrollment had actually grown, to 5,932 students.

But "what remains a challenge is cost," Judy wrote in an April 2021 blog post. "In large part because of the way higher education is funded in Vermont, CCV is the most affordable college in the state but among the most expensive community colleges in the country.

"Similarly, Vermont has one of the highest high school graduation rates in the country, yet one of the lowest rates of continuation to postsecondary education and training. While cost is not the only factor behind this statistic, with the price of a CCV course approaching $1,000, we can't ignore that it is a significant barrier.

"As the state emerges from the pandemic and we work to help Vermonters get back on their feet," the president wrote, "CCV is focused on this question: How do we ensure that students of all ages and backgrounds have the ability to pursue education and training beyond high school? Helping Vermonters prepare for promising jobs, and helping employers meet their workforce needs, starts with looking critically at the cost of college."

Judy noted the positive impacts on enrollment of two initiatives during the first pandemic year. First was the McClure Foundation's gift of a free CCV course to every member of the spring 2020 high school graduating class. That helped to double the number of recent high school graduates who enrolled at the college in the fall, with more than three-quarters of those students saying they planned to continue at college. Second was a workforce-training program, backed by federal Covid relief funds, that provided free classes and training at the state colleges to nearly five hundred Vermonters whose jobs were affected by the pandemic.

"Students from all 14 counties took advantage of this opportunity," Judy wrote, "and the average age of new students who enrolled was 42."

"... The question for many Vermonters as they consider the value of higher education," the president concluded, "is not whether they will choose between CCV, UVM, or a private college or university; the question is whether they will choose between CCV and nothing. Rebuilding stronger in the wake of Covid-19 means making postsecondary education accessible to all Vermonters, and it begins with finding creative ways to reduce the barrier of cost."

'Change and innovation are needed'

Back in 1998, the Vermont Legislature created a Commission on Higher Education Funding, which soon reported that state funding for Vermont's public institutions of higher education ranked forty-ninth in the nation.

State funding was this low even though, said a 2008 summary of the commission's work, "a high school diploma was no longer sufficient to enable a person to earn a living wage; employers need a highly skilled workforce to fill jobs; the 'traditional' college student is no longer under the age of 22; Vermonters are burdened by high tuition and higher debt loads; Vermont colleges and university are struggling to fund their core services; and a 'disconnect' exists between the needs of its citizens for education and training, and the state's financial investment in post-secondary education."

Ten years later, said the 2008 summary, "the reality is that all of the Commission's findings are still true, but the situation has worsened.... Vermont's ranking is still 49th in the nation in its support of higher education. Tuitions have increased substantially since 1999, and our students are laboring under a debt load that has doubled since 1994."

Measured in inflation-adjusted dollars per full-time equivalent student, Vermont state funding for all public higher education declined by 23.4 percent between 1980 and 2020, according to a 2020 report by the State Higher Education Officers Association. In 2020-equivalent dollars, the state's funding per FTE student, the report said, was $4,425 in 1980, $3,339 in 2010, $2,956 in 2019, and $3,387 in 2020.

Even before the pandemic struck, Vermont's three residential state colleges had been struggling for years to stay solvent amid the low state support, declining enrollment, and rising competition from online education providers. Now they faced bankruptcy. When then-Chancellor Jeb Spaulding proposed in spring 2020 that some of those campuses be closed, his suggestion was attacked, it failed, and he resigned.

The Legislature then created a new Select Committee on the Future of Public Higher Education in Vermont. Its fifteen members included the new VSC chancellor, the presidents of UVM and VSAC, legislators, academics, and leaders of businesses, nonprofits and the state's education and labor agencies. To chair the Select Committee, Republican Gov. Phil Scott chose CCV President Judy.

The Select Committee presented its recommendations in April 2021. They were dramatic.

"The Vermont Legislature should recognize the gravity of the fiscal crisis facing the Vermont State Colleges," its report declared. It recommended that CCV — whose finances, it noted, had remained "relatively balanced" during the pandemic — be maintained as a separate college while Castleton University, Northern Vermont University (formerly Johnson and Lyndon state colleges), and Vermont Technical College would become a single institution, with their multiple campuses but with unified leadership, policies and procedures.

The panel urged a new injection of state support to accompany "coordinated and comprehensive" changes within the new institution. The Legislature responded by approving nearly $89 million in a one-time boost of state support for the VSC System, most of that coming from federal Covid relief funds.

The three residential colleges had strong, vocal supporters and decades of history; Castleton, the oldest, became a college soon after the Civil War. But the VSC board quickly adopted the reform plan.

"Change and innovation are needed," wrote VSC Board Chair Lynn Dickinson in *VTDigger* in July 2021, "to seize this once-in-a-lifetime opportunity to create the student-centered and future-oriented higher education system that expands access to education across the state while meeting the needs of our current and future learners, the state, and our financial stability." That September, the board voted to name its new, unified system Vermont State University.

In recommending that CCV continue as a separate state college, the Select Committee said that Vermont should "ensure that CCV continues to focus on its mission to provide Vermont residents with affordable access points to postsecondary education throughout the State, and to develop and deliver responsive workforce-relevant education and training programs."

During the intense, suspenseful period when the Legislature and the Select Committee were pondering the future of the state college system, quite a few Vermonters spoke up for the institutions they valued. One of those was Tammy Howard Davis.

A Rutland native, Davis had been working for twenty-four years as an academic coordinator at CCV's Rutland center. The letter she sent to her state representative has since been widely shared within the CCV community. Excerpting it might be the best way to sum up, for now, the ongoing story of this very uncommon college.

> ### Tammy Howard Davis
>
> Imagine having a dream of a college education but lacking the self-confidence and belief in self-worth to walk through an educational institution's door. This is the fragile demographic that I am referring to, these are the people we serve, and this is the poverty cycle I am referring to.
>
> In sharp contrast, imagine finally enrolling in a class or two and being the first one in your family to ever walk through a college door. Imagine hearing from someone at the college level that you have potential and yes, it is in you to do this. Imagine the feeling of nervous excitement that would come over one as you do your first set of homework. Imagine modelling the role of pursuing education to your children as you do homework together. Finally, imagine having hope for a better future. These are the feelings and experiences of many CCV students. CCV changes lives, one at a time.
>
> ... I have boxes of notes and letters thanking CCV for "everything." I keep a board in my office dedicated to student appreciation letters that serve as a reminder of our work at CCV. There are so many examples I could share:
>
> - The single mom who completed the manufacturing certificate and gained a well-paying manufacturing job, enabling her to save their home from foreclosure.
>
> - The gentleman struggling with unemployment and lack of housing, who wandered into our lobby and is now in management with a degree in business.

INVENTING THE FUTURE

- A young lady from an area high school who was an addict by the time she was in her junior year of high school, but who is now finishing her master's degree in psychology at Northern Vermont University.

This is what we "do" at CCV. We build people and we build futures. We strengthen foundations.... Every day, every week, every month and year after year, CCV opens its doors and provides access to those in search of bettering their lives.

Afterword

In spring 1971, when the just-born college was first known as the Vermont Regional Community College Commission, Richard Eisele was among those who volunteered to teach its very first courses. Twelve students signed up for his class on "Understanding Human Behavior." Almost all were women. One evening a week, they met in the basement of the Bethany Church in Montpelier.

"At that time, there was no formal registration, no tuition, no teacher pay, no grades, and no credits," Eisele later wrote. "This amazing experiment in community education was strictly a matter of matching adults in the community who wanted to learn something with other people from the same community who had the appropriate talents to teach them. How cool was that?"

Eisele joined the college staff in 1975 and stayed until he retired in 2005; but he continued to teach courses, from that earliest start all the way until three years before he passed away in July 2021.

On a warm sunny Saturday in August 2021, several dozen longtime staffers, leaders, teachers and friends of CCV gathered with family members and more friends of Dick Eisele for a potluck picnic in his honor. In an open-sided pavilion at Montpelier's Elm Street Recreation Area, when the meal was finished and the time came for tributes, Don Hooper stood up to speak.

In those beginning years, Hooper had been the person hired to recruit teachers in the Montpelier area. None of the instructors, back then, would be paid.

"I used to say, 'I didn't hire teachers, I cajoled them into doing their community service,'" Hooper said. "I found my way to Dick Eisele, and he had such a calmness and a presence. He was at that time the guidance counselor at the Waterbury elementary school — and term after term, he did that for money and gave up one night a week to teach for free, long before he became a career employee at CCV. He was a godsend."

Peter Smith, the college's founding president from the 1970s, had returned to Vermont to reunite with old friends and attend the memorial. When he took a turn to speak, he said, "The way the college has evolved, the people, over these fifty years — there is consistency, the values are extraordinary, but it has evolved and changed as well. There's some magic in that, and in the middle of it are people who were there for twenty-five years, thirty years. What this institution has become is in so many ways because of those people who committed their lives to it.

Dick Eisele

"This guy was a rock," he said of Eisele. "He was there all the time, forever. To me he symbolizes those of you who didn't just come and go, like some of us did — but who stuck around, to make this college what it is today."

Acknowledgements

I'm incredibly grateful to all the people connected to the Community College of Vermont, past and present, who gave me their time and told me their stories. I owe special thanks to Tim Donovan, past president of the college, and to Joyce Judy, the current president, for their patience and care in answering my many questions, pointing me toward people to talk with, and generally helping this book come to be.

I'm also especially grateful to Peter Smith, founding president of the college, for his recollections and encouragement in getting this project off the ground; to Larry Daloz, for his invaluable contributions to Part One; to Megan Tucker for her help in digging up vintage photos; and to both Megan and Mary Ellen Lowe for collecting the CCV Stories, which appear today on CCV's website and were indispensable to making this a chronicle told through many valued voices.

Emerson Lynn and Barbara Brittingham were supportive and encouraging, and I much appreciate the endorsements they gave this book, as did Tom Slayton, the justly admired dean of Vermont journalists. Barbara Benedict and Carolyn Weir of the J. Warren and Lois McClure Foundation were really helpful, as was Aimee Stephenson, who introduced me to the fruitful jumble that is CCV's attic archive in Montpelier. I learned so much from my conversations with past CCV presidents Myrna Miller, Mike Holland and Barbara Murphy, and from the video-recorded interview that Tim and Megan did with Ken Kalb before his passing.

This book benefits enormously from Kate Mueller's expert copyediting, and from having been visually crafted and designed by Mason Singer of Laughing Bear Associates in Montpelier. Mason has given world-class design to book after book coming out of Vermont; his contribution to our state's sense of community and our shared memory is real, and it will last.

Overall, the extraordinary spirit of creativity, commitment and caring humanity that has shaped CCV through the work of so many people, over more than 50 years, came through in all the conversations I had with so many people involved with the college. A most heartfelt *thank you* to everyone.

Doug Wilhelm

Photo credits: Photo of Peter Smith on page 18 by Ray Ellis; of Peggy Williams on p. 43 by Jamie Hyde; of Ken Kalb on p. 139 by The Foto Shop; of Eileen Chalfoun on p. 175 by Peter Wrenn, and of Barbara Murphy on p. 206 by Alan Jakubek. All other photos were sourced from the CCV archives or provided by the subjects, and are used with permission. Thanks also to Jeff Danziger, for permission to include two of his editorial cartoons.

Doug Wilhelm is the author of 18 previously published books. His most recent novel, *Street of Storytellers* (Montpelier: Rootstock Publications, 2019), was awarded three national honors and one New England gold medal for independently published books. His middle-school novel *The Revealers* (New York: Farrar, Straus & Giroux, 2003) has been the focus of reading and discussion projects, most of them all-school reads, in more than one thousand schools across the U.S. and internationally. A former Vermont reporter for the *Boston Globe,* Doug and his wife, Cary Beckwith, live in Weybridge, Vermont, where he is a full-time self-employed writer.

www.ingramcontent.com/pod-product-compliance
Lightning Source LLC
Chambersburg PA
CBHW071853290426
44110CB00013B/1129